A WOMAN'S ODYSSEY INTO AFRICA:
TRACKS ACROSS A LIFE
Hanny Lightfoot-Klein

SOME ADVANCE REVIEWS

"I read the book from page one to the end in one night and could not put it down. A ray of hope for women who feel resigned to unfulfilling lifestyles, a breath of fresh air for all who wrestle with midlife issues, and a marvel for those who admire Western individualism."

Heino F. L. Meyer-Bahlburg, PhD
Professor of Clinical Psychology in Psychiatry
College of Physicians and Surgeons, Columbia University

"A stunning double helix of a story. One strand of the helix is the odyssey of her African adventures. The other strand is the odyssey of her personal demon who catapults her, at age fifty, into Africa. The African strand becomes a metaphor of redemption from the haunts and ghosts of childhood and young womanhood. The tales of this feminine Ulysses are told by a virtuoso performer of the narrative art."

John Money, PhD
Professor of Medical Psychology & Pediatrics, Emeritus
Johns Hopkins University

"Her adventurousness and courage make this extremely readable story a source of inspiration to others who may well be equally desperate to change the course of their lives. Her profoundly human account is also a tale of high adventure, one which makes for engrossing and altogether enjoyable reading."

Ashley Montagu, PhD
Cultural Anthropologist
Princeton, New Jersey

NOTES FOR PROFESSIONAL LIBRARIANS
AND LIBRARY USERS

This is an original book title published by Harrington Park Press, an imprint of The Haworth Press, Inc. Unless otherwise noted in specific chapters with attribution, materials in this book have not been previously published elsewhere in any format or language.

CONSERVATION AND PRESERVATION NOTES

The paper used in this publication meets the minimum requirements of American National Standard for Information Sciences — Permanence of Paper for Printed Material, ANSI Z39.48-1984.

A Woman's Odyssey into Africa
Tracks Across a Life

HAWORTH Women's Studies
Ellen Cole, PhD and Esther Rothblum, PhD
Senior Co-Editors

New, Recent, and Forthcoming Titles:

When Husbands Come Out of the Closet by Jean Schaar Gochros

Prisoners of Ritual: An Odyssey into Female Circumcision in Africa by Hanny Lightfoot-Klein

Foundations for a Feminist Restructuring of the Academic Disciplines edited by Michele Paludi and Gertrude A. Steuernagel

Hippocrates' Handmaidens: Women Married to Physicians by Esther Nitzberg

Waiting: A Diary of Loss and Hope in Pregnancy by Ellen Judith Reich

God's Country: A Case Against Theocracy by Sandy Rapp

Women and Aging: Celebrating Ourselves by Ruth Raymond Thone

A Woman's Odyssey into Africa: Tracks Across a Life by Hanny Lightfoot-Klein

Women's Conflicts About Eating and Sexuality: The Relationship Between Food and Sex by Rosalyn M. Meadow and Lillie Weiss

Anorexia Nervosa and Recovery: A Hunger for Meaning by Karen Way

Reproductive Hazards in the Workplace: Mending Jobs, Managing Pregnancies by Regina Kenen

Women Murdered by the Men They Loved by Constance A. Bean

A Woman's Odyssey into Africa
Tracks Across a Life

Hanny Lightfoot-Klein

Harrington Park Press
An Imprint of The Haworth Press, Inc.
New York • London • Norwood (Australia)

ISBN 1-56023-007-X

Published by

Harrington Park Press, an imprint of The Haworth Press, Inc., 10 Alice Street, Binghamton, NY 13904-1580

Cover design by Marshall Andrews.

Library of Congress Cataloging-in-Publication Data

Lightfoot-Klein, Hanny.
    A woman's odyssey into Africa : tracks across a life / Hanny Lightfoot-Klein.
      p. cm.
    ISBN 1-56023-007-X
    1. Sudan — Social life and customs. 2. Lightfoot-Klein, Hanny — Journeys — Africa. 3. Sexologists — United States — Biography. I. Title.
DT 154.9.L54 1991
916.2404'4 — dc20
                                     91-19531
                                         CIP

To my Implacable Demons,
To Laurance the Loveable,
To John, my Benevolent Ogre,
And to Lightfoot, my Indian Grandfather,
Who taught me how to Live.

ABOUT THE AUTHOR

Hanny Lightfoot-Klein, MA, is an independent researcher under the auspices of the American Foundation for Gender and Genital Medicine and Science. Ms. Lightfoot-Klein studied female genital circumcision during three year-long treks through Sudan, Kenya, and Egypt; she lived with families of all social levels and geographic areas and interviewed over 400 people in all walks of life in regard to psychological, sociological, historical, sexological, medical, religious, and legal aspects of female circumcision. An avid writer, Ms. Lightfoot-Klein has published many articles in the *Journal of Obstetric Gynecology and Neo-Natal Nursing, Medical Aspects of Human Sexuality, Journal of Psychology and Human Sexuality, Journal of Sex Research* and several British and German publications as well. She is a member of the Association of Women in Psychology, Society for Sex Therapy and Research, National Women's Studies Association, and the Society for the Scientific Study of Sex. Her first book, *Prisoners of Ritual*, was also recently published by The Haworth Press, Inc.

CONTENTS

Letter from Kadugli

Daniel, my dearest Sonshine,

Sweet heaven! Surely this must be the end of the earth! Have I fallen off yet, or am I about to fall off? If only it were not so inhumanly hot! If only I were not so abominably homesick! It has been almost a full year since I have seen my kiddies and nearly as many moons since a letter has gotten through to me! This engulfing loneliness does not hit me often, but when it does, suddenly and completely out of the blue, it is like a sledgehammer, straight to the gut. Where does it come from? I was so *happy* yesterday!

But I am getting ahead of myself. Yesterday? Oh yes, I was coming back to Kadugli from Kelek, a village in the mountains. There is a lake of sorts at Kelek. Its waters are impossibly clouded, slimy and filled with animal ordure. Great herds of cattle and goats wade into it every morning and evening to drink, while water for human consumption is ladled out no more than a hundred yards away along its banks, as if it were any less polluted there! I have cursed the weight of my full water bottle all too often, but what a treasure it becomes in places such as this!

And what a village! Absolutely untouched! It is altogether innocent of the ubiquitous plague of plastic bags. There is not a single soda can. I was carrying a stack of book matches, donated by a kindly stewardess in Khartoum, and they caused quite a stir. I tried to explain that they could be very useful during the rainy season, but the irresistible magic of this marvel proved to be too much. Whenever I gave a pack away, having first demonstrated its powers, its recipient merely sat and lit one match after the other until they were all gone. Perhaps it is best that way. Quite obviously they have ways of making fires even during the rains and have no need for my matches, except as a wonderful entertainment!

They call me *Chiwadja*, white woman, and when they ask my

1

name, I say that it is *El Shadida*, the strong woman. I don't feel too strong at the moment, I must confess. I feel weepy and abysmally lonely. *This* too shall pass. It shall, it shall. It always does, eventually, with the next step, the next day, the next adventure. All that I need to do is to hoist my pack upon my shoulders, put my left foot in front of my right one, then the right in front of the left one and just keep going. It is a formula that never fails me.

The ride to Kelek was not too bad, but I've learned to make allowances for the discrepancy between theory and reality here. In theory, the lorry leaves Kadugli at 3 p.m. and gets to Kelek at 5 p.m., and there should have been ample time for me to pitch my tent before dark. So far, so good.

In actuality, the driver did not leave until 6 p.m. and after the usual breakdowns and visits with the relatives in the villages along the way, we finally wheezed into Kelek at midnight. But it was all quite wonderful, for all along the way there were gifts of dates and peanuts for me at every stop, invitations to tea and lemon juice at every village, and many exotic sights to see.

And so, there I was at 12 p.m. trying to pitch a tent. The ground was hard as stone, and for the life of me I could not sort out that monster of a tent in the feeble moonlight. Oh well, no matter. The sleeping bag would have to do. But it does get cold here! The mercury creeps well beyond 110 degrees during the day, but at night it must be in the vicinity of 40 degrees.

A word about roads. (There will be a brief pause while I giggle hysterically.) There is no such animal, of course. There is, however, a path of dried lorry ruts, a legacy from the rainy season, and these are great sport when the springless vehicle descends into and climbs out of the many dry gullies that have to be crossed.

Another source of amusement one can count on is getting the lorry started after it breaks down. Everybody, and I do mean *everybody*, has to pile off the freight and push. It usually goes for one or two hours before it breaks down, unless you are exceptionally unlucky.

I have no idea how this letter will get to you. Perhaps someone here will journey to Khartoum soon. Perhaps not. It is a three day trip by lorry, one hour by plane. In Khartoum the bearer will have to find someone who is leaving for Europe or the United States. It could well take a month, three months, or no more than a week to reach you.

Here in Kadugli there is another little America, enclaved in an octagonal structure known as the "Round House." The inhabitants are quite a bit easier on the nerves than the petty bureaucrats vaguely connected to the American presence in Khartoum. I am not too clear about what they do here, and know only that they are engaged in some agricultural project. Right now they are all in Khartoum and are graciously allowing me to use the house.

The house is a marvel of modern technology in that it features a refrigerator, a flushing toilet, a washing machine, ceiling fans, real beds with mattresses, furniture, a shower, and an electric stove. However, there is rarely any electricity to activate this miracle. On lucky days it comes on for one or two hours, but lucky days are rare.

Today the water came on for half an hour, oh joy and gladness! When I got back from Kelek yesterday—filthy, grimy, and covered with dust—there was no water at all, and no houseboy to be found. It finally occurred to me to check the refrigerator, and I was over-joyed to be rewarded with a bottle of warm but drinkable water.

It is amazing how quickly you learn to adapt. You don't just plunge into the shower when the water comes on. You make sure that you fill a couple of buckets first, just in case the water suddenly goes off again just as you are about to wash the shampoo out of your hair.

The journey back from Kelek was gloriously bizarre. I managed to obtain a ride on a lorry carrying a school excursion back to Ka-dugli. Imagine, if you dare, the highly specialized, concentrated lunacy of 50 junior high school aged pubescent African males, stuffed into a lorry that sensibly can hold about 20, crashing through the roadless mountains on a vehicle with no shock absorb-ers, and *your mom*.

There is only one way to get through that type of thing. You must make some rather considerable shifts in your nervous system. If you are capable of making those shifts, it is not only possible to survive here, but everything becomes a challenge, a crucible in which all of your dross is eventually burned away, bit by bit. Having been a runner helps. It has taught me how to process the physical pain that is an integral part of all travel here.

Meanwhile, culture shock continues. The Sudanese mentality is not an easy one to fathom, simply because they are so far ahead of us in certain aspects of their human relations and so far behind us in technology. The thing that one must constantly remember is that these are extremely *moral* people, in the best sense of the word.

There is one concept that one had better learn very rapidly in this barren, waterless land, and that is the concept of *fee* and *mafee* — there is and there isn't. When things are mafee they are mafee without hope of redemption or remedy. If water is mafee, it is mafee. If transportation or medical help or comfort or reprieve are mafee, they are *mafee*. Telephone? Mail? Airplanes? Totally mafee. And that does something to your head. You must develop an acceptance, and you had best do so very quickly if you have any hopes of remaining sane. After all, there still is a half hour of water per day, but you had better learn to take it as it comes. Culture shock? Oh yes. Culture shock *fee*!

It's pretty different in Khartoum. In spite of all the moaning and complaint that one hears at the American Club, that city does have a small handful of reasonably decent restaurants, and the Western sector boasts two or three swimming pools, all fed by the waters of the Nile. Also along the Nile stand a small number of swank hotels that are microcosmic enclaves of Western luxury and quite naturally of the kind of mindset that goes along with them.

But out here, along the borders of mafee, everything balances delicately on the knife edge of subsistence.

As I write this to you, one of the houseboys is standing behind me, looking over my shoulder. The houseboys all think that I am a *dictori* and that I am writing a letter to Washington. Every morning I join them in the courtyard where they have built a fire and are heating water in their battered kettle. I bring along my treasured tin of English tea for us all to share, and we chat. I am finally beginning to get a real feel for the language.

At Kelek I saw them slaughter a bull which they had tied between two trees. It took several minutes. I don't think I will ever be able to eat beef again. They hit him in the head with clubs and then cut his throat, which gushed an incredible fountain of blood. I wanted to run away and hide, but made myself watch it from beginning to end. This is no place for someone who is afraid of seeing blood. It flows constantly, like a river, far more freely than water does.

On my first night in Kadugli I stayed with the wife of a doctor to whom I had been written a letter of introduction by a nurse in Khartoum. The doctor, whom I had hoped to interview, had just left for Port Sudan. His wife took me in and treated me like a long-lost friend even though I had descended on her, completely unheralded, around 1 a.m.

The next morning she was wearing a simple sleeveless house-dress and I could see that all of her upper back and arms were severely marked with scars — random, not ritual scars, as though she had been horse-whipped. I could not help myself; I had to ask her how she had gotten them. She merely laughed and told me that when she had been a small girl living in a village, her mother had beaten her with a donkey whip if she did not mind her.

I accepted her explanation, and I cannot help but wonder what the entire story is. Those scars are quite impressive. Some of them are seven or eight inches long and by the looks of them, she must have been cut quite badly by the whip. People don't usually beat their children here. You very rarely hear a child crying. I wonder what area she hails from. Perhaps she simply had some singularly bad luck. Some people do. Yet, what a warm and loving woman she is! I wish I knew her story.

Today, wandering through the hills, a Land Rover complete with one English botanist, a Sudanese assistant, a driver and, miracle of miracles, an empty seat for me and an invitation to join them for the day, suddenly appeared. What a wonderful piece of luck, to get a feel for the region without any wear and tear on myself in traveling through it! It gives me a chance to learn more about the Nuba.

An interesting subculture, the Nuba. They are a real nature tribe in the process of transition. The Sudanese government forces these people, who until quite recently went naked, to wear a badly cut and thus obviously uncomfortable garment known as "missionary shorts" to cover in these people what the government considers offensive to display. To make this edict more palatable, the shorts are made of wildly colorful fabric.

The Nubans keep their bodies meticulously clean but have absolutely no concept of how to deal with clothes, and it is quite obvious that these missionary shorts are never washed. To top it off, this garment is made of cheap, synthetic cloth which does not breathe. It is not too difficult to envision its unhealthy effects on the Nuba in this tropical climate.

By some queer quirk of fate, a shipment of wildly colored leg warmers has also found its way into Nuba and so these improbable garments complete the high fashion look, which is enhanced still further by their custom of inflicting extensive decorative body scarring.

The dominant Islamic culture obviously regards the Nuba as an inferior subspecies. The two cultures coexist, with all the trade and property, such as they are, being in the hands of the former. They own the lorries, the watering places, the granary, the bakery ovens, and the school. The Nuba exist somewhere along the fringes. They dig their own water holes, which are shallow, muddy, and full of pig excrement. The children's bellies are distended by parasites, and infant mortality, according to what the British botanist tells me, hovers around 50%.

The botanist is quite an interesting specimen. He believes himself to be the luckiest and also the happiest man in the world. He spends his day collecting samples of leaves, seed pods, and flowers, which he sequesters in plastic bags and then labels carefully. He tells me that he can imagine nothing in this world that he would rather be doing. Half of his time is spent at the University of Khartoum, the other half on field trips to remote areas.

Africa obviously agrees with him. He too loves the freedom of trailing through the landscape, being entirely his own man. His wife and three children live in Khartoum. His children love it there; his wife is only barely able to tolerate it. He realizes that regarding this family, there will come a time when he will have to make a choice, that he has already made without knowing.

We came upon a superb flowering tree in full bloom. It is covered with enormous orchid-like flowers that emit a powerful, heady scent. Its flowers are so spectacular that I am about to pluck one so that I may examine it more closely, but he stops me. The natives call this marvel the "Poison Tree," and its sap is so toxic that if it remains on your skin it will eat right through it. He pulls on a pair of protective gloves and plucks a blossom for his collection, all the while humming happily to himself. It is difficult not to envy his personal world of perfection.

Africa is like that. You either love it or you hate it. Those who love it may well find themselves in the grips of an obsession that is so powerful that everything else in their lives pales by comparison, and only those who are similarly obsessed can understand their passion.

Three days later, in the village of Reika: I have fallen in love once more. I am living at the house of the local merchant, in the women's quarters, along with his three wives. He is neither very young nor particularly attractive, so there appears to be little reason for jealousy among them. They get along exceedingly well together and share everything: work, food, care of the children, and each other's company.

Between them they have eight little children, six of them girls. Only one of these has been subjected so far to what they euphemistically call "female circumcision" here, and oh good heavens, how different her eyes are from those of the other, untouched ones! Something happens to the eyes. I have seen it so many, many times! It is as if the whole eye goes flat—literally, morphologically *flat*! And something is absent from those eyes. It is as if the light has been snuffed out, a fire has been extinguished. It is unmistakable.

I have fallen in love with all of these exquisite, frail birds of children who hang like strings of pearls from both my hands as I go walking. But there is one in particular, one who is always the very first to find my hand, one who reads my every wish from my face, one who sits by the hour studying my every move as I write. Oh, how I wish that I could rescue her! How I wish that I could take her to a place where she will be safe from the ordeal that awaits her! But of course I am totally powerless to do so, and that is the unremitting torment that I must live with here.

My entourage of small girls has learned to say "little squirts" to me because, I suppose, I must be saying it to them constantly. This morning while their mothers were otherwise occupied, they solemnly took me aside, lifted their dresses and showed me the underpants they were wearing. I accepted their gesture as the ultimate expression of trust and sisterhood, and when all of them looked at me with an urgent air of expectancy, I lifted my robe and showed them my own underpants. They seemed at least to be quite satisfied with this. Yet I cannot help but wonder what it is that they really wanted to see. When I recall my own seething curiosity at that same age, I have a fairly good idea of what it may have been.

At a time within living memory, the climate of the Nuban hills was moderate, humid, and ideal for plant and animal life. It is now oppressively hot and dry in the daytime and ever colder at night. I could see clearly the process of desertification from the air. A Norwegian anthropologist who sat next to me on the flight pointed it out to me. Wherever there is human habitation, there is a circle of totally denuded land that surrounds it. As the population increases, more and more of these circles are created until they overlap and blend, and the end result is overpopulated bare desert. It is frightening to behold.

One week later, back in Kadugli: Interesting commentary on the Sudanese personality. When I returned to the round house, I found that all of my belongings, which I had left in a locked room, have been expertly rifled. All of my clothes, papers, snapshots, films, tapes, medications and toiletries, pulled out and carefully inspected. My money belt, which I had hidden in a lead film shield envelope, has been gone through with a fine-tooth comb. No effort has been made to reassemble my belongings or to try to cover up the search that has taken place. I unhappily contemplate the open zippers and unbuckled straps on my strewn-about possessions, wondering where to begin reassembling them. The houseboys and watchmen seem to have evaporated into thin air.

After perhaps two hours of inventory, I have discovered to my great puzzlement that nothing whatsoever has been taken. Not a penny, not a piaster, not a picture, pill, or piece of underwear. Obviously it has all been the doing of one or all of the houseboys, for no reason other than irresistible curiosity, or perhaps merely boredom.

For two days I glare at them, and do not come out into the courtyard with my tin of tea in the morning. I do not speak to them, while they contritely tiptoe around, averting their eyes and leaving me peace offerings of buckets filled with water. On the third morning I relent, and we all have tea together once more.

In the interim, two Welsh teachers have come by and told me that there is a young woman who works with them at the secondary school who is too ill with hepatitis and anemia to be moved to Khartoum. She has been receiving blood transfusions twice a day. Nearly everyone here has had malaria, and is therefore useless as a blood donor. I offer them a pint of my type O blood, with the provision that I myself will supervise the sterilization procedure of whatever instruments will be used on me.

The next day they come by once more and report that their friend's condition has improved to the extent that they can risk flying her out. There is an airstrip here, and there are AID and UNICEF emergency taxis for authorized personnel and those who are able to pay disproportionately large fares. I fit neither category. Total, unencumbered freedom has its price!

Some of the researchers connected with the round house have returned. There is Frank, an American anthropologist, and two British animal scientists. No water has come from the taps in two days, so we take their Land Rover to Miri, some distance away, where there is a dam and a fairly substantial reservoir of clean water. What an ideal place this would be to camp for a few days!

A slight distance away a troop of baboons is visible in the branches of a small grove of trees. I can see them quite clearly through my binoculars. Suddenly a shot rings out and one of them plummets to the ground. Then a second shot, and another one falls. The remaining animals scatter. I can see them disappearing into the shrubs.

A few minutes later the proud hunter appears, dragging the two carcasses. His leathery, much-creased skin is blue-black, he is dressed in rags that might at one time have been a uniform, and he sports a multi-stained army hat of considerable vintage. Proudly, he displays the proof of his prowess as a sharpshooter, a young male and an old female. He has cut their throats in partial deference to his religion, which mandates this method of slaughter, but also forbids the eating of these animals.

I am drawn into stunned contemplation of the beauty of their curiously human faces, their expressive features, the sensitivity of their aspect even in death. That my first sighting of primates in the wild should end like this! The hunter points to my camera, then to himself and his quarry. He strikes a pose, aiming his ancient and utterly improbable weapon at the two corpses at his feet. Because it creates an activity that takes my mind off my deep emotional turbulence, I snap his photo.

He begins to skin the carcasses, which thereby look even more human, and invites us to share the meal he is about to prepare. We decline as graciously as possible, saying that we have already eaten. Here, before you partake of the flesh of a creature, you must first be willing to look your potential meal in the face, and these two faces are far too human in aspect for comfort.

Back at the round house, I spend hours in conversation with the various scientists who come and go and who seem to see considerable merit in my strange research. It is obvious that they do not regard me as a "weirdo," as do some at the American Club in Khartoum. Scientists come from all over and each is deeply involved in some kind of exciting field work. They are an interesting and varied group of people, and for the first time since I became involved in my own studies, I feel comfortable and among peers.

Frank, the anthropologist, is a former professional opera singer, whose chest measures an amazing 58 inches. He sings to me entire arias from Wagner, Verdi, Puccini, and oh, sweet heaven, Mozart! His brilliant, powerful voice reverberates through the Nuban hills. What an unlikely setting for such a wealth of musical riches!

Frank has the gift of seeing auras. Mine, he says, is very clearly perceptible. He has seen only one like it before. It is predominantly violet, shading into blue, with red, spike-like outcroppings, and it is flecked with gold. His interpretation of my aura is that it belongs to a person who has suffered considerably. The predominant color, violet, is a delicate, vulnerable spiritual color which is based on blue, a color which he interprets as connoting stability. The red, spike-like outcroppings he perceives as suffering and the golden flecks as humanitarianism.

For whatever all of that may be worth, our intensive conversations have provided him with enough information to have enabled him to come to these conclusions by different routes. The interesting things about his strange gift are that he claims to see auras even on photographs, and that he does not regard his talent as a form of extrasensory perception, because it comes to him through his ordinary, everyday senses.

One week later: What a bummer! Time to return to Khartoum! I can hardly wait to go back to the American Club so that I can hear the latest horror story about how the service at the Hilton is going downhill, and the latest undue hardship story among the lesser lights at the embassy.

The last time I came back from one of my excursions into the interior, some of them insisted on knowing who was funding me. Although this is essentially none of their business, I am rather proud of the fact that I am merely a retired school teacher who is altogether self-supporting and self-motivated, and I told them so. They absolutely refused to believe me, and really got quite belligerent in the course of the conversation. It seems to be impossible for them to grasp that I would actually come to Sudan of my own accord, and repeatedly at that, and actually even use up my own savings, when the likes of them have nothing better to do to keep from going crazy than to count their hardship pay. Eventually, of course, they worked it out. Frank gleefully informed me that a rumor has spread through the entire American community that I am in reality an Israeli agent, whose mission it is to sow dissent among the Arab states! Oh Joy!

How the slough of boredom threatens to engulf and drown those of petty mentality. And I thought that I was too far out of step for anyone even to take notice of me!

That's really a good one for you. Your mother the hitchhiker, your mother the sexologist, your mother the desert rat. And now, by gum, *Your mother the spy!*

First Steps

I was at one time an English teacher in one of New York City's high schools, located in the depths of the inner city slum. Like most of these nightmarish schools, it featured massive doses of all the madness that such a setting can engender. Drug dealers roamed its halls with little constraint, conducting business in locker rooms, stairwells, and lavatories. Gang rivalries erupted regularly into violence, and chain whippings or knifings were so commonplace that they made no headlines.

The years of working in an amalgam of institutionalized bedlam, concentrated masses of personal desperation, rampant demoralization, violence, and hypocrisy have left me with some indelible images. One entire memorable year, for example, a pile of human excrement was deposited somewhere in the building every single school day. It would make its appearance, perhaps along the halls, by the blackboard in a classroom, on a shelf in the library, by the door of the teachers' lounge, or on a tray in the lunchroom. The "Mad Shitter," as he came to be known, was never apprehended, but mercifully disappeared forever when the school year ended.

In the year that followed, another form of pervasive madness became the order of the day in the form of frequent, seemingly casual attempts at arson. Small fires would be started in trash-littered corners or wastebaskets or classroom lockers almost daily, as if to dispose of at least some of the garbage that was heedlessly flung about everywhere. These small fires were always discovered and quenched quickly, but they left everyone tensely alert and with a relentlessly nagging sense of unease. No one questioned that they were the manifestations of a diseased mind, and that there was real danger.

The grand finale, after this series of insignificant blazes, occurred toward the end of the school year, one day early in June. We were well into the last period of the day when I happened to glance out of my third floor hall window and was horrified to see that the entire empty and presumably locked classroom across from mine was ablaze. I quickly herded my class down the nearest stairwell, pulling the fire alarm as I went.

As I watched the last of my students disappear safely down the stairs, one of the assistant principals (a truly splendid example of the school's administrative staff) who happened to be passing came rushing up to me and began to berate me loudly. I had no right to dismiss my class! He had not yet given the order to evacuate the school and I could be sure that he was going to report my insubordination to the principal! I took time only to guffaw incredulously into his face before I ran down the stairs and into the street, where I joined my students in watching the ensuing full-scale evacuation of the building. Within a few minutes a half dozen fire trucks arrived on the scene, and the fire, which was as yet safely contained within the room, was swiftly put out.

The assistant principal later shamefacedly approached me and requested with an unaccustomed humility that I ignore the scene that had taken place between us. True, I had totally defied his treasured authority, but upon calmer reflection he had obviously realized that reporting my insurrection would only have made him the laughingstock of the entire school. In keeping with the bizarre, Kafkaesque madness of the entire system, this same man was to become principal of the school only a few years later.

One morning, my departmental supervisor was taking inventory in the stacks of the book room adjoining her office, when she heard its heavy door open and a moment later snap shut. She was cornered by an armed youth and raped.

She was not able to register his partially masked face clearly, but was under the distinct impression that he had been a one-time student at the school. After he had raped her, he disappeared into the milling crowd of students changing classes in the halls, and was never apprehended. She fled the school in a state of acute shock and none of us ever saw her again. The lurid details of the case made their way into every newspaper in the city.

It is notable that in a school where teachers were physically attacked or ripped off with depressing regularity, nothing untoward ever happened to me in the 15 years that I taught there. Part of this was no doubt simply luck. Part of it also was due to the fact that I enjoyed a rather enviable popularity for all but the very last years of my teaching career. Maybe also it was in some measure due to the fact that I had inherited or learned some of the lunatic bantam rooster courage in the face of threat that characterized my father, and it is likely that word got around that I had best not be messed with.

I recall one particular incident when I had just undergone one of many operations to my knee that had been ruined in an accident many years before, and was navigating around the classroom in a hip-length walking cast, helped by a crutch. Suddenly the door of my classroom burst open, and four toughs exploded into the room. Two of them took up guard at the doors, while the remaining two busied themselves with brutalizing a lock affixed to one of the lockers against the back wall.

I had never seen any of them before, and so I loudly demanded that they explain what they were doing. They totally ignored me, concentrating intensely on their individual tasks. Loudly I asked again. The one that seemed to be the ringleader deigned to look up in my direction at this second insistent demand for attention, jerking his chin in my direction. "Don't bodder me, Teach!" he dismissed me contemptuously.

I was beginning to see red. This was *my* classroom these goons were invading! I picked up my crutch and began to advance toward them, supporting myself by the desks with the other hand as I went. "You have no business in my classroom! Get away from that locker!" I hissed at them from between suddenly clenched teeth.

"Fuck off, Bitch!" the group's spokesman snarled, renewing his efforts to rip open the locker.

I was barely able to register that my students were cowered in their seats before I was galvanized into instant outraged action. Brandishing my crutch above my head like a war club, I lurched forward screeching, a plaster cast clad fury of terrifying aspect. The invaders managed only one startled look at my face before they took to their heels and fled *en masse*. My students sat, averting their eyes. When the bell rang, they filed out quickly and in silence.

There are some memories of the school that I will always treasure. There was a time during the late 1960s when I became part of a wonderful, newly formed, experimental program. It sought out a small group of entering, disadvantaged minority students who in some way demonstrated a spark, a drive, or a talent which promised to enable them to succeed academically, given a leg up.

The administrators of this small "school within a school" were helpful and permissive to the utmost and obtained for me the books and materials I chose to work with. Classes were limited in size and invigoratingly lively. The sense of freedom I experienced in being able to teach exactly what and how I pleased caused me to rush to school an hour early each morning and made me loath to leave it at day's end. I glowed with inspiration and my lessons became daily marvels of invention.

I spent most of my class time motivating students to write and teaching them to tell their stories, and in the process of teaching them, I also learned to become a writer and a storyteller. I fully believe that if you pour your heart and soul into teaching something to others, you will eventually learn how to do it well yourself.

It was a love affair that was to last for several years. I never tired of spending weekends taking my students on trips, to plays, exhibits, concerts, and happenings. I brought along my own two far younger children and they gleaned, along with my students, an aspect of education that none of their own teachers could offer them.

The success rate of the program proved to be significant and a large percentage of the students in it ultimately finished college. Eventually, like all good things that happen in big, unwieldy, and uncaring institutions, all the good people were usurped and replaced by not-so-good people. These laid claim to their turn at taking over what had after years of hard work become a smoothly functioning system. The success rate of the program declined, funding was withdrawn, and bit by bit its soul died. All that eventually remained was a standard remedial reading program that did not work particularly well.

Inevitably, of course, I burned out. The deteriorating conditions in the school made my own position in it more and more ethically untenable to me. I carried on a vain struggle against the many personal emotional defeats and bouts of debilitating illness which came to characterize my life. Eventually I gave up. The fires in me died and I succumbed progressively to a deepening depression.

When a sabbatical leave unexpectedly became possible to me, an old dream I had had many years before suddenly leaped once more into clarity. I recalled that when I had first begun to teach, I had met a young biology teacher at the school, and finding things in common to talk about, we had become friends. A few years later he had set out to realize his lifelong ambition to travel around the world. It was something that quite a few young people were doing at that time and they managed to do it, somehow, on surprisingly little money. They took with them only what they were able to carry on their backs and set out, learning the ropes as they went along.

When my friend returned once more to the school after his two year journey, wildly bearded, proudly clad in his travel-worn, threadbare rags and glowing with achievement, I was amazed to see how much he had gained in personal stature in that time. He now exuded an aura of serene self-possession, something that had been painfully absent in him before. He was a far, far happier man and he was full of wonderful stories of adventure.

I envied him. Oh, *how* I envied him! I longed to make such an odyssey into the remote corners of the world, but the straps of my own life's harness were soon to tighten ever more cruelly about me, and in time all such longings were stifled and forgotten.

By the time my chance to obtain a sabbatical presented itself, I was already 51 years old. My children were grown, releasing me from my most significant responsibility. My marriage to their father, a desperately unfulfilling alliance of many years' standing, was in its final stages of disintegration. A variety of health problems, which had for many years virtually crippled me, had recently been resolved surgically, and the acute depression from which I had suffered for an even longer time was, for the moment at least, in remission.

I applied for the sabbatical, fervently hoping almost against hope that it would be granted. To my great surprise and elation, it was. My direction now lay clearly ahead of me. I knew that at that relatively late stage in my life, it could only be now or never.

I purchased a backpack and made preparations to leave.

Two weeks before my projected departure, I sustained a skull fracture. This unfortunate happening, which was to affect my life in a number of untoward ways, very nearly put an end to my hopes for freedom. But something in me has never allowed me to give up once I start something, and in my mind, my journey had already begun. After I had left the hospital I resumed my preparations, and only four weeks later I was able to board my flight to London.

For the first month I adhered to the safety of bus travel and lodgings in youth hostels while I toured castles all over Scotland, but I tired of this very quickly. I observed that many of the far younger travelers were hitchhiking casually through England, from one hostel to the other. Gathering courage, I approached a number of them and asked them to show me how to go about it.

Like most travelers of this type that I was to meet along the way, they were most pleased to demonstrate their expertise and to share information. The basic guidelines for safety were quite simple. Like all city areas, the greater London region tended to be difficult and a bit tricky, so it was best to find more conventional modes of travel there. Anywhere else along the English countryside, daylight hitchhiking was notoriously pleasant and extremely safe.

As far as at least parts of the Continent were concerned, one had to keep in mind that men of certain nationalities tended to hold attitudes toward lone female hitchhikers, which differed considerably from those apparently held by the easygoing and friendly British. If one was enterprising, however, one could always find ways that were completely safe. It was not necessary to stand by the side of a road, flagging down cars.

Every long-term hitchhiker developed an individual system, and mine eventually became quite sophisticated over a period of years. For example, lorries with only one driver waiting in line to board ferries could always be counted on to take you aboard in the role of second driver, which had the added advantage of saving you the price of the ferry. Once aboard, it was not difficult to find someone at the lorry drivers' special table, or if this failed, among other passengers, who was en route to your destination. Quite often, after a driver took you aboard, he would then go out of his way to help you find further passage.

From these drivers I also eventually learned to go directly to lorry loading stations and to inquire at their offices whether anyone was loading up and about to leave for my destination. If the expediters were not busy, they were more often than not willing to make the necessary arrangements. On several occasions when their loading station could not accommodate me, they even phoned others and had someone take me there to make certain that I would not get lost.

I would then have a chance to study my driver before I even approached him personally, and by the time I actually entered his lorry, half a dozen people knew that I would be riding with him, so I was quite sure that I would be perfectly safe.

The more I learned about the ways and means of this far more interesting and adventurous mode of travel, the more completely I shook off what had at first been a most tedious dependence on bus schedules. I experienced my first heady surge of freedom.

I crossed the English Channel and began to travel with lorry drivers whose routes traversed all of Europe. For several months I roamed around the Continent in this fashion, eventually drifting further and further south as the weather turned cold. By the end of November, I had reached Greece.

In Athens I read an American newspaper for the first time in several months. I found that I would have to alter my tentative plans to continue overland through Turkey and Iran, en route to India. The year was 1978 and political relations with Iran had become unstable. A week or two later, they deteriorated completely.

By this time I had already learned to roll with the punches when plans went awry. I made my decision to continue yet further southward. I obtained a cheap night flight to Cairo and my African adventure began.

Once in Africa I drifted further and further south until I had reached Khartoum, the capital of Sudan. There, entirely by chance, I learned about the custom of female genital excision, which is still performed on small girls and adolescents in the greater part of Africa. I discovered that Islamic Sudan was the most tenaciously defended stronghold of this strange custom. A particularly extreme and damaging version of the procedure was ubiquitous there, even among the most highly educated class.

Appalled and fascinated at the same time, I began to gather information about the practice from anyone who was willing to speak to me about it. I quickly created for myself the role of itinerant American journalist. The only accoutrements needed to be convincing were a notebook and a readily poised pen, and in an African setting, these were potent charms indeed.

I traveled around the country by whatever means of transportation I could muster. Eventually, as I gained in experience, a true but heretofore unexpressed bent asserted itself, and my studies in the unique field of anthropological sexology were born.

After six months of all-consuming, intensive study I returned to Athens. I traversed the entire length of Europe via lorry once more, as far as the Arctic Circle. In the solitude of a Norwegian fishing village, I wrote my first article.

Later, in Stockholm, I showed what I had written to a Swedish woman with whom I had formed a friendship. She telephoned the newspapers, asked for an editor interested in Third World women's affairs, and arranged for an interview the next day. My story appeared in *Svenska Dagbladet*, the country's largest newspaper, a week later.

This set the pattern for me. I spent the next several months hitchhiking from one major European city to the next, calling up newspapers as soon as I arrived in order to find a vehicle for my story. The editors with whom I spoke were likely to be helpful in a number of ways. If an editor's newspaper was unwilling to handle my story because of its unconventional nature, I was generally passed on to an editor in the service of a publication where my chances were better. In this way the article eventually found its way into print and I thereby succeeded in publishing my material in five West European countries.

Sometime in the course of the day, while these arrangements were being negotiated, someone invariably asked me where I could be reached by telephone. I would answer candidly that I had not yet found accommodations and was seeking a place to stay. Because of the humanitarian overtones of my involvement, and no doubt also because my highly unusual lifestyle appealed to their imaginations, they would then get me in touch with a women's commune or bookstore, and lodgings were swiftly found for me. Sometimes they themselves simply took me home. I eventually became so proficient at finding free transportation and shelter that over a period of years I had to resort to the conventions of ordinary travel and lodging only when I once more reached the United States.

When my sabbatical was over and the new school year was about to begin, I reluctantly headed back to New York to resume my old job. I planned to teach for another year, only long enough to finance another journey to Sudan. Although I had known that readjustment to my old work routine would be difficult, the actual shock of reentry exceeded all my apprehensions. Having led a splendidly free gypsy life for a full year, I had totally outgrown the straitjacket of the school's farcically self-defeating routine. Every successive day back in the odiousness of its system only increased my torment.

By the time eight months of the school year had passed, I was once more in a state of deep depression. Other residual effects of my skull fracture had by then become so acute that I realized I was becoming unable to function much more than minimally in my work. I resigned my job, accepted my minuscule pension, breathed a vast, ecstatic sigh of relief, and walked out of the school forever, utterly free.

Over the next three years I continued to travel as before. During this interval, I returned to Sudan twice more for two additional six-month periods of solitary field research. My powers of observation and reasoning sharpened, my line of questioning grew more incisive and direct, my journeys from Khartoum into the interior became progressively more daring and prolonged.

I have been asked what drove me ever back to Sudan, when I well knew after my first experiences there what hardship awaited me. I can only answer that I was a woman possessed. The plight of the women and children whose lives touched mine and whom I studied and wrote about would not let me go.

As far as the hardship was concerned, I grew to love the personal challenge it presented. The closer I pushed myself to the everyday endurance level of the native Sudanese, the prouder and more accomplished I felt. I gloried in cleansing myself of all the decadence of Western civilization.

After my third and final journey to Sudan, I felt that I had learned most of what I had set out to learn. I spent the next 14 months in Kenya, searching out some final bits of information. At this time, I became deeply engrossed in writing about my experiences. On Lamu, a small island near the port of Mombassa, I completed the initial draft of my first book, *Prisoners of Ritual*. Its contents are best described as the observations of a deeply enthralled and driven amateur ethnologist. The subject of the book was my Sudanese odyssey, and it gave a detailed and painstaking account of a taboo practice hitherto only glancingly explored.

Eventually, on Lamu, I became increasingly aware of what one of my friends in Europe had astutely observed to be my inexorably growing hunger to once more have my own key to my own door. I realized that the time had come for me to return home and to seek some kind of permanence. I flew back to the United States, swiftly relocated out West, and started a new life.

When *Prisoners of Ritual* was published, the Decade of the Child was just starting. By then I had begun to lecture to various scientific and humanist societies about what I had found in Africa and written about in my book.

I encountered a great deal of curiosity about the personal aspects of my odyssey through Sudan. What had suddenly precipitated me, as a middle-aged woman, into such a highly unusual undertaking? What exceptional factors in my background had set the stage for my fascination with this subject, and given me the tenacity to explore it to the extent that I had? How had I dealt with the hardships of my journey and its dangers? What had been my most exciting adventures? And, most of all: Had I not been afraid?

It was of course inevitable, in attempting to answer these questions not only for those who asked them, but for myself as well, that fate should lead me gently into the fulfillment of yet another destiny. I found myself evolving into a storyteller. Eventually the outlines for *A Woman's Odyssey into Africa* began to take shape.

In every storyteller's mind, there adhere indelibly some of the images encountered in the work of other weavers of tales. Among such images, it is these that have precipitated most clearly in mine:

- The multitudes of blameless lunatics and near lunatics that wander about in Kurt Vonnegut's pages, clinging precariously to a tenuous survival in the face of a colossal and implacable cosmic lunacy.

- Bernard Malamud's Matchmaker and the young rabbi who approaches him, seeking salvation from his bleakly unfeeling and empty existence. The matchmaker shows him pictures of variously unsuitable women, all of whom the rabbi declines to meet. He accidentally drops the photo of an angelically lovely young girl, which he tries to hide from the rabbi. The younger man is instantly smitten and importunes him to arrange a meeting. After many refusals and subterfuges the Matchmaker reluctantly agrees. The girl who waits at the designated street corner is none other than the desperate Matchmaker's own fallen, estranged and innocent daughter. As the rabbi rushes forward, clutching a bouquet of flowers, the Matchmaker, hiding in an alley, silently breathes the Prayer for the Dead.

- And, most haunting of all, Karen Blixen's tale: The Great Diva Who Has Lost Her Voice wanders about the world in self-imposed exile. In her wanderings she is overtaken by darkness in some mountain region. She seeks shelter in a hut, the abode of a very ancient man, who is obsessed by a soul-wrenching horror. He shares his simple meal with her and relates his terrible history. At some time during his youth he had become marooned, and fearing death from starvation, he ate the flesh of his already dead friend's hand. The Diva lies down on the old man's bed with him, offering her breast and a mother's forgiveness, restoring him to humanity.

As a storyteller now in my own right, it is my hope to convey to the reader, and most particularly to women of my generation who have failed to realize their own potential, that even a life of quiet desperation is not beyond redemption. It does not matter at what late stage one finds the empowerment to change it.

Change starts with reassessment of the distortions in self-image one has been programmed to accept. It starts with an inner rebellion, a realization that something has been amiss and a desire to set it right, if only to leave a better heritage for one's children. And then, most important of all, it begins with one single, wild, breathless moment, where one picks up an unaccustomed load and steps off into the unknown. . .

The Flight from Egypt

My solitary journey had begun early in September. By the time I reached Egypt three months later, I feared that I would die of loneliness. I began to fall prey to an almost palpable anxiety which threatened to paralyze my very breath.

The strangeness of Cairo's teeming squalor served only to increase my sense of desolation. The wretched hostel where I found lodging proved also to be a den of thieves where strangers were robbed routinely.

I was warned by a young Dutch traveler that the crowded bus en route to the pyramids at Giza was famous for its pickpockets. I distributed my valuables under my clothes and clamped my small pack securely under my arm. Pressed tightly against sweating bodies in the packed, fume-spewing bus, I believed myself to imagine that hands were delicately exploring my body. When the bus arrived at its destination, four European travelers discovered that they had been stripped of their wallets and other valuables. From me the thieves had gleaned only an empty eyeglass case and some blank slips of paper that their touch must have deceived them into believing were bank notes.

The hostel, when I returned to it after a day of scrambling around the pyramids, was in a state of extreme agitation. A three-story brick building some 200 feet behind it had collapsed without warning, as though struck by lightning. Travelers were assured that there had been no casualties since it had happened during the day and no one had been in the building at that time, but I failed to believe this. Through the cloudy, barred window of my dormitory room I could see a number of distraught people picking forlornly through the rubble, and could not help but wonder bleakly what they were searching for.

I sought out a small, dank hotel near a mosque in the hopes of feeling safer there. The proprietor had a kind face and his wife smiled at me shyly as she picked up my pack and carried it to a dark, grimy room. Speaking no English, she pantomimed that she would wash my laundry and assign the task of watching it while it dried to her two daughters, so that no thieves could steal it. When I requested tea, one of the little girls brought it to me on a tray, stealing shy but curious glances at me from under her eyelashes. I knew that I would be safe with these people.

Five times a day, the loudspeakers of uncountable mosques all over the city competed vociferously with one another, calling the faithful to prayer. At sunrise the amplifiers in the turret of the mosque next to my hotel insisted on obeisance from the followers of Allah at such tremendous volume that it catapulted me out of a dream-laden sleep and nearly deafened me. As I lurched into the hall to the water faucets, I passed the hotel sweeper, lost ecstatically in prayer on his shabby mat.

I found a group of young Europeans with whom to safely wander the teeming streets at night. We scoured the narrow alleyways in search of diversion. The music of a distant festivity beckoned, and we followed it until we came to a canopy strung across an alleyway between two rickety buildings. A wedding was in progress. As soon as we approached, we were eagerly surrounded by some of the guests and led to greet the bridal pair.

The groom wore an obviously vintage, ill-fitting suit of the kind fashionable in America in the 1940s. Expressions of determination and uncertainty alternated on his sallow, nervous face. The bride was dressed in traditional Egyptian garb. She had blotchy skin and did not look at all healthy. The knuckles of her work-worn hands were stiff and swollen.

I looked at her and at her sweating groom and had a premonition that she would not have an easy time of it with him. On an impulse, I took off a gold band which had been my wedding ring and gave it to her as a gift. Although I knew that she would not be able to understand the words, I softly said in English, "May you have better luck with it than I have had."

One of my companions, an American government clerk who had just been evacuated out of Iran and was going on an overland journey to Kenya before returning home, shook her head incredulously. "How can you give away your gold?" she asked in disbelief. I had divested myself of nearly all my valuables before leaving. Jewelry carried on a journey such as mine only mocked the poor and sent out invitations to thieves. "I have no need for that ring any longer," I shrugged, "and I have nothing else to give the bride." "Why give her anything at all?" she scowled. It wasn't worth the effort to explain it to her. I let the matter drop.

A festively emblazoned belly dancer of somewhat advanced years mounted the podium on which the bridal pair was sitting and began to rotate her enormous belly sensuously and with great skill. There was much clapping and ululation by the women, while the faces of the men darkened with lust.

The ceremonies progressed, the wedding contract was signed and witnessed. When the moment came to exchange the rings that finalized the marriage, there was a terrible moment of panic. The groom could not force his golden band over his bride's badly swollen knuckle. For fully five minutes he struggled to wrestle it onto her finger. Sweat ran in torrents from both of their faces while they gibbered accusingly at one another. Hysterical relatives wrung their hands and shrilly screamed advice. Finally, lubricated by the greasy sweat of fear, the knuckle yielded and the ring slipped into place.

Tension eased immediately from everyone's face and the festivities continued. I saw that the bride was secretly cradling her abused hand, but her face revealed only relief and satisfaction. The belly dancer resumed her undulations and women came down the stairs from one of the buildings with large trays of food.

An almond-eyed, barely pubescent girl had been edging toward me timidly and finally seemed to gather the necessary courage to pluck my sleeve. I smiled, and with shy pride she showed me that she too knew the movements of the dance. The last time someone had danced for me, it had been my own Stephanie, my child, my heart of hearts. For a moment, I felt my eyes cloud with unshed tears. Then I reached up and touched the little dancer's face endearingly. Emboldened, she took my hand and pulled me along the stairs to the second floor. She showed me two tiny, barred rooms and a windowless kitchen, indicating that this was her home. She pointed to her festively dressed mother who squatted on the kitchen floor, loading trays with food for the wedding downstairs.

I noted that men were periodically coming and going along the stairs, continuing on to a floor above. At first I did not pay a great deal of attention until I saw a man beckon to me enticingly. I shook my head, but he beckoned urgently once more. When I turned away, he shrugged and disappeared up the stairs. Within five minutes he came back down, an unmistakable look of satiation on his face. When he saw me looking at him, he grinned foolishly, spread his hands, shrugged once more, and went back to the wedding. Another man appeared. He too tried to induce me to follow him up the stairs. Again I shook my head, and he in turn disappeared into the darkness above. After four minutes he also returned, only to be followed by yet another man.

By this time I had figured it out. Whatever was to be found on the third floor was obviously one of the amenities of the wedding, and whatever it was I failed to cooperate in, was taken care of there.

I tired quickly of the noise, filth, and brutality of Cairo. I tired of men who tried to entice me into their hotel rooms on any foolish pretext whatsoever. The lure was generally an exchange of money, and the rates they promised were ludicrously favorable even on the black market. These transactions had to take place in secrecy, they would whisper, and their hotel room was always available and conveniently nearby. Most of all, I tired of the arrogant conviction which all of these men seemed to share, that women were by nature so greedy and gullible that they could not fail but succumb to such a temptation for easy gain.

From a bus I saw a man beating a donkey that had fallen from exhaustion. Enraged, he was aiming his heavy club with great deliberation at the emaciated joints of the dying beast. I shrieked at him wildly as the bus careened by and fought to reach the door, but to no avail. Donkeys all over the city were flogged without mercy, as they mindlessly struggled to pull weighted-down carts, harnesses dragging across bare flesh where their hide had been chafed away. Soon I could stand it no longer and fled once more southward, up the Nile to Aswan, close to the Sudanese border.

In Aswan the faces were darker, softer, and more open. I found lodging at a small inn in the native quarter, and felt secure there. The Nile rolled by majestically a short distance away, and I sat on its shores for long healing hours, watching the water birds as fleet *falukas* sailed swiftly by.

I avoided the tourist hotels that were reputed to exist some miles downriver. Occasional adventuresome Westerners from that other world ventured only briefly into the quarter. A trickle of backpackers from all over the globe came and went daily. They caused little stir and blended easily into the landscape. In the alleyways and markets of the town I began to experience a different pulsation, and I realized that what I was feeling was the slow, patient heartbeat of Africa.

It was not long before this tranquility began to mock me. Finding no meaning to my life and driven by inconceivable loneliness, I fled yet further south on the riverboat that traveled along the Nile to the Sudanese border.

This boat consisted of four ancient barges lashed together and filled to overflowing with human freight and with animals trussed for transport. It wended its slow and dreamy way through Lake Nasser and along a narrowed Nile, whose built-up, dune-like shores had been rendered lifeless and barren by the massive Aswan Dam downstream. The fertile Nile valley had disappeared. Empty sand dunes bare of all traces of vegetation loomed on both shores for mile after hopeless mile and day after tedious day. Horrified, I stared in numb disbelief. My precipitous, haphazard journey in search of meaning had become a descent into hell.

At the end of four days, the barges docked at Wadi Halfa on the Sudanese border. By this time the entire boat was rank with ordure, and as we were being herded like cattle down the gangway, a clean up crew was already at work spraying DDT over its every surface.

As our papers were being checked at gunpoint by uniformed officials, all African aliens entering the country were separated and forced to take yellow fever shots. All of these injections were administered by the same enormous, death-dealing hypodermic needle. The needle was returned after each use to a glass half filled with some liquid that I presumed had at one time been disinfectant, but which had long since become ominously viscous, gray and opaque.

Mercifully, I discovered, all Western passengers were exempt. I had my certification that I had received a yellow fever injection before leaving the United States some months before, but there was no guarantee that any of the officials at this border station would be able to read it.

Some hundred yards away in the totally barren desert a single railroad track stretched off into the distance, and perhaps a quarter of a mile further, the train that would take us to Khartoum stood waiting. Passengers were hastening toward it, and I too panted forward as fast as I was able. When I reached it I clambered hurriedly aboard.

Garden

In the desert
Where the train stops
There is a circle of stones.

Within this circle of stones
There stands a small plant
With five leaves.

That is the only living green
For hundreds of miles around.

* * * *

One of the most profound communications I have ever experienced with another human being took place on the journey from Wadi Halfa to Khartoum. The ancient, rickety train plods its ramrod course through the desert along a single track of rails laid down under British rule during the time of colonial occupation. Scorching winds whip the desert dust under a broiling and merciless sun.

The terrain that stretches for a distance of some hundreds of miles is totally featureless. An unbroken, desolately flat 360° horizon without end numbs the incredulous eye. There are no trees, no shrubs, no grass, no living creatures anywhere. There is no bird song. There are not even insects, except for the flies that the train itself carries with it. These separate groggily from piles of human ordure mounting in the stinking latrines and try to cling to nose, mouth, and eyes in their frantic search for moisture.

There are no boulders, rocks, or stones—only wind-driven, swirling dust. The desolation, monotony, and emptiness of this desert defy all comprehension, all imagination. The mind of the traveler wrestles vainly with the construct that it still finds itself on earth, not on some alien nightmare planet.

I had been told at the outset that the journey from Wadi Halfa to Khartoum would take 22 hours. It does not take long to realize that all schedules are meaningless formalities in Sudan. Again and again the locomotive labors, wheezes, and then comes to a hopeless halt. The train sits motionless for long hours under a seemingly vindictive sun, waiting for the repair car to arrive. Metal blisters the skin that touches it, time stretches on meaninglessly, the mind wanders into a different reality.

Sometimes the train sits on a siding at a tiny desert stop where two starkly barren mud huts and several earthen jugs partially filled with water stand all alone along the side of the track. It waits interminable hours for the train coming from the opposite direction to arrive so that it may resume its plodding journey along the single track.

When this other train finally arrives everyone spills out of the compartments, and for a number of minutes there is a carnival atmosphere while the passengers of both trains joyously greet and embrace one another and relay messages to heaven only knows what remote outposts. Then the locomotive starts up, we cautiously ease off the siding, and continue ponderously onward through the vacuum of desert ahead.

Night falls and a harsh, freezing cold descends. In the packed compartments people grasp at elusive snatches of sleep. There are bodies crouching on and between the sagging seats, wedged tightly under them, spilling precariously out of the impossibly tiny baggage racks. In the scanty aisles outside the compartments yet more sleeping bodies are wedged, crouching and stretched out, their heads wrapped tightly against the dust swirling along the ground, looking like so many mummies.

The nature of reality begins to alter in my mind. I find myself slipping into a reality that I recognize from an earlier experience. It is fully valid, but altogether outside the realm of everyday perception as I have come to know it. The past experience is the birth of my son.

The two of us labored unsuccessfully to separate from one another, without the help of analgesic, for nearly three days, and we both came very close to death. At some point during that time I found my incorporeal self exteriorized calmly somewhere near the ceiling of the room, gazing down on the writhing body beneath me and feeling great compassion for it. In that reality I contemplated not myself, but an unrelated being lying below me.

During my voyage through the desert, I crouched painfully for several days in the narrow aisle next to a village woman. We slept, as much as we were able, leaning against one another's bodies for warmth in the night after the train had lost its daytime heat to the desert frost. She had enormous, suffering, courageous eyes, and wide tribal markings of a finger's width had been gouged deeply into her cheeks. The English colonials called this particular config-uration, common throughout Northern Sudan, the "one-eleven scar" because it consists of three straight vertical cuts extending from the lower lid to the chin line.

Our journey stretched on into four or five days, and during this time we told one another about our respective lives. I did not speak her dialect and she knew not one word of English, but we confided many things to one another in that different reality, and we felt as close as if we had been sisters. We communicated by means of gestures and facial expressions and tonal inflections, with which we revealed our deepest feelings to each other.

Sometimes we merely looked into one another's eyes and experi-enced another type of communication that exists only in very trun-cated form here in our everyday Western reality. In the West we tend to avoid one another's eyes, perhaps fearing what we will re-veal with ours and what we will find or fail to find in the ones we probe.

In Sudan, the eyes in every face I saw were to meet and hold mine. For the first time in my life, I experienced the heady freedom of being allowed to gaze into a face and search a soul to my heart's content, as it was also searching mine. I felt a sense of trust and security such as I had never known before. My eyes became my credentials and their eyes my passport to safety.

No words enable me to relate what was said to me by the eyes of my Sudanese sister, because I would now have to speak in a differ-ent language from the one I then employed. Our shared reality was such that words were of no significance. I can only recount that we were able to understand what the other had suffered, the joys she had known, the intensity of her love for her children and what she

had learned from life. By some means, which I no longer comprehend in my present, everyday reality, we told one another all of
those things. I do recall quite clearly that there was an intense feeling of love between us, such as exists between women who are truly
of one soul.

When we parted, we each placed our right hand over the left
breast of the other, felt one another's heartbeat, and touched cheeks
in the way that women express kinship for each other in Sudan. We
gazed deeply into one another's eyes for one last time and went our
separate ways. Our paths never crossed again.

A Sudanese Proverb:
When Allah Created Sudan,
Allah Laughed

In April of 1989 *The Wall Street Journal* carried a front page article announcing that Khartoum had just been declared the number one hardship post in the world. While this saddened me, I was hardly surprised by such a statement. I had spent enough months in Khartoum to be acutely sensitive to the relative luxury in which Westerners lived there when one considered the plight of the Sudanese by comparison. I had bridled at the ill grace with which they angrily tolerated what they felt to be an affront to what they deserved in life, while the gently smiling Sudanese gracefully endured their own impossibly difficult lives with serenity and an imperturbable patience. For most Westerners, living in Khartoum was a constant nightmare, for to them everything untoward that happened assumed the dimensions of a disaster that had been directed at them personally.

It is small wonder that tourists do not often venture into Khartoum. Anyone without a strongly defined sense of purpose will find little to do there, nothing to see, nowhere to go. Airline schedules are meaningless, mail never arrives, gasoline is unobtainable. The most ordinary amenities that have always been taken for granted are totally absent. Intense heat fries the brain and saps the body of all energy. Incessant stinging, wind-driven dust from the desert clogs the lungs. The monotonously stark ugliness of the streets affronts the senses. The stink of feces is everywhere.

Nothing works. Everything mechanical breaks down and remains broken down, because there is no one there who can fix it. Potholes in the totally unpaved roads may be large enough to swallow a small car. Dead donkeys and camels rot in the street. There are daily interminate power failures.

A cumbersome, nonfunctional bureaucracy clogs all initiative. Bored government officials, their desks embellished with telephones that have not worked in years, lacking even paper to shuffle about, chat idly and consult their nonfunctioning watches to see whether it is time for the next tea break.

Heaven help those who become sick. Nothing else will. The university hospital is surely the seventh canto of hell. There is no bed linen in the teeming, filth-clogged wards and like as not no sterile cotton, no adhesive tape, no disinfectant, no analgesic, no penicillin, no hope for ever leaving there alive. Operating theaters are regularly closed down with infestations of tetanus. The lights go off in the middle of operations, which must then be continued under the feeble beam of flashlights with dying batteries. Only muddy, undrinkable water comes from the taps — and all too often none at all.

To the culture-shocked Westerner, Khartoum is truly hell on earth.

With predictable regularity, the thin ranks of Americans and Europeans who are compensated with maximum hardship pay for serving in this nightmare capital are thinned out yet further when its members go quietly and sometimes not so quietly mad. Some who have been assigned to Khartoum have been known to never even leave the ramshackle airport. They simply take one look and catch the first flight that leaves the country, escaping to *any* place it happens to be bound for.

Among those who remain, there is also a handful of strong and courageous souls, not at all abashed by this hardship. They seem rather to court it and to thrive on sometimes considerable deprivation. They love the gentle warmth of the Sudanese. They are moved by their beauty of spirit, their incredible generosity, the depth of inner goodness evident in their limpid, soulful eyes.

It is a mindset that cannot be forcibly created. It stems from an inner, highly individual motivation and it can only be cultivated and strengthened where its germs already exist. These "Africa Freaks" are a different breed altogether. They return to the Western world only with the greatest reluctance, and when they do, suffer massive culture shock upon reentry. I quickly and eagerly join their ranks.

*　*　*　*

In the fierce heat of early afternoon the train from Wadi Halfa finally wheezed into Khartoum. Reeling and half mad with sleep deprivation I staggered along the tracks under what had become an unbearably heavy pack toward the hostel reputed to lie nearby. Two or three other packers were hastening groggily in the same direction, and I struggled to keep up with them.

The hostel consisted of a large fenced yard of mostly bare ground, two trees, a few anemic shrubs, some dripping faucets surrounded by small patches of grass and a box-like concrete structure containing dormitories for men and for women. I took one look at the stained, ominously sagging cots crammed into the debris-littered women's quarters and quickly opted for the lawn outside. I found a sparse shady spot under one of the trees, lay down on the hard, baked ground, and fell instantaneously and stuporously asleep.

By the time I awoke, it was dark. I was comforted to find that I had been joined under the tree by another woman who had spread her modest mat and sparse belongings near me. She was older by a good number of years than I, and looked as if she had done some far and hard traveling. It was the first time in the five months that I had been on the road that I had seen anyone older than myself who had chosen to journey in this fashion and I was instantly intrigued.

When she saw that I was awake, she smiled and offered me a piece of bread. She was a doctor from the Albert Schweitzer Institute in Gabon. She had journeyed overland on the top of lorry freight all the way from the equator in West Africa to Cairo on the Mediterranean Sea in order to learn the techniques for making papyrus at the Papyrus Institute located there. She planned to take her newly acquired skill back to the leper colony in Gabon in order to pass it on to the lepers, so that they might support themselves with it.

She had worked with Albert Schweitzer when he was still alive and spoke of him with great veneration. The insight and wisdom of the native medicine men in Gabon also had impressed her deeply on the many occasions she had had to observe their unique healing techniques. They knew many things, she said, of which Western medicine had no conception. There was much that could be learned from them.

She continued her journey back to Gabon the next morning and a handful of new voyagers arrived at the hostel. Among this extremely youthful group was an American black man in his late thirties who, it turned out, had traveled extensively in Africa before. Ravenous for information on how I myself might proceed, I engaged him in conversation.

He was on his way to the jungles of Zaire in hopes of collecting masks and other art objects. Sudan was not to his liking, he said, shaking his head sadly. It was brutal what they did to women there. I looked at him questioningly.

"Oh, don't you know about it?" he asked. "You must understand that I have been intimate with quite a considerable number of women here, and that it has been done to all of them. They raze off their sex organs when they are little girls, and then sew shut what is left. It's really pretty terrible."

I stared at him, horror-struck. "But surely this is still done only by the most primitive tribes, out in the bush?" I pleaded in numb disbelief. He shook his head emphatically. "It is done by everyone," he insisted. "Even educated people do it. Of course, no one will speak to you about it. They will all deny that it is true, but I warrant that there is hardly a woman to be found in this city that has not been dealt with in this way. They call it 'Pharaonic circumcision' and they do it to keep their women chaste."

I regarded him sardonically. "Obviously, it does not always work," I remarked. "Women are women," he shrugged, "just as men are men. You cannot change the natural order of things."

I became aware that the workings of my mind, reeling under the frightful information that had just been thrust upon it, were separating into two remarkably distinct levels. One part entertained in numb horror the full implications of what the American had just told me. The other part excitedly recognized with great clarity that I had found what I had been questing for; an instantaneous, crystal clear sense of purpose; a drivingly urgent narrowing down to focus; a task to which I knew I might well dedicate what remained of my lifetime.

It did not take me long to discount the American's warning that no one would speak to me about this strange and terrible custom. He failed to foresee that I possessed an enormous advantage: I was a woman. While this subject was beyond discussion with a Western man, even by those Sudanese women he had slept with, no such taboo existed in relation to me.

The first educated man that I was able to approach some days later for help in learning more about the subject, wrote out letters of introduction for me that would begin the chain of open doors that I would eventually find and enter all over the country. I began to interview women and men in all walks of life throughout Sudan, carefully piecing together, bit by bit, the fragments of a hidden picture that had never before been revealed so clearly to anyone from an alien culture.

Costi

I sojourned briefly under my meager tree in the hostel. It was only on subsequent journeys to Sudan, many months later, that I was to discover the early morning luxury of the deserted winter pool at the somewhat shopworn Khartoum American Club, as well as the cool oasis of the Hilton Hotel lobby that I was to claim eventually as my "personal office." But more of that later.

The hostel had little charm and did not invite lengthy stopovers. Most travelers stayed only long enough to make arrangements for permits and transport to someplace else, a process that was often dragged out by a sluggish bureaucracy into many tedious days and sometimes weeks.

I had heard that by far the most exciting but also arduous journey was made by steamer up the Nile. This boat wended its slow way to Juba, which lies close to the border of Uganda. It was said to depart every two weeks from Costi, a reputed day's travel from Khartoum by train.

This twelve-day journey, I was told, was not without considerable risk of contracting one of many possible serious diseases. Travelers could even be overtaken by death along the way. When the boat made its stops at riverside villages in the depths of the interior, it was not unusual to leave behind for burial the bodies of its dead. Yet those few Westerners who had made the journey spoke of it with awe. It had been by far the most unforgettable experience of their lives.

I bought a rail ticket to Costi, which lies some distance to the south of Khartoum along the Nile. As might well have been expected, the train once again broke down repeatedly. The projected day's journey dragged on into a second and finally a third day.

Each evening before nightfall, I wandered about the train, exploring different compartments. In one of them, a feverish woman lay nearly stuporous in the arms of her sister. The sister indicated that the woman's head was causing her great pain. She pleaded with me for medicine that would lessen her suffering. I told her that I was not a doctor, but that I could give her some aspirin that I carried with me. I poured out water for her from my canteen and watched as she gently coaxed her sister to swallow the pills.

The next morning, as the train was about to pull into Costi, I decided to visit the compartment once more, hoping to find that the sick woman's condition had improved. I was shocked to find that a long line of people had formed outside in the narrow hall, all waiting for the *dictori* to make her appearance.

As I tried to push my way toward the compartment, children were held up to me; patches of skin were bared to reveal abscesses, hands clutched at different parts of anatomies to show where the pain lay. I tried to communicate that I was not a dictori as they believed me to be, but to no avail. I fled into the compartment and found that the feverish woman, as might have been expected, was no better.

My "patients" remained waiting stoically in the aisle outside, and when I reluctantly emerged from the compartment, the scene that had taken place before was repeated. I wanted desperately to be their dictori and heal all of their ills, but I had no power or means to do so. In desperation I tried once more to convey this to them, and failing to do so, fled in despair.

In Costi I found a small group of European backpackers squatting on the ground near the station. They too were in search of lodging and I hastened to join them. We found an inn near the main market in which cots were set up in rows along a shaded courtyard. Most of its patrons were Islamic men who lost themselves fervently in prayer whenever the call rang insistently from loudspeakers of the many mosques. They seemed to find little else to do as they awaited the arrival of the boat from Juba and spent the rest of the day sitting quietly on their cots. I was quartered along with other women in a barred dormitory room that lay at the inner end of the courtyard.

Costi was hot, dank, fly-ridden and rank with putrefaction. Still, there was something about it that arrested the imagination. It was an altogether different Africa from the one that I had experienced so far. Here the darkest, most hidden mysteries of the Nile beckoned seductively. I wandered over to its waters and watched, concealed, as naked, half-submerged tribesmen washed their splendid, black-gleaming bodies in its waves. Unfamiliar vegetation grew lushly along its bank and bright water birds dodged and bobbed along its muddy edge.

Among the beggars in the marketplace there were many lepers. Other supplicants were in advanced stages of crippling and frighteningly deforming diseases such as I had never seen before. Blindness seemed to be endemic.

The boat to Juba lay docked some distance away, awaiting departure four days hence. Its dented, peeling sides and filth-encrusted decks reeked with rot. I viewed the prospect of boarding it with growing trepidation, achingly weighing in my mind the siren's powerful lure of adventure against an equally strong fear of lurking, unknown dangers.

On my second day in Costi I began to feel a growing malaise and within hours succumbed to the heavy lethargy of a fever. My head throbbed as if it would burst, my body raged with thirst, and I could do no more than lie panting on my cot in the fetid, steamy dormitory room. Two kindly Syrian women with soft, petal-like hands brought me water to drink and helped me lurch, weak-kneed, to the latrine.

After two days the Syrians suddenly disappeared. By this time my life-saving antibiotics had taken hold and I was weakly testing my rubbery legs around the courtyard. I asked the innkeeper what had happened to the women. "I turned them over to the police. They were prostitutes," he answered sternly. I tried to question him further, but he would tell me no more.

Greatly troubled, I asked two young Australians in the courtyard if they could find out anything about the fate of the two women. They were packing their gear in preparation for leaving on the boat but left their task to go asking around the inn. They returned, saying that they too could get no answers.

I found myself too weak to search further. At that point I came to the heart-wrenching decision that self-preservation must become the better part of valor. I had to return to Khartoum where at least some form of rudimentary medical care would be available. The innkeeper found a man with a donkey cart who transported both me and my pack to the station and I lay waiting along the tracks for the train to arrive, sorely dreading the long ride back.

The train, scheduled to arrive at noon, rolled in reluctantly at sundown. I feebly pulled myself together to search for a compartment. Luck was with me. At the first door I opened, seven young, fresh female faces turned toward me and bade me welcome. The women were students from Khartoum University on their way home from a field trip. Their chaperoning professor joined us a moment later and passed some minutes in polite conversation. Then he retreated to the greater comfort of an adjoining private compartment and left us alone.

Obviously aware that I was ill, the women coaxed me to lie down on one of the benches. Two of them shared the other bench, while the remaining five bedded down on the floor, three in the narrow aisle and two wedged under the seats. They fell asleep almost instantly, and I mercifully found the strength to smother my feelings of guilt over taking such shameless advantage of their easily proffered hospitality.

Miraculously, the train did not break down. I dozed during most of the day and by early evening was feeling well enough to answer some of their curious questions about myself. The freedom of my solitary travel frightened and intrigued them equally. They knew little about the lives of women in other lands. "I think that my own country is far kinder to its women," I said. All of them remained sadly silent, except for one, who looked steadfastly and courageously into my eyes. "Sudan is a bitterly hard country for women," she said. "Women suffer very cruelly here."

I felt that this was a woman whom I might ask the questions for which I had so burned to find answers, but just as I was about to ask them, the professor entered and told us that we would arrive in Khartoum within the hour. By the time he left us alone, weariness had overcome me once more and the opportunity was gone.

When the train pulled into the station I thanked the women for their kindness, we bade one another farewell, and I somehow managed to stagger back to the hostel where I lay weakly under my tree for another two days, before I finally began to regain my strength and it became apparent that I would be all right.

Two years after this abortive adventure, I was joined in my solitary early morning swims by a middle-aged American woman who sat alone by the side of the pool at the American Club. She spent most of her day tensely sitting there, evidently knowing nothing else to do. She was waiting for the return of her husband, who had taken the boat from Costi to Juba. She herself felt absolutely no inclination toward adventure, and the Khartoum American Club already stretched to the utmost her tolerance for primitive conditions. She was a soft-spoken, rather timid woman with an air of quiet desperation which was to grow more and more intense over the months.

By the time I was ready to leave once more for Europe, she was desperate. She had waited for more than five months, her visa was about to expire, and she had had no news of her husband.

I have little doubt that she never saw him again.

The Barbaric Practice

British colonials referred to it as "The Barbaric Practice" and fought against it with great moral fervor, and unfortunately at that time, little understanding. As might have been expected, no tangible good came of their effort. People all over the world have their own individual, culturally ingrained customs and the righteous indignation of foreign rulers, as history has shown, generally does not suffice to shake them loose, no matter how humanitarian its intent. In the case of Sudan, the only demonstrable result of the honest efforts of British reformers was insurrection among the populace.

In 1956 Sudan, like other African nations in that momentous decade, fought free of colonial domination and regained political sovereignty. Its newly formed government formulated a body of Sudanese laws, and among these was an edict to end this tenaciously defended, culturally embedded practice which had so disturbed the British. This law, however, proved to be no more enforceable than the one that had been imposed under colonial rule.

Just when, where, or how the custom had its beginning is unknown. Few clues have been uncovered that tell us much about the history of the "Dark Continent" in areas where no ancient written records exist. There is mention of the practice in the writings of the Greek historian Herodotus as early as the fifth century B.C., and from this we know that it in fact arose somewhere in the depths of antiquity. Beyond this record, nothing else is certain about its earliest origins.

There is some reference in the writings of the Prophet Mohammed, whose teachings formed the basis for the Islamic religion in the seventh century A.D., which indicates that he may have attempted to ameliorate the performance of The Barbaric Practice. Even so immense a power as the Prophet's word brought about no change. Custom in Africa is stronger than domination, stronger than law, stronger even than religion. Over the years customary practices have been incorporated into religion, and ultimately have come to be believed by their practitioners to be demanded by their adopted gods, whoever they may be. This has happened in various parts of Africa among essentially animistic converts to Islam, Christianity, and Judaism.

There are numerous theories concerning the origins of the practice, and some of them have a certain charm. One of them argues, for example, for the validity of the Islamic legend that Hagar, Abraham's concubine and Ishmael's mother, was its very first victim, and that this gave rise to The Barbaric Practice when she perpetuated it later on her own daughters and granddaughters.

The argument does hold a certain merit when one considers the social milieu of Biblical times in the Nile Delta, a milieu which has not changed to any great extent in places like Sudan or even Egypt, where the institutionalization of the patriarchal family continues to be as powerful as ever. It is a system that divides women into classes of "respectable," which is to say, conforming, male-protected, chaste women; and "disreputable" or unprotected, low class and slave women.

In an age when virgin daughters were a valuable family asset, to be honorably sold only in an *unsullied* condition to the families of prospective bridegrooms, proof of their premarital virginity, and continuing married virtue became so important to women that it is quite likely that they resorted to any means, no matter how drastic, that would enable them to demonstrate it.

Throughout the centuries slavers, marauders, and bandits have roamed the Dark Continent. Only the protection of a male-defended family compound offered any kind of security from these predators to unarmed women and their children. "Respectable" women grasped eagerly at clearly visible symbols, such as the veil, to indicate their worthiness of this life-sustaining protection. These symbols distinguished their anxiously defended status from the feared and truly terrible lot of slaves, prostitutes, and outcasts, who were subject to unchallenged rape, abduction, and murder.

Would it be any wonder, under circumstances such as these, for a woman like Hagar, who had been elevated from slavehood to the relatively far more secure status of a concubine, to willingly submit to the sacrifice of her sexual organs as proof of her subservient respectability? And would it be any wonder that she would then subject her daughters to the same procedure to safeguard their virginity and enable them to offer living proof of their full deservingness?

But that is all within the realm of speculation. It does not really matter with whom The Barbaric Practice actually began. What matters is that female sexual mutilation is to this very day ubiquitous in the greater part of sub-Saharan and central Africa. The number of affected women has been variously estimated to be 30 million, 80 million, and over 100 million, and the relative accuracy of these figures is sometimes hotly debated. This always strikes me as being as pointless as arguments about the precise accuracy of statistics on the numbers of human beings destroyed in the Holocaust. A precise statistical accounting is not really the crucial issue. All that we need to know in either instance is that we are talking about the destruction or torture of *many millions* of human beings.

Pharaonic circumcision has not changed over the centuries and is generally performed in Sudan on little girls between the ages of 5 and 9. All of the external genitalia save the skin of the large labia are excised, and this is sewn together down to a minute opening, barely adequate for urination and menstruation.

The object of this mutilation is to dampen the girl's sexual drive by removing her most sexually sensitive parts. It is believed that this will cause her to remain chaste and thus safeguard the honor and integrity of the family. An indelible lesson is unquestionably reinforced upon her small and defenseless body almost beyond the reaches of our imagination by the pain of this generally unanesthetized procedure. Through it the little girl learns, by force and beyond all redemption, her role of total submission to the society. The sewn remnants of her labia form, in effect, an artificially created chastity belt whose intactness at marriage is guarantee to her bridegroom and his family that her virtue and the honor of his family are secure.

This incredibly bitter pill that these small girls are forced to swallow is generally sugarcoated by great festivities surrounding the day of circumcision. The child is the center of all attention and receives many desired and unaccustomed gifts. She has been told that she will be purified of a dangerous and unclean thing that is festering between her legs, and that when she has been made rid of it, she will be pure and sweet-smelling and pleasing to the man that is to be her husband. She is told that the day of circumcision is the most important day of her life, for it will ready her and make her worthy of marriage.

It is for this reason that little girls inevitably look forward to their circumcision with a mixture of eagerness and dread. What small child can resist the lure of presents heaped upon her, and what small child does not strive for the security of approval? What small child is not intimidated when she is told that her body harbors a repulsive and unneeded piece of flesh that is dangerous to everyone she loves, makes her stink, and will cause her future husband to reject and denounce her? And yet, what small child is not terrified to know that she will be cut, that she will bleed, that she will scream with pain as she has heard her predecessors scream?

When it happens, it happens swiftly. She is seized and held down by several women who pinion her arms and legs to the ground. The operation is generally performed by midwives under the direction of women elders who, if they have produced sons for their husbands and survived their own reproductive years, wield tremendous power over younger women in the family. Men are not involved in these practices at all, but little actual choice regarding their performance exists for women. An uncircumcised girl will simply not find a man who is willing to marry her, and a family that leaves its girls in what is considered to be a scandalously dishonorable condition is despised or even cast out by the community.

In a society where all women have been dealt with in this manner in early childhood, their condition is naturally regarded by them as nothing other than normal. The agonizing pain a woman must face when her bridegroom penetrates the wall of flesh that has been created to safeguard her virtue is perceived as entirely natural if she knows of nothing different.

The terrible births, in which dilation is made impossible by hardened scar tissue which endangers the lives of both the mother and her infant and which must be cut open and then resewn, are unquestioningly accepted as a woman's inescapable lot in life. It is a rare occurrence when even an educated woman questions her circumcision as being anything other than in the natural order of things, and this is hardly to be wondered at. One needs only to consider the lamentable fact that the United States of America is presently the only country in the world where routine nonreligious foreskin circumcisions are performed on the greater majority of all male neonates in its hospitals. While the magnitude and potential harm of this operation cannot be likened to the one performed on little girls in Sudan and other African countries, one cannot help but marvel at the fact that *no other* technologically advanced country on the planet any longer finds medical reason for performing these unquestionably painful operations. On the contrary, many medical authorities in other countries have spoken out quite forcefully against them, as for example those in Scandinavia.

Quite universally, medical opinion and popular custom agree in the rest of what we regard as the civilized world that these penile circumcisions are unwarranted, superfluous, and even dangerous. They are reluctantly performed in other countries only in rare, isolated cases where some sort of mitigating pathology exists. Yet *we* continue to routinely perform these procedures on our male infants, even in the face of opposition from some of our own highly respected medical authorities.

This strange custom of ours escapes all scrutiny by most of us. We regard circumcision of our newborns as being completely acceptable, exactly as female circumcision is regarded as being normal in Africa.

It might also be pointed out that as a society we have for some time accepted the dictum of medical authorities that the female reproductive organs are unnecessary to normal functioning of the human body once they have performed their primary purpose of bearing children. As a consequence, our country boasts the highest rate of hysterectomies performed anywhere in the world. Until very recently, surgeons have routinely excised perfectly healthy ovaries when a problematic uterus required surgical interference. Then it was belatedly discovered that such removal caused osteoporosis in women who had been subjected to it.

I must confess that my indignation at this particular routine procedure reflects an intensely personal bias. After this had been perpetrated upon me without my having been previously consulted, my own surgeon rather blithely stated "This is a procedure that we do to save you the possible later need for another operation."

I sincerely believe that this man did not bear me any malice, and that he thought that what he did was in my best interest. He was merely misguided. Nonetheless, I must live with the knowledge that I too have been needlessly sexually mutilated. My intense futile rage over this has been one of the demons driving me back to Africa again and again.

I must add here that if we were to carry our national passion for prophylactic sexual surgery to its absurd conclusion, we might also remove the breasts from all adolescent females to save them from the eventuality of contracting breast cancer later in life. Breasts are, after all, not necessary to the survival of the individual. And why stop at penile circumcision? Why not obtain sperm samples from all adolescent males, to be frozen for later use in artificial insemination? Then we can prophylactically remove their penises and thus protect them against the eventuality of contracting penile cancer in their later years.

Before we pass judgment on those who inflict the tortures of The Barbaric Practice in Africa, or on those who simply submit to them without rebellion we might do well to first examine our own cultural practices and our *own* barbarities.

Sex Education

When I was 14 years old and anxiety was battling with curiosity in my adolescent mind regarding the changes that were taking place in my pubescent body, I asked my parents a few tentative questions about sex. I got the customary runaround. My mother's answers featured resentful, mumbled evasion, my father's profoundly cynical or piously moralistic pronouncements made me feel depraved for having asked. Thus I learned from my progenitors only one thing, and that was to ask no further questions of them on this subject.

I tried my luck with the encyclopedia. It featured sterile diagrams of human anatomies, chastely labeled with words that I could not understand. At best it gave me some sort of rudimentary vocabulary, but no way of relating it to what was happening to my body or to my feelings.

Next I explored my father's medical books and journals. Although these did not answer most of the burning questions that beleaguered me, I found the pictures of naked bodies in them both fascinating and reassuring. Not only did they acquaint me with at least the rudiments of what a male organ looked like, (since I had never seen an adult one), but I discovered to my great relief that the strange changes that were taking place in my own organs were not the formation of some kind of abnormality or tumor, but this was what a normal adult female could expect to look like.

Beyond this I learned little since the language employed by these highly specialized publications was altogether outside of my limited scope. However, there was among them a small, somewhat more popularized journal published for doctors by a pharmaceutical company which carried information that I could sometimes understand and which was sometimes vaguely related to matters that interested me. I began to eagerly await its appearance on my father's desk each month, and always searched it from cover to cover.

Among the articles that I found in this booklet was one by Ashley Montagu, the noted anthropologist. It dealt with the history of male circumcision practices that could still be found among primitive peoples in various parts of the world.

I had heard the word "circumcision" many times and had been told that it was this that made Jewish men special, but I had no idea of what this actually involved. I had some vague knowledge also that it was done to the male genitalia, and I felt acutely slighted because my brother had been subjected to something that made him special, while I had not been deemed worthy of such an honor, being a mere girl.

The pictures of uncircumcised male genitalia in the medical books, along with a vague recollection of what my brother had looked like when we were still very small and were bathed together put things into perspective for me. The detailed anatomical descriptions and depictions of the loathsome horrors imposed on the penises of struggling aboriginal youths filled me with nausea and drove forever underground any feelings of covert envy for my brother's special condition. For the first time in my life I felt relieved to have been born a mere girl, unworthy of this awful thing that made boys special.

This article made an indelible impression on me. For many years it remained in the subconscious file of my mind. Fully 45 years later, I recognized instantly both it and the publication in which it had appeared while leafing through a relatively sparse file on the history of circumcision at the library of the Kinsey Institute for Sexual Research.

A somewhat strange and terrifying event that had happened when I was 14 years old had also lain deeply repressed in the recesses of my subconscious mind. It leaped into instant awareness when I was first told about Sudanese female circumcision by the art collecting Africa traveler in the Khartoum hostel.

My father had at one time been a ship's doctor and had traveled along the coast of the Mediterranean Sea. Although he had never penetrated into Africa more deeply than the Moroccan seaport, he had learned of some unusual African practices there and had one day told me about them. This was during that period of my life

when my father's feelings for me were undergoing a transformation
that I was at that time totally unable to fathom.

"Africa!" he snorted, laughing suddenly in a chillingly nasty
way, "That's where they cut women's sex organs off!" There was
something so savagely vindictive and woman-hating about that
laugh that it frightened me beyond all words. I withdrew into myself, remembered only that I adored him blindly, and quickly obliterated what had just transpired from my mind.

Many years later when I was teaching English, I received a lesson on how desperately eager all adolescents are for any useful
information concerning sex. Among the routine vocabulary and
spelling lessons required of me by the administration, I embedded
one in which I taught correct anatomical terminology pertaining to
the sex organs, ways and means for warding off unwanted pregnancies, and other subject matter of similar ilk. I answered any questions that my students wanted to ask me, and as I was known among
them to be a scrupulously straight shooter, there was no dearth of
direct questions. To justify inclusion of this lesson into the English
curriculum, I wrote a long list of difficult, pertinent words on the
blackboard and had my students copy it. This would be tangible
evidence that I was indeed teaching them vocabulary and spelling,
should a supervisor come into my room to check on my activities.

I would announce this lesson the day before I planned to give it
and on the day of its actual presentation would find all sorts of
students who were unknown to me sharing the seats with members
of my own class. The strangers were generally the boyfriends or
girlfriends of my pupils. Although I realized that they were probably cutting another teacher's class, this was nothing out of the ordinary for them in the course of a day so I asked no questions and
allowed them to stay.

Toward the end of the term when tests rolled around, I invariably
found the same results. Students who had previously been unable to
define or spell the simplest two-syllable words correctly, wrote out
and lovingly gave articulate definitions of every single word I had
given in that lesson.

This happened every time without fail. Actually, it is unlikely
that they have forgotten to this very day how to spell gonorrhea,
gynecologist, diaphragm, or spermicide correctly. In an age where

education in America seems to be dropping to a lower and lower performance level, this certainly says something about students' true ability to perform when they have been given motivation to apply themselves.

*   *   *   *

It was a never-ending source of wonderment how doors somehow unfailingly opened wide for me at my very appearance in Sudan. Perhaps I owed this phenomenon to that minute group of dedicated and loving Western medical professionals who, without fanfare or strivings for personal glory, worked doggedly for the betterment of the populace in the hospitals and dispensaries. It was a thankless job at best, with endless hardship and frustration, the most necessary materials being in short supply or totally unavailable.

Perhaps, when I appeared at the gate of a hospital, I was automatically presumed to be one of them. Perhaps also I developed a presence of my own. Perhaps it was only the simple watchman's automatic response to a wristwatch, a pair of adequate shoes, and skin tones of Caucasian origin. Being unable to read a letter of introduction, he must have had to develop his own methods for judging merit or character. All I know is that whenever I approached the barred gate of a hospital where perhaps a hundred women were clamoring for admission, a path was cleared for me, as if the Red Sea itself were parting, and I was allowed to pass.

It was in this way that I entered the portals of the small gynecological hospital of Dr. Aziz in Port Sudan. I carried on my person a letter of introduction, which had been written for me by a mutual friend. Such letters of introduction were always inscribed in elegant Arabic script, and although I collected a fair number of them in the course of my travels, their content has remained an enigma to me since I am unable to read them. At first I ascribed near magical qualities to their content because it seemed that by virtue of being able to present them, whatever I asked for was granted to me.

Later I learned that it was granted with equal facility even without the letters. Whatever magic took place occurred between me and those whom I importuned and was based, no doubt, on what we emanated toward one another.

Gynecological practice is at best the most urgently needed and at worst the most horrendously frustrating medical specialty in Sudan. To a man like Dr. Aziz, who had received his training in England, it must have been doubly so. His years of exposure to medical practice in the Western world had given him a basis for comparison. He had had the opportunity to carry on his chosen profession under a more normal set of circumstances and was bitterly frustrated by the circumcision-induced abnormalities that confronted him daily in Sudan.

Such insurmountable obstacles to effective medical treatment thwarted and angered him, as it did all of his overtaxed staff. It was all too often impossible for them to arrive at a simple diagnosis. The tightly sewn genitalia of a patient were frequently too closed off to allow even the insertion of a speculum. Diagnosis had to be based on educated guesswork and often the only way to obtain the information needed to treat a patient was to operate.

He had such a patient being prepared for an exploratory procedure at this very moment, Dr. Aziz told me when I interviewed him. He suspected that there was a good-sized uterine tumor pressing on her bladder and that he would most likely have to perform a hysterectomy. He asked me if I wished to observe the operation.

This was the first time that such an opportunity had presented itself to me, and choking down my trepidations, I gratefully accepted his offer. I had only recently been gutted of my own reproductive organs and was therefore tremendously interested in seeing a similar procedure performed. I explained this to him.

"You are offering me a wonderful opportunity," I said. "Only last year my own uterus and ovaries were removed, and I am naturally extremely curious to observe such an operation." By way of long habit, Dr. Aziz asked me for further medical details. A large, fibrous uterine mass had increased rather rapidly in size, I told him, and a prompt hysterectomy had seemed indicated. "But your ovaries?" he questioned. "Were they affected as well?" "No," I replied. "The surgeon told me afterward that they had been quite healthy."

Dr. Aziz frowned. "Then why did you allow him to remove them? That is something that should under no circumstances have been done!" He seemed extremely agitated.

"I was not asked," I admitted. "When I came out of the anesthesia it had already been done. When I protested, I was told that it had been a quite routine procedure."

"That is barbaric," Dr. Aziz pronounced severely. He shook his head in vehement disapproval. "That is absolutely barbaric."

It was a moment of the most splendid irony.

As Dr. Aziz made ready to leave for the operating room, I felt myself inexplicably shying away from my next request. I was often overtaken by these sudden self-doubts. Who, after all, was I to pry so clumsily into people's most private lives? But as I looked around me in the dismal hospital I took heart and forced myself to go on.

"Do you think you could give us permission," I asked haltingly, almost overwhelmed by my own audacity, "I mean, would it be possible for us to take a photograph of what this mutilation looks like?" I gestured toward Dale, the young man with whom I was briefly traveling, who had been sitting quietly in a corner of the room with his camera, listening to the interview. "My partner here is a medical student and a photographer as well."

"Of course," Dr. Aziz nodded, as if this were the most matter-of-fact request in the world. "The patient will already be under anesthesia. You may take a picture before I begin the operation."

We were escorted to the scrub room and outfitted with surgical gowns, masks, and rubber boots. Dale, who had witnessed operations before, excitedly murmured the benefit of his experience to me as we were washing up. "The toughest part to watch is the first incision," he said. "After that you tend to lose yourself in the fascination of what is going on and you will probably not find it hard to watch. But if at any time it begins to bother you or if you feel faint, simply pull your eyes away and look at something else. Look at Dr. Aziz, look at the nurse, look at the patient's face or at her feet or hands. Look anywhere except at where the surgeon is working. You will find that after a few moments you will have regained your composure and that it no longer bothers you to watch the operation."

We followed Dr. Aziz into the small operating room. I had expected to be prepared for the sight that I imagined would confront me there, but I was wrong. The young, silken-skinned patient lay already anesthetized on the table, her face covered by the anesthetist's mask. Her feet, no more than two paces' distance from the entrance to the room, had been placed in stirrups, and the area between her legs lay fully exposed, shockingly close to my startled eyes.

For a moment I was wrenched back violently into that other reality and I saw only the lifeless, barren desert, bisected neatly by a thin line of railroad track. Then the image changed, and I was looking at the anatomical deception of a Barbie Doll, whose featureless pubis gave the lie to answers that a child expected to find there. I felt tears blur my eyes and when I shook my head to clear them, faced the reality of the unconscious young woman who lay breathing shallowly upon the operating table before me.

"It is sad, is it not?" I heard Dr. Aziz ask. Mutely I nodded.

Dale, meanwhile, had set up his camera and was swiftly and expertly taking his photographs. When I look back upon this scene, I feel no guilt at having stolen these photographs from this nameless woman, for in my memory of her, she has no face. If we had seen her face, it might have been altogether different.

The operation proceeded, and at the first incision I was glad of Dale's advice. I concentrated on the delicate proportions of the young woman's limbs and when I was able to look back at the procedure being performed on her lower abdomen, I found myself both detached and intrigued. Dr. Aziz maintained a running didactic commentary on what he was doing, as if we were his apprentices. In the next half hour I learned a great deal about female anatomy, the properties of living tissue, and the incredible art of surgery.

When he had finished the operation, Dr. Aziz said that he would show me one more thing. A small girl had been brought into his hospital two days before, delirious with raging fever and hemorrhaging furiously after a badly botched village circumcision. In an attempt to save her, she had been subjected to two continuous days of transfusion. The bleeding had been arrested, but she was still delirious.

He explained that such a child being brought into the hospital at all was a rare occurrence in Sudan. Because of the laws prohibiting pharaonic circumcision, little girls were generally allowed to die rather than risk exposing the performing midwife to punishment by the authorities. It was once more a question of family honor. Transgression of this rigid code risked ostracism. The death of the child, when it occurred, was accepted by her parents as resulting from the inscrutable and all-merciful will of Allah.

A delicate, wild-eyed, flinching child, her legs flexed unnaturally wide, was brought in on the arms of a gentle, motherly attendant, who placed her tenderly upon the examining table with the greatest care. Dr. Aziz lifted the covering cloth so that we could see what had been done to her, while the girl's frail little arms made feeble motions at warding him off.

Her entire abdomen and thighs were massively swollen and engorged. At the site of the operation, dark sutures were barely visible in the swollen flesh. Otherwise nothing of any note could be seen.

As if trapped in some inexorable nightmare, I stared numbly at her face. Her violated eyes froze my blood.

I signaled to Dale to take her photograph. I have no excuse to offer for this. I have often weighed in my mind the potential good that the uses of this picture may be able to do in the cause of ending this cruel practice, against the possible additional cruelty that we may have inflicted on that child by this act. I have never been able to arrive at a balance. It is something that I did, and this is a fact that I must live with.

I take some measure of solace from the fact that I am not the only one who needs to cope with such a memory. At his hospital in Omdurman Dr. Salah invited me to attend rounds, and in the course of these cautioned his students and interns against announcing too glibly a diagnosis of pregnancy, when there was any reasonable doubt whatsoever that this was actually the case. Pregnancy tests available in Sudan were often unreliable and deceptive and this could lead to the most tragic consequences.

He related the case of a girl who had been brought to him when he was resident in an outpost hospital, some years before. The girl's lower abdomen had been distended in what appeared to be pregnancy and the man who brought her to the hospital demanded that she be examined. The pregnancy test proved to be positive and Dr. Salah, assuming the man to be the girl's husband, congratulated him on his wife's pregnancy.

As he related the rest of the story, Dr. Salah's face darkened while he stared into nothingness with haunted eyes. "The man I had presumed to be her husband proved to be, in actuality, her brother," he recalled tonelessly. "He was gone the next day, leaving the strangled body of his sister behind. When we did an autopsy, we discovered that she had not been pregnant at all. A tumor-like mass of urinary and menstrual debris had accumulated behind her tightly sewn bridge of scar tissue, simulating pregnancy."

He looked around at his students and then straight into my eyes. "I will never be able to forgive myself for that terrible mistake," he said, shaking his head as if to rid himself of an oppressive ghost. "I must live with it for the rest of my life."

As I grew to know the Sudanese doctors, my respect for them became ever deeper. I constantly marveled at how they somehow continued to function with remarkable competence under conditions that would have driven most people mad.

I had occasion to seek out the services of a Port Sudan dentist when a large filling fell out of one of my teeth, leaving only a throbbing shell. I was sent to him by Dr. Sidahamed, who had graciously extended his hospitality to me. The dentist's waiting room was packed to overflowing with patients, but as usual I was treated preferentially and was invited into his treatment room almost immediately.

It was only the throbbing of my tooth and Sidahamed's earnest assurance that this was the best dentist that could be found in Port Sudan that kept me from fleeing the room instantly when I actually saw the man. His smooth, child-like face gave him the appearance of being no more than 16 years old and it was only the obvious delicacy and sensitivity of his hands that made me force myself to sit down in his chair.

There were, of course, no such amenities as novocaine. There was no running water or antiseptic cotton. His machine, although unquestionably the most up-to-date available in all of Port Sudan, was a relic of another age. I remembered being subjected to such a torture device in my early childhood.

I must reluctantly confess that in a country where women bear pain with incomprehensible stoicism, I acquitted myself rather badly. I had recently suffered a skull fracture and merely having my head touched filled me with unbearable anxiety, not to mention the grinding pain generated by the impossibly dull burr of his drill. Every few seconds as he worked, I pulled his hand away, being able to bear it no more.

It required a full hour to complete the filling and I am forced to admit that he did look at me rather strangely when it was finally done and I apologized and thanked him. I was unable to induce him to accept any payment whatsoever. Desiring only to flee as swiftly as possible, I thanked him once more and hurriedly edged my way out through a waiting room full of incredulously staring patients, nursing my throbbing ego.

When I returned to Europe I wrote a card to my dentist in New York, telling him of the incident. Some months later he had occasion to examine the tooth when I consulted him for a checkup, which he confessed he had been burning to do. He pried around in my mouth for some moments in total silence, then sighed in blissful admiration. "Wonderful," he marveled, "absolutely wonderful. I only wish I had done that tooth myself."

*   *   *   *

I sometimes wonder how Sudanese women must feel when they are exposed to the peculiarities of our own medical system. I know that they laugh among themselves and try to make light of the horror that their condition elicits among medical caretakers here. To them, after all, it is a completely normal thing, hardly even worthy of note.

There seems to be an unfailing response that they can count on when they are first examined. "What happened to you?" they are invariably asked by the uninitiated doctor or nurse. "Were you in a car accident?" They think that this is deliciously funny, of course, and giggle about it among themselves. Whenever one of their number readies herself to enter a hospital to give birth, the rest of them impishly advise her, "Be sure you tell them about your car accident!" And they laugh.

Personal Demons

His name was Natan, and by a perverse kind of logic, his youthful contemporaries called him "Satan." When he at one time confided this to me, he confessed also that it had been a source of considerable torment to him to be thus branded. The names by which we are called all too often shape our destinies. Here, as in a Greek tragedy, are the Satanic Verses of *his* destiny.

It was he who spawned me and he who helped me spring into the world from out between my mother's legs. His was the first face that I saw as I was propelled precipitously out of her womb with widely open eyes, unexpectedly and at high noon, while their midday meal grew cold upon the table.

I have little doubt that she was more than glad to be rid of me, for I had been an unwelcome and unwanted tenant. She promptly and with evident relief turned me over to what developed into a panoramically changing succession of underpaid, abused and surly servants, whose unloving ministrations allowed my infant head to bounce about on my vulnerable neck like a ping-pong ball.

It was my misfortune not only to have been conceived far too soon after my brother's entry into the world, but to have been born unequivocally resembling my swarthy father. She had wished for a child that resembled her own blond and blue-eyed father.

I was born hirsute and remained so for most of my life, to my constant torment. It blighted what was noted by many to be an otherwise remarkable physical beauty. It was the result, I was later to understand, of a fetal environment saturated with a surfeit of adrenal hormones—a symptom of great stress, and no doubt distress in my discontented young mother.

What was the source of her distress? By the time that I was conceived, one year after the inception of a hopelessly ill-matched marriage urged upon her by her own mother and three months after the birth of my brother, she and Natan/Satan hated one another with a ferocity that bordered on dementia. Over the years they tried several times to separate, but economic necessity brought on by our eventual flight from the political horror of Nazi Germany did not allow it.

She granted me the grudging favor of her breast, from which I protestingly sucked the poison of her anger and revulsion. Mercifully the milk dried up soon enough, while the mainsprings of her anger and revulsion continued to overflow.

I can only conceptualize what he must have felt toward me in those early years. Most assuredly, a significant part of his feelings for me during my infancy were those of love and tenderness. He pitied my abandoned state. There was also a woeful component of his own grinding need to find some kind of solace for the wounds his ego had suffered in his own infancy.

I recall the furry comfort of clutching the hair on his deep, barrel-shaped chest and the warmth of his hands as he held me, his disconsolate and bereft infant daughter, close to his body.

I know little of my mother's childhood. She remembers her cheery and somewhat simple father with great affection. Her own mother was the last and sixteenth child of a 53-year-old, physically depleted woman. She was talented, neurotic, and emotionally crippled by periodically recurring episodes of delusional depression, which resulted in repeated periods of institutionalization, and electroshock therapy. My mother's feelings of contempt and embarrassment over her mother's "weakness" seem never to have left her.

I do not recall my mother ever beating me, while my father, under her insistent goading, frequently did. However, she belittled and demeaned me verbally without end. I became her scapegoat. I remember seeking vainly to escape from her relentless teasing in my earliest childhood. The teasing changed in time into a chronically angry, cruelly demeaning stream of ridicule. She, in her turn, became the subject of a constant bombardment of bitter sarcasm from my father. The all-encompassing atmosphere of hatred that saturated every aspect of my childhood devastated my budding psyche.

For some reason, my innocent and sickly young brother elicited only the profoundest anger and contempt in my father. He had wanted a son who projected his ideal image of an aggressive and superlatively masculine male, and this was not what he had gotten.

All of this bitterness ensued even before I was able to understand language, at a time when my cues came only from their facial expressions and tonal inflection. This was my family life. During my entire childhood, I was entrapped within this tragic saga of disappointment and unresolved rage.

I can only speculate on how the script by which my father lived his life originated. I know, for example, that he had been the fourth and last born son of a well-known and highly respected rabbi and newspaper editor, and that he was born just before the turn of the century in a medium-sized town in southern Germany.

He never spoke of his mother or his parental home in tones other than the greatest reverence. Yet it always struck me, even when I was small, that when his mother had been widowed and crippled by a stroke, he hardly ever undertook the day's journey to visit her, while he unfailingly found time to vacation alone in Italy.

His mother was considerably younger than the rabbi, an intelligent, beautiful, and personally ambitious woman who had been bitterly thwarted in her own self-realization. Being a product of her time and her society, she had to contend herself with the prime achievement that was then open to her, which was becoming a rabbi's wife and serving as the bearer of his children. It was a role she had evidently learned to play quite well in time, but under whose limiting yoke she continued to chafe.

By the time she had given birth to three sons, she desperately longed for a daughter. When she found herself pregnant for the fourth and last time, she assembled a layette for the girl she so coveted. Alas, this too was not to be granted to her. The last of her brood proved to be yet another male child. Weeping with frustration, she dressed him in the frills and laces she had prepared for a daughter.

On the eighth day of his youngest son's life, the rabbi took the boy and circumcised him. He gave him the name of Natan. Natan was to spend his entire first year dressed as a little girl, while his mother continued to weep. Finally, when he had outgrown his little dresses, bonnets, and pinafores, his mother dried her tears and bowed to the inevitable. She acknowledged his unwelcome maleness by allowing him to wear the castoff trousers of his elder brothers.

There were two significant roles in his life script which he continued to unreel for all of his measured days. One of them was The Enemy. Whomever he cast into this role became the object of his most vitriolic and vindictive hatred. The other was The Loved One, who had to be protected against The Enemy at all costs. I was fated to be cast by him in both of these roles in the course of his lifetime.

By the time I was born, my mother had already been cast in the role of The Enemy, and I quickly became The Loved One. This role was neither easy nor comfortable to fill. It demanded unconditional subservience and slavish loyalty. This was the ever renewable price of admission into a world where one was worthy of human touch. Even the slightest deviation was instantly interpreted as "proof" that one had "joined the other side" and allied oneself with The Enemy.

My greatest joy when I was a small child (and there were few) was to be allowed into his bed on Sunday mornings, where he would listen to my childish prattling and make me giggle and play innocent games with me. On Sunday mornings he belonged to me alone. As luck would have it pedophilia was not in his nature, so our innocent games did not become overtly sexual, although they must have been, within the unhealthy character of this warped triad, the foundation of what was later to become my own tyrannically sensual and erotic nature.

In my innocently childish mind, they fostered the forbidden fantasy that I would someday, when I had grown to womanhood, be his wife and that he would then be mine alone to love. Such fantasies are hardly unusual in the psychic life of even the most normally developing child. Quite generally they run their course and find channels that are more socially acceptable, but mine was hardly a developmentally healthy environment.

I recall only one overt episode of childhood sexuality. It happened when I was six years old, during one of my many bouts of respiratory illness. I was left alone, in bed, for long periods of time. Our little wire hair terrier wandered in and out of the room, keeping me company.

One morning I awoke to a warm and thrillingly pleasant sensation. It took me a moment to understand what was happening. The little dog had burrowed under the covers and was licking me in a private and secret place. Enthralled, I allowed myself to enjoy what I instinctively knew to be a forbidden pleasure.

The next day my father brought a strange doctor to examine me, and one week later, without any explanation, my mother took me on the train to a sanitorium, several hundred miles away, and left me there.

I was overwhelmed with guilt and remorse, certain that my terrible secret was known and that I had been banished forever. In my several months at the sanitorium, I had only one visitor. It was my blessed one-armed uncle Leo. He had felt enough compassion for me to drive the entire distance alone. From my parents I received not even a letter.

At the end of my long and fearful exile, my father came to fetch me. He said nothing of the episode with the little dog and acted, in fact, as if he knew nothing about it. But I knew better. I had received the indelible lesson that he irrevocably owned me, and that my punishment for the least transgression would be total abandonment. I had been given warning.

The little dog too had been punished. He limped about, one of his hind legs in a cast. I was told that he had fallen off the second story balcony into the garden below, but I felt certain that his leg had been broken when my father beat him, as he sometimes did.

As I grew into adolescence I began to lust increasingly for the world, yet knew that the only lust that I was allowed to feel without endangering my role as Loved One was for my father.

I can speak only for myself here. I cannot speak for him, nor what forbidden fantasies his own mind may have entertained. By the time I turned 14, he had begun to invade my erotic dreams from which I would awaken, horrified and full of revulsion at their undisguised and overt character.

In my youthful inexperience I was unable to recognize that as my body ripened, his behavior toward me had evolved into naked seductiveness, and had grown redolent with sexual suggestion and innuendo. Because this created a flattering intimacy within an illusion of safety and because I felt that it gained me the highly desirable status of an adult, I was eager to respond. At the same time I suffered intensely from guilt and self-revulsion at what I believed to be entirely self-generated forbidden longings. Being a product of my time and upbringing, normal sexual experimentation with boys my own age was of course strictly forbidden to me.

He had little interest in my education although, having been born with my eyes wide open, I early manifested a rabid curiosity. This tended to charm him when I was small, but as I matured and began to develop a capacity for analytical and logical thinking, this pleased him not at all. His attitude in regard to women's education was that it was altogether wasted on them. The only exception was the kind of education women could obtain in schools for nurses or secretaries where they would be taught useful, which was to say, subservient and thereby safe, skills. Intellectually accomplished women, who must have posed as great a threat to his sexuality as his mother had done in his infancy, infuriated and frightened him.

The life that he obviously envisioned for me was light years removed from everything I secretly and avidly longed for. The very last thing in the world that I wanted was to be a woman like my mother, furiously entrapped and spewing a powerless vehemence.

I thirsted for my father's freedom. And more than that, I lusted increasingly for his power, because while she could dance and trample furiously upon *my* vulnerabilities, he himself remained impervious to her. He was a man and could choose to do as he pleased. He was the ruler of the household and of everything in it. I was his property, little more.

His power over me was such that I was sure that he had the ability to read my thoughts. If I were to have allowed my mind to imagine *her* as anything more than an object worthy of loathing for even a single moment, I would have risked losing irrevocably my only source of affection and support.

And yet, at 14, as I felt a new and different kind of threat beginning to engulf me, the courage of desperation somehow overwhelmed me unexpectedly. He came upon me as I was weeping and asked what was the matter, and suddenly it all came pouring out of me in a torrent. I felt that I was going mad, I could no longer bear to live in such a home where constant war was raging; something had to change. I could not stand any more of her vicious lashings out — and then, with sudden great clarity and purpose, as my entire body began to shake and tremble: *"But you must change too, you must* stop antagonizing and demeaning her constantly, or nothing will ever be better for any of us in this house."

I could almost hear something shattering. I do not know whether it broke inside of me or in him or if it broke between us. I vaguely recall that he raised his arm to strike me, but that his hand never connected with my face. As I saw it return slowly to his side, I frantically searched his face for a trace of warmth or compassion. His expression revealed only steely contempt. To soil his hands by touching me, it said plainly, even with a blow, was irrevocably and forever beneath him. His eyes were still focused on me, but it was as if no one was there for him to see. I had ceased to exist. He turned on his heel, walked out of what to him was an empty room, and pulled the door shut behind him.

I remained standing there in a state of acute shock, desperately struggling to come to terms with the inexorable: I had irrevocably destroyed the only thing in my life that gave it meaning.

For many days I crept about, rank with self-loathing, while he remained oblivious to my despicable existence. I fully believed that nothing short of actually ridding the earth of the blight of my being would ever cleanse me of the horrendous sin I had committed. While he lay basking in the sun on the roof of our apartment building, I stood at the edge and contemplated plunging to the sidewalk far below. I discovered that I was too cowardly to fly, like a doomed bird, into that final nothingness, and this served only to compound my self-revulsion.

I was prepared to capitulate, beg for forgiveness, grovel for mercy. Despairingly I tried to cling to a last hope that he would find it in his heart to allow me to dwell, repentant, somewhere at the outer boundaries of his benevolence. In a last ditch effort to reconstruct my ruined life, I began to rehearse a small, stiff speech to which I hoped he would deign to listen.

"Daddy," it began, "I know that nothing will ever be the same between us, but I realize that I must apologize." Beyond this opening statement, my recollection fades mercifully into vagueness. I rehearsed my recantation over and over in my mind, until I had hopes that I could recite it without breaking down.

After enduring two weeks of his steely and all-encompassing indifference, while my mother continued to mock me, I felt as if I no longer existed. Trembling with anxiety, I slunk into his office, waited until his reception room was empty of patients, and haltingly whispered my request for an interview to his nurse.

As I entered his consulting room, I saw that he was standing by his desk and that he was looking coldly in my direction and completely through me. I closed the door and tentatively approached him. Halfway across the room I stopped, my gaze riveted to the ground.

"Daddy," I began, and then, in a scream of desperation, as a wave of pain rushed up to engulf me: "I am *sorry!* I am so *sorry!* I will *never, never* do it again! Please! Please! *Forgive me!*"

He rushed forward, enfolding me in his arms. I heard him ask tremulously, in a soft voice, "Baby, why did you wait so long?" I remember crying for what seemed like a long time in his embrace until I finally realized that he had indeed granted me a reprieve, that everything, after all, was not lost, that something, somehow could be salvaged.

But later I gradually began to realize that something else had also happened. True, like Gallileo, I had recanted, as if on penalty of death. But I knew of a certainty, somewhere in my heart of hearts, that the earth was neither flat nor the center of the universe. I knew that it turned on its own axis and that it revolved around the sun, and I knew that I would never again accept that it did otherwise.

My emotional enslavement to my father was to last for many weary years to come, but his absolute right to dominance, by virtue of his benevolence, was now somehow no longer intact. The episode had driven my fear of him far closer to the surface of my awareness, and on some level I realized that although his blank rejection had reduced me almost to a state of the walking dead, I had, after all, survived.

*   *   *   *

The choreography of our ballet of sexual seductiveness and counter seductiveness grew more intricate within the next few years. He had at least two mistresses and several transient relationships that I knew of, while my own opportunities for sexual experimentation with young men of my own age were truncated by taboo.

While his own sexual relationships with other women no doubt eased his imperatives in my direction, he now began to cast me more and more in the role of confidante. He related stories of the sexual escapades he had had in his youth. He gloated angrily about women he had known, who had freely indulged in sex. He dismissed them contemptuously as having been no better than pigs. He bragged of deceitful conquests. He even bragged of rape.

His little games, only a step removed from becoming overtly sexual, grew stranger and stranger. Through his mistress, who also used me as her confidante, I learned about some of his imaginings in which he "allowed" me to perform servile sexual acts on him, ostensibly to alleviate my own torment. He became progressively obsessed with my virginity and beleaguered me constantly with religious dictums and observance, designed to enforce women's fourth-rate citizenship.

When I turned 18, I told him that I could live with the conditions in my home no longer and that I intended to leave. He pleaded with me like a lover. He needed me. He would divorce my mother if I would consent to stay and be his housekeeper.

This was not how I envisioned my future. I wanted to find love. I planned to enter college. I told him that I had to get away not only from my mother, but from him as well, if I were to preserve my sanity. He alternately threatened and pleaded with me. I experienced a growing revulsion.

He sent me to a colleague at one of the city psychiatric hospitals, a lesser light, who told me that what I was contemplating was highly abnormal for a woman and that were I to carry out my decision, I would live to regret it. He then showed me the highlights of his ward, the hydrotherapy room with its restraining harnesses and the cubicle where electroconvulsive shock was administered. Fumes from his two rows of rotting teeth wafted sickeningly in my direction as he grinned obscenely. "This is how I bring my more recalcitrant patients under control," he bragged.

It was then that I realized that I must truly leave, and that I must leave quickly. I knew that if the controls slackened and fantasy somehow became reality for my father, I would be hopelessly trapped. No one would ever believe me if I then betrayed him and told the truth of what was going on between us.

My dear little grandmother was already dying in the obscenity of a state hospital psychiatric ward. I feared that my protestations would simply be discounted as the fabrications of a congenitally defective mind. It would be easy for him to have me committed if he should need to do so. If I did not escape him, I faced the risk of spending the rest of my days in the unspeakable back ward horror of some state hospital.

I made my escape and moved to another city. For some years he tried by every possible trick he could devise to induce me to return. I suffered horribly from guilt and anxiety but managed to elude him.

Much as I tried, I was still unable to free myself from his power which continued to control me, even at a distance. The potent threat of religious vengeance remained. If I married outside of his religion, I would lose my place among the living. My loathsome existence would henceforth be remembered only by the Prayer for the Dead. From earliest childhood on, it had been impressed upon me that if I were ever to marry outside of his religion, his will, his dictates, I would be banished to the realms of death forever. No matter how I struggled, I could not overcome my infant fear.

Eventually he divorced my mother. They remained embittered enemies for the rest of his life. A year later he married his new housekeeper, a disturbed and pathetic survivor of the Nazi concentration camps. She was only in her late thirties and still of reproductive age. She had been married once before. Her husband of some years standing had fallen victim to the Nazis.

To his great delight, my father discovered when he married his new wife that she was still a virgin. When he glowingly uncovered this fact to me, I asked him neither what had caused this unusual circumstance, nor why this sad fact should occasion such joy in him. I felt only relief that he was happy.

She was a simple-minded and singularly devious woman who spent most of her leisure time playing with dolls. She wanted desperately to have a baby, a little girl, but my father, by then already in his fifties, refused categorically and to her great chagrin to engender any more progeny. Thereafter, she filled the role of Loved One that I had so willingly vacated some years before. My brother, who had returned from the war and lived with them for a period of time while he completed his schooling, was swiftly shunted into the role of The Enemy.

To my knowledge, he had done nothing to earn this. Quite to the contrary, for the rest of my father's life my brother labored slavishly to win his approval. The reason was quite simply that it was his turn to fill the slot left empty by the departure of my mother. Nothing my tormented brother could do would alter his condition. Eventually he married and engendered progeny, but this did nothing to change his status. He remained in the totally undeserved role of The Enemy until many years later, when an even more unkind destiny released him.

I too married eventually. My marriage was a tortured and punishing one, and because it left me still deprived of touch and kindness, I gradually drifted back under my father's control. I lived once more for the scraps of affection he cast my way, and slavishly accepted his edicts regarding the religious upbringing of my children, although this violated everything in which I personally believed.

Periodic, dutiful visits with the children were obligatory. The all but openly overt demand implicit in these visits was obeisance, and they took place under the ever-watchful and only marginally tolerant eye of his wife.

He confided to me that he loved her and that he was, for the first time in his life, completely faithful. He could not understand why he was becoming impotent with her. There seemed to be no health problems that should cause this.

As they grew older and his wife left her reproductive years, she felt more and more deprived in her barren state. The balance of power in the relationship began to tip in her favor as she came into a large inheritance. Her rage and growing vindictiveness directed itself toward his own progeny, and finally burst out of all containment. She could not tolerate the thought that he should have deprived her of her chance to be a mother, while he himself had grandchildren. She demanded vociferously that he give them up.

My unfortunate brother, meanwhile, had fallen victim to a terrible affliction which left him crippled for the rest of his life. It became impossible for him to fill the role of the confused and supplicating Enemy, and so the role was left once more vacant. What happened next was inevitable.

At this time, my marriage became so troubled and I suffered so acutely from depression that I had begun to look for love with other men. Filled with confusion and guilt, I turned to my father, wishing somehow for his forgiveness and approval. I felt a great need to talk to him, if only to make him understand what was happening to my life.

My stepmother had the habit of listening in on all of his telephone conversations on another extension. It was known among his patients that she did this, and many had left him for a less compromised doctor/patient relationship with other practitioners before his retirement several years earlier.

I visited their home with my children, and in the course of my visit begged to speak to him for five minutes alone. As I spoke, I saw a well-remembered steeliness from a time long, long past come back into his eyes. His wife angrily left the room, to listen, I was well aware, at the door. I told him that my marriage was all but over and that I had taken a lover.

Incongruously he answered. "Well, now you know what it is like. Don't expect me to help you. You *had* your chance with me. It is too late for you now."

I had not expected this. It had been too long ago. More than 30 years had passed. "I do not expect you to help me," I said. "It is only that I desperately need someone to talk with."

"So now you have talked with me," he snapped. Then he added, "I know you are trying to separate Leah and me. But you will not succeed. Leah and I are one."

"Why would I want to separate you?" I asked, taken aback. "What could I gain by such a thing?"

"Then you could have me all to yourself," he flung at me contemptuously.

"What *for*?" I asked again. "Whatever would I want you for? I am glad that you have one another, to love and care for each other. I am overwhelmed with responsibility as it is. I do not need you to take care of too!"

"Oh," he said, confused for a moment, "I thought you wanted me for yourself."

"No, Poppa," I said. "You thought wrong."

Seemingly mollified, he called his wife back into the room.

Aside from her obvious display of having suffered great wrongdoing, the rest of the visit proceeded almost normally by comparison.

When I telephoned several days later, however, I realized that I had been irrevocably dumped into the conveniently vacant role of The Enemy. I suspected that it was to be mine for the rest of his life, for I could think of no one else who was left to fill it. I refused, however, to play the role of anxious, guilt-ridden supplicant, as my brother had done so well for such a monstrously long time. After two or three more calls, closely monitored by his wife, I simply gave up.

Thereafter, I heard only episodic reports from distant relatives. I was being maligned for my ingratitude and for cruelly withholding my children. I vainly searched my memory for something to feel grateful for. My nearly grown children at no time evidenced the least desire to spend time in their grandparents' company, having known no love from them and realizing, no doubt, that they were wanted only to serve as pawns. None of us would play Natan's game, and this became his greatest source of wrath.

In the three years that followed, I heard accounts of violent fallings out between him and people who had long been his staunchest and most steadfast friends. The rifts that were thus created proved always to be irreparable. They were the result of his embittered defense against his erstwhile allies' altogether imaginary attacks on his unity with The Loved One.

The last time I saw him was at a family wedding, one year before the beginning of my African Odyssey. A friend of the bride's mother, obviously innocent of what had transpired between us, took my hand as I entered the room and exclaimed, "Your father is already here!" She pulled me to where he and Leah were standing, and left me there.

He had aged since I had last seen him. His stocky, powerful frame had begun to shrink and I, long since the taller of the two, towered over him by at least half a head. In a sudden rush of tenderness, I held out my hand. He grasped it in both of his, and for an irrational moment, I thought that he would pull me toward him to embrace me.

Then his face contorted with hatred and he squeezed my fingers viciously with all the power remaining in his body. He pushed downward, trying to force me to my knees. My long pent-up out-rage lent me strength. I did not give even an inch. Detached, I watched his vain struggle, smiling mockingly. He could not have helped but read my expression, which said all too clearly, "So *that* is what you still want. After all these years!" He panted with exer-tion, his face turned red with effort, and finally, unable to make me yield, he gave up in frustration. His hands dropped uselessly to his sides.

"Goodbye, Daddy." I said softly and turned away. I felt drained of all feeling. There was no anguish left to conquer.

Several months later, the telephone rang. It was his sister-in-law, who informed us that he had died of a heart attack. My presence, she said, was unwanted at the funeral. I answered quite truthfully that I felt absolutely no desire to attend it, and hung up.

I sat for a long moment, thinking. So it had all finally come full circle. A vast wave of anger gathered and threatened for a moment to overwhelm me. Then my breathing evened, and I stood up.

"It's all finished," I said aloud. "The rest of my life is mine, old man. The rest is *mine!*"

Then I went out to run. Although I did not yet know it, I was on my way to Africa.

Charade at Wad Cherrifay

In the days when British colonials ruled in remote outposts of Africa, they dressed every night for dinner in spite of the brutal heat. Sometimes this exercise in formality helped to keep their threatened sanities intact. It was a device for clinging to a structured way of life that had meaning to them, and a desperate attempt to ward off their feelings of alienation in a setting to which they did not feel they belonged.

Some "went native" and forever forfeited the privilege of belonging to the culture from which they had originated. They were shunned or they were pitied, but it was generally agreed that they had succumbed to madness.

Madness and death are often your only steadfast companions when you travel in Africa, and they are never far from your side. Your world consists of a constant panorama of faces and scenes that fill your avid eyes with wonder and discovery, but no matter how great the excitement of exploration, they leave you somehow empty and wanting. The greatest joy of solitary adventure is the heady freedom to move only to the beat of your own drum. Its greatest scourge is gnawing loneliness and a constant wrenching hunger of the flesh.

Passing, generally ill-matched affiliations may provide an occasional temporary distraction, but the wound continues to fester. All too rarely a brief friendship develops, there is a moment of emotional support, and then the wind seizes you once more like a driven leaf and has its way with you.

Kassala lay along the Ethiopian border, and at night the boom of artillery rang out from the mountain where the civil war with Eritrea continued to rage. Desperate young Eritrean refugees roamed the town in search of employment under the suspicious eye of noticeably nervous officials in uniform.

When I passed a photographer's shop and on a sudden impulse

importuned him to move his cumbersome blunderbuss of a camera outside to take my photo, an agitated man in uniform materialized out of seemingly nowhere and excitedly demanded to see my papers. Photographs anywhere in the town were forbidden, he shouted, and all ordinances were strictly enforced. Startled, I hastened to apologize and was relieved when he allowed me to leave when he had finished shouting at me.

In the marketplace I met a quietly plain and inconspicuous American woman, clearly even at first glance a seasoned Africa traveler. She was buying spinach and my experienced eye quickly noted that her frail, thin body carried a small but advanced pregnancy. Her name was Ros, and she had indeed been traveling through Africa for five years. In Kenya she had met and married a native Kenyan, an architect by profession, and had lived with him in a village hut as his African wife. She had devoted herself to teaching the women of the village sewing skills so that they might become self-supporting. Her efforts had come to naught. The women's hands were far too often so swollen by the beatings regularly inflicted on them by their husbands that they were unable to hold a needle.

Although it was obvious that she was unduly modest and self-effacing to the utmost, her wifely role eventually became impossible even for her to tolerate and she had fled from the village some six months before. I asked her how far her pregnancy had progressed, and she expressed surprise at my question. It had not occurred to her that she might be pregnant, she said. She had not menstruated for over seven months, but had attributed this to the trauma she had undergone and to her consequent debilitated state.

I placed my hand upon her belly and felt the fetus stirring in her womb. I guided her hand to what I was feeling. She sighed. Yes, she had felt it before, she said, but she had thought it was no more than a digestive upset. I looked into her frightened, apologetic eyes. "Ros," I said, "you *must* have some prenatal care. You cannot go on denying this reality any longer. You must make plans. Your baby will soon be born."

There was a long moment of silence while she studied her feet. Then she sighed again. "I will eat lots of vegetables," she said. She bought some spinach and then showed me where there was a tea shack that sold yogurt.

We agreed that it would be to our mutual benefit to travel together for a while. The presence of another woman was clearly stabilizing and reassuring to her and I realized that there were many things that she could teach me. Among the skills that I was to learn from her was how to obtain free and safe lodging at police stations. Hospitable boarding schools were also not hard to find, she said, and if either of those alternatives proved to be wanting, cemeteries were unfailingly safe in an emergency. No African would dare enter a cemetery after dark. It was best to stay away from hospitals, she added, even as a last resort.

Although I generally preferred the relative quiet of a police station to the tumult and assault on my eardrums created by the incessant shrieking of "What is your name?" at close range by overly enthusiastic pupils in a school yard, I never found myself in a situation where I had to resort to a cemetery.

Later in my journey I was to meet yet another American woman who had traveled through Sudan alone. She felt safe only in cemeteries, and for good reason. In a village police station near Wau, in the South, she had been brutally assaulted and raped by the drunken chief of police himself.

Kassala lay at the foot of a mountain, which consists of a single absolutely smooth block of granite. It rises inexplicably from the perfectly flat surrounding desert to a height of 3,500 feet, having been flung up by some cataclysmic act of nature. From this mountain, water trickled into deep wells through a seemingly impossible system of pipes laid by Italian engineers. These created a lush oasis within a sunbaked, windswept desert. The deadly monotony of this desert was broken only rarely by the thunderous passing of great herds of camel, their colors ranging from pure white to sand to nearly black, who were urged along by Bedouin drivers on Arabian steeds. Some distance further, we were told, there lay villages and fertile, irrigated fields.

We left our heavy packs safely locked in the police armory and began to walk along the base of the mountain. The terrain was bleak and strewn with rocks. We plodded along in the desert heat until we reached a village. In the square, a lorry seemed about to leave. We asked the driver where he was going, and he said that his destination was Wad Cherrifay, only 45 minutes further along. For a few piaster, we bought passage on top of his boxed freight and within the hour we were on our way.

A short while later, the desert gave way with abrupt suddenness to lushly green fields that flanked the dirt road. We became aware of the buzz of insects and the lyric music of birdsong. There was moisture in the air and the musky odor of rich, black soil filled our nostrils like rare perfume. We drew deep breaths of luxuriant air into our lungs, ridding ourselves of days of accumulated desert dust with each exhalation.

When we reached Wad Cherrifay we explored the marketplace for some minutes and then made our way to the police station to announce our presence in the village, as official procedure demanded. Our arrival had already been heralded. On the porch of the station two cots, each covered with a sheet the color of royal purple, had been set up for us.

As we entered the courtyard of the station, the chief, a fine-looking man with an arresting smile, strode purposefully toward us and vigorously commenced a formal greeting which consisted of the booming recital of a seemingly endless stream of phrases calling down upon us all the blessings of Allah. Ros, who spoke Arabic quite well, graciously muttered the appropriate responses, while all I could do was to smile with pleasure, thank him repeatedly, and shake my head at the enchanting wonder of it all. He was such a splendid specimen that I was half in love with him by the time he had finished. It did not escape my notice, however, that all of his subordinates stood quite rigidly at attention during this entire marvelous performance, and I decided then and there to be altogether decorous in my demeanor so as not to dissuade him in any way of his obvious impression that we were personages of some significance.

After we had been regaled with tea served in china cups matching the unparalleled splendor of purple sheets, we were taken on a tour of the area. The chief strode at the head of our little procession while Ros and I, surrounded by most of his staff and several other functionaries, followed. One of these, a youth with a coarse, unattractive face eager to display his rudimentary command of English, had apparently taken it upon himself to serve as my personal guide and to call my attention to a number of details that he obviously felt

I should not be allowed to miss. He told me that monkeys came out of the mountains at night and took fruit from the orchard. He showed me where lightning had split a tree.

Then, as we walked along, he plucked a large, oval seed pod from a shrub growing along the road, opened it, and proudly showed it to me. I was about to admire its delicately configured interior when with a sudden violent gesture he scooped out its contents, dashed them to the earth, and ground them under foot. Then, with an expression of satisfaction, he tapped his knuckles against the hard and bare inner walls of the pod.

I blanched. What had I just witnessed? Was my mind playing tricks? Was there any meaning to what he had just done or was my sudden feeling of horror no more than a product of my own fertile imagination?

"What is that plant?" I frowned, trying to curb my disquiet. "It is a Sudanese plant," he answered proudly. Then he flung the pod aside and spat. This gesture only increased my agitation. But surely, I tried to reassure myself, it had no significance. Sudanese men spat whenever the impulse seized them, which was often, in their yards, on the road, out of train windows, even on the dirt floors of their huts. But what meaning had there been to that little charade? Or had there been no meaning at all? I knew no more than that *I* had perceived something of note, but what had this scene meant to *him*, or what had he intended to convey by it? I could not shake my feelings of unease, but I also had no stomach to question him further.

Later, when Ros and I were walking alone, I plucked another seed pod, opened it, and showed it to her. "What does this remind you of?" I asked. She looked at me and smiled, half embarrassed. "It truly is amazing, isn't it," she said, "how the organs of plants sometimes mimic those of humans in appearance. It does look just like a woman's vagina, doesn't it?"

At least I knew that I had not imagined that part of it. But what had that callow youth been trying to convey? I found that I could not bear to think about it, and tried vainly to force such disturbing thoughts out of my mind.

After a restless night, I set out to explore the area on my own the next morning. The cumulative rigors of travel had caught up with

Ros and she opted not to join me, preferring to remain in the sheltering shade of the police station. I wandered toward the mountain, feeling driven to climb into its heights. I could see from a distance of some miles away that there was a narrow, scalable pass in the sheer rock so I left the fields behind and headed steadily in that direction. By late morning I had found the pass and begun to climb.

Smooth rocks along the steep grade provided a surprisingly steady footing. Occasionally my ascent was aided yet further by deeply entrenched shrubs which served as helping handholds. For some time I pulled myself slowly but steadily upward in the hot sun until I saw above me a kind of cave consisting of a flat ledge shaded by an overhang four feet above it. Faint with heat and thirst, I made my way toward it and edged into its soothing shade.

I drank the last of the water from my small canteen and lay viewing the scene below me. A narrow circle of green broken occasionally by a cluster of village huts lay around the base of the mountain and ended with unequivocal abruptness. Beyond it an infinity of featureless, barren desert stretched to the horizon.

A gentle breeze had sprung up. I felt deliciously alone and free. An irresistible impulse to shed the oppressive confinement of my decorously concealing clothes, demanded even of Westerners by the propriety of Islam, suddenly seized me. I hastily stripped them off and lay concealed and naked on the cool, sheltering ledge, experiencing the African wilds as a natural being for the first time. It was as if I had entered heaven. Sighing contentedly, I let the gentle winds play over my skin. My eyelids became more and more heavy and I fell asleep.

When I awoke, the sun had sunk closer to the horizon. I gauged the distance below me, hastily donned my clothes, and began my hurried descent, punished by a fierce afternoon sun. The wind had completely died down. In the oppressive heat, my sweat-drenched clothes clung to my skin. My throat and lips grew parched with thirst and I had to concentrate on picking my way carefully along the rocks as I grew progressively more lightheaded.

Somehow I lost my way and suddenly found nothing below me but a sheer cliff from which I found it impossible to descend. In panic I quickly retraced my steps, fearful that I would not reach the plains below before the onset of darkness. Aggressive baboons were reputed to roam the mountains at night and cold winds rose from the desert to assail the inhospitable rocks.

I reached the plains just as night began to fall. A sliver of moon rose on the horizon and in its pale, silver light I picked my way across the plain, back toward the lushness of the irrigated fields and the villages beyond. As I approached them I began to hear a great, drumming heartbeat of a sound whose insistent magnitude kept growing as I approached it. I found myself suddenly at a water-filled ditch and next to it a throbbing pump pulsed out water. I sank to my knees and drank long and deep of the crystal clear, sweet gift of life that was spilling out of the mountain.

When I had drunk my fill I again followed the road, as if walking in a dream, to a second pump and then yet another. At each I knelt with renewed thirst and drank greedily. Each time I rested for a long moment, my whole body attuned to the great heartbeat. I gradually felt clarity returning to my mind and strength to my limbs.

When I left the third pump, I began to hear a more measured, insistent kind of drum and followed its heavy beat until I emerged at a village clearing where a wedding celebration was in progress. In the center of a square ringed by spectators, several men were dancing vigorously with enormous, heavy swords, engaged in mock battle. A young man, obviously the bridegroom, sat surrounded by village elders on a low platform, watching them intensely. In a circle somewhat removed from this scene, a group of women were shuffling one behind the other in a slow dance, their hands upon one another's shoulders.

I spotted Ros sitting quietly on the sidelines. When I went to join her, she expressed relief at seeing me. "They came to ask me several times where you were," she reported. "I told them you had gone walking. They seemed quite upset that you had gone out on your own."

I nodded, for this was something that I had long since come to expect. Yet I flew in its teeth rather sooner than later wherever I went. The sheltered role of the well-protected woman of Islam was a straitjacket that I hastened to shrug off at the earliest opportunity, and this was somehow always inexplicable to my self-appointed guardians. Why could I not simply sit and take my rest as they so well meaningly bade me do? Why did I venture alone into the marketplace or up the mountain or along the rivers where they could not protect me? It was as much beyond their comprehension as it was beyond my ability to submit.

As we watched the dances, I asked Ros if she understood their meanings. She was not sure about that of the women, but ventured to guess that their dance simply afforded girls a rare opportunity to put themselves on display for potential husbands who might then importune their families to arrange a marriage. Unmarried girls generally had to remain inside the confines of their courtyards and could only rarely be seen outside.

As for the men's dance, she did know the object of the mock sword battles. These were designed to instill the bridegroom with vigor and courage, which he would need to penetrate his bride. The wedding generally went on for a week while this difficult task was accomplished by him.

The bride was nowhere to be seen and I asked Ros whether she did not consider this strange. "Not strange at all," Ros sighed, shaking her head. "She is without doubt cowering in her hut, fearfully awaiting her husband's next onslaught. It is not likely that she feels much like celebrating."

After some hours we left the wedding and walked back to our regal beds. The next morning we thanked our hosts profusely, accepted their relieved help in finding a lorry that would take us back to Kassala, and departed.

In Kassala Ros and I once more went our separate ways. She had friends among the Eritreans and assured me that they would look after her until her return to Khartoum. I found a lorry and continued on my way.

Her baby, in fact, was born only six weeks later. Her letter to me containing this information and sent by way of the Khartoum mails reached me in New York six months after it had been posted.

Small Sins

I have seen over a hundred photographs taken of our family during my childhood, and in many of them my mother's hands rest on my brother, but never on me. The closest she came to touching me may be seen in a family portrait taken just before we left Germany. The photographer had tried to pose her with her hand on my shoulder, but the hand had curled under and away in loathing of its assigned task. The expression on her face in this picture is sullen and angry.

My father felt sorry for me and defended me against her bitter wrath when I was small and malleable and adored him slavishly. He only began to hate me when I developed a will of my own, ultimately so much so that he left me out of his own when he died. Strong-willed and self-assertive women terrified him, which is why, I suppose, he was often so vicious and vindictive toward them in his relationships. He used to brag to me of his more ugly conquests, and I suppose that this was meant to frighten me, and make me toe the line.

When I try to forgive him, I imagine what it must have been like to compete against four more powerful males in his nuclear family for the love of his disappointed mother, and how desperately he must have had to fight for his masculinity when he served in the Kaiser's army in World War I.

It is ironic yet perversely logical that he never spoke of his mother without the greatest reverence, and that the rest of womankind elicited only his profoundest contempt, revulsion, and lust.

When I try to remember why I loved him so slavishly for far too many years of my life, I can say in my defense only that he touched me when there was no one else to touch me. When I try to remember other good things about him, I can recall only that he had a magnificent singing voice that could shatter glass, that he was a gifted orator, that he was able to cry, and that, being a small man, he had the mindless, gutsy courage of a bantam rooster.

I did not find it easy to form a self-image that I could live with. My father did not consider an education necessary for a girl, and I quite disagreed. I moved to another city, found a job, and somehow slugged my way through college. I came to be a loner and a rebel, and I don't think school ever taught me anything that I did not want to learn.

At 20 I began to explore my erotic potential, but my experiences were marred by guilt and fear. I could love men, but I could not love myself. I finally married a man who seemed to be as unlike my father as he could possibly be. At first, at least, he admired and enjoyed my intellect. Before long I learned that he was also sorely threatened by my capacity for initiative, which he admired but also envied, and more devastatingly, by my sensuality. He could not touch me nor stand to be touched by me. In marrying him I had fallen into my own trap. I had finally escaped my father only to find my mother all over again.

It was a trap from which I found it impossible to extricate myself for many years. I came to accept it, along with my then inoperable knee condition, as my inevitable fate. It was only many years later when I commenced to commit my small sins that I began to see the possibility of some hope for a different kind of life.

I have always chafed under authority. Maybe this has been true because I see so clearly the self-righteous pomposity and hypocrisy that often hides under its cloak. I have committed my small sins against authority with relish and élan, and I have generally managed to get away with them. There lives in me a small imp, generally a quiet and well-behaved tenant, but on occasions it gets raucous and takes over the whole building. Its favorite targets are petty bureaucrats and tyrannical teachers.

In Africa, where no one knows very much about what is going on in the rest of the world, petty officials are easily impressed by important sounding names and official-looking documents, no matter how worthless they may be. Sometimes one may have to create such a document at the spur of the moment to get out of a jam or to obtain entry into some difficult place.

In my travels I collected a rather impressive array of potentially

usable stationery, which included sheets from the British Broad-
casting Corporation, the University of Frankfurt, the Faculty of
Medicine of the University of Khartoum, Gutenberghus Bladene (a
Scandinavian publishing house), the Lockheed-Georgia Company,
and the Sudanese Ministry of Information. I always managed to talk
myself into or out of just about anything, and so the need for forg-
ing credentials never arose. Nonetheless, I felt a great deal more
secure knowing I had the insurance of those blank pages at my
disposal.

When in Khartoum I needed documents that would gain me entry
to medical installations and give me permission to take photographs, I was told by my gynecologist friend that I would have to
apply to a high official in the Ministry of Health. He also told me
that this man was an absolute dunce, that every academic examina-
tion from high school on had been taken for him by someone else,
and that every academic paper required by the university had been
written for him as well. He was barely literate, and his advanced
degree was meaningless. He had acquired his position of power
only through membership in a very influential family.

This official proved to be exactly as he had been described. He
glared at me arrogantly and demanded to know how it would be to
his advantage to grant me access to medical installations. I answered quite honestly that my proposed research was apt to bring
about material contributions from Western countries which would
improve the health of women and children in Sudan, and that this
would reflect most positively on his ministry.

"How do you know that I will not take the money and build a big
house for myself?" he taunted.

"I wouldn't know that at all," I answered, "but I would assume
that the aid will come in the form of teaching materials and similar
matter. Besides," I added, as my imp began to dance up and down,
"I can tell that you are an honest man."

"We have had a lot of material aid sent to us," he confided.
"We have warehouses that are bursting with oral contraceptive pills
that arrive weekly. Actually, we have run out of space in which to
store them, and they now rot on the docks in Port Sudan."

"Why don't you distribute them?" I asked, taken aback.

"The transportation and distribution problems are very great in this country," he said, and I knew that this was true, so I nodded. "Actually, what I would like to have some help with is a pet project of mine," he continued, "and that is infertility among the tribes in the South. There is such a tremendous rate of venereal disease among them that the sterility rate is well above 30 percent."

My imp was turning cartwheels. "I have an idea," I suggested. "You write a letter for me requesting aid with your project, and when I get back to the West, I will try to find an agency that is interested in increasing the population growth in Africa." He agreed that this was an excellent idea and set about writing the required letter immediately. In return for my promised efforts in behalf of his pet project, I obtained my permits.

Things were quite different in Atbara. My day in Atbara was not a day for even the smallest of sins. I was on my way to Kassala, along the Ethiopian border, and I had stopped in this small desert town along the Atbara River to change trains. I was told that I would not be able to make connections until the next day and that I would have to report my presence at the police station.

I wandered in the direction that had been indicated to me and found the station easily enough. It sat isolated in the desert, outside of the town, and was a typically unadorned, no-nonsense structure left over from English colonial days. As I walked toward the entrance, I saw a group of mournfully huddled old women squatting in the dust and immediately next to a barred, cage-like cell. In it sat about a dozen gentle-faced old men in white Islamic garb. Their hands and feet were heavily shackled with incongruously modern stainless-steel manacles.

I greeted the old women. They moaned sorrowfully and raised their withered arms to heaven. I walked over to the cell and shook hands with the old men sitting nearest to the bars. Whatever could they have done to warrant such treatment?

"Why are you here?" I asked them. They raised their patient eyes to heaven. "It is the will of Allah," they murmured in resignation.

I entered the police station and was shown by a very nervous soldier into the inner chambers of the chief of police. The chief was sitting at a ludicrously elevated magistrate's bench that looked like something out of a stage set for a play by Kafka. He was imposingly large and corpulent, intimidatingly stern, and altogether frightening. He descended from his bench with measured tread and invited me to join him for tea. He warned me that there was a dam some distance up river and that I was not to go near it. His soldiers had orders to shoot on sight anyone who came within a mile of it. I thanked him quietly for the warning, adding that I had no interest whatsoever in seeing the dam. My imp was impressively silent and was nowhere to be seen.

When I finished my tea, I asked him about the shackled old men in the cell. What had they done? "They are murderers," he intoned sternly. I could hardly believe my ears. Those sweet old men, murderers?

"It hardly seems possible," I marveled aloud.

"Yes, they are murderers," he reiterated, and then added severely, "or *suspected* murderers." My imp crouched quietly in the corner, trying to look like furniture. My imp is nobody's fool.

He poured more tea which was far too sugary for my taste, but I drank it dutifully. Then he ordered an armed soldier to take me on a tour of the town. I left quickly, greatly relieved to escape that oppressive room. The patient, gentle eyes of the shackled presumed murderers and suspected murderers followed me sadly as I hurried past their cell. There was nothing I could do.

In Nyertete, at the foot of Jebel Marra mountain in the West of Sudan, my imp had better luck. I knew that there would be a small government rest house where lodgings were reputed to be available. Government rest houses all looked very much the same in Sudan. They were spartan structures that had been erected in remote and scenic regions of the country by the English some decades ago during colonial occupation. They had since fallen into utter neglect and disrepair, boasted no furnishings whatsoever, and lodgings for the traveler consisted of no more than sleeping bag space on a generally littered stone floor, often among an indeterminate number of other wayfarers. The tattered remains of long defunct screens embellished shuttered windows. The heavy concrete structures themselves were still more or less intact, and some sort of water could generally be found reasonably close by.

I arrived in Nyertete at about noon. Its beehive market was buzzing with activity and I wandered about its extravagant displays of

brilliantly colored wares of grain, fruits, and vegetables at a leisurely pace. Eventually I was lured in the direction of the irresistible aroma of baking bread, and a short distance away, next to a
primitive mill with huge grinding stones, I saw an enormous, dome-
shaped oven in which bread was browning. I sat down to wait. My
patience was duly rewarded and I bought a loaf from the baker. The
bread he handed me was so hot that I was unable to hold it, and as
everyone nearby laughed, I quickly set it down on a large rock to
allow it to cool.

As I finally sat contentedly munching my prize, I noticed a group
of young men and women, shepherded by some older men, exploring the market. Several of them were carrying what looked like art
materials, and I inferred that they were students on some sort of a
field trip, along with their chaperones. I followed them into one of
the tea shacks, and soon discovered that they were indeed art students from the University of Khartoum. They had made the journey
on top of a lorry in several days of arduous travel across a broiling,
dusty desert. They had just returned from a week in the mountains
and had moved into the government rest house. The next morning
they would begin their return journey. Among these students I noticed a man with an arresting, craggy face, several years older than
the others. He was studying me with intense, luminous eyes, and I
was soon drawn into conversation with him. He explained that he
was a teacher of art who had recently returned to his studies at the
university in order to obtain an advanced degree. He was particularly interested in secular Western art, the teaching of which was an
entirely new concept in Sudan.

We talked for some time. Eventually everyone began to drift in
the direction of the government rest house, located perhaps a mile
down the road. The teacher picked up my backpack and offered to
show me the way. I had been talking to him about the great art
museums of Europe, and his luminous eyes never left my face. As
we left the tea shack we were joined by one of the chaperones, an
elephantine man with a booming voice. He wore a great flowing
robe, and undulated along beside us for several minutes. Then, satisfied with the evident propriety of our conversation, he fell,
wheezing, behind.

The government rest house consisted of two fair-sized rooms and one rather small one. The latter had been assigned to female students, although they far exceeded male students and professors in number. The room was already crowded to overflowing with sleeping mats and makeshift pieces of luggage but I was graciously welcomed. In a matter of fact way they all compacted their gear just a little bit more in order to make room for my sleeping bag.

I took in the situation at a glance: Twenty closely packed bodies sleeping in one tiny, airless room that would be claustrophobically shuttered and barred. My face began to twitch with anxiety and I secretly plotted my escape. I left my pack and sleeping bag near the door and went in search of water.

The sparkling waters of a creek bubbled along the rocks about one-tenth of a mile away and I saw that a friendly looking tree formed a kind of shelter some distance off downstream. I went to investigate and found it to be a perfect spot with soft, level ground where I could lie comfortably. This, I decided, would be my haven for the night.

As I returned to the path I found the art teacher, who, having filled some large containers with water, was waiting for me. It occurred to me that he might have followed me and that he had observed my explorations. I quickly consulted with my imp, but it merely shrugged its shoulders.

Back at the rest house a feast was being prepared, and in true Sudanese fashion, I was smilingly welcomed and urged to partake of it. The art teacher carried with him a stringed instrument that resembled a lute. On it he played a curiously accented, trance-inducing music such as I had never heard before.

At sunset everyone prepared for evening prayers, and while they were thus occupied, I quietly whisked my sleeping bag out of the cluttered dormitory room and hurried down to the shelter of my tree. Darkness fell swiftly, and before long a pitch-black, moonless night descended. Wispy clouds obliterated even the stars, and I could hardly make out my hands in front of my face. I leaned against my tree, breathing the cool night air, ecstatic at having escaped that terrible room.

I heard soft footsteps and felt the art teacher sit down beside me. For a few minutes we sat in silence, then his hand found mine and he gently stroked my palm. "When I woke up this morning," he mused, "I had the feeling that this would be my lucky day." Again I briefly consulted with my imp and it gave me its opinion that I was long overdue for a little recreation. I turned to face the art teacher. "Perhaps it will be," I murmured.

What ensued then is best described as one of the more pleasant aspects of my particular field research. It was especially noteworthy for its swift initiation devoid of any further introductory refinements. In this way, a change of heart was clearly outside the realm of possibility. Under the cover of darkness and an open sky, it lasted for an impressively long time.

After two hours had passed most agreeably, he said, "I must return to the rest house, or they will begin to search for me. I will tell them that I have spent the time with you, and that we have been conversing."

I agreed that this would be a good thing for him to do, and then I was alone once more under my tree. The clouds had begun to dispel, and soon a brilliant array of stars covered the sky from horizon to horizon. I gazed at them for a while, and then I closed my eyes and slept the sleep of the truly virtuous at heart.

I awoke in the gray of dawn, rolled up my sleeping bag, and walked back to the rest house. As I approached the entrance, my way was blocked by the elephantine chaperone who swooped down on me like a mammoth avenging angel.

"Where have you been?" he demanded in a resounding voice that threatened to shake the foundations of the building and certainly awoke anyone that was not already awake. "I have been told that you did not sleep in the room with the other women last night! Where did you sleep?" My imp, which had been blissfully curled up in a corner, woke with a start. I motioned it to remain silent, and answered pleasantly, "I slept under a tree."

"You slept under a tree?" he fumed. "How did you dare to do such a thing? You did not have my permission!"

"It is my custom to sleep under trees," I said calmly. "I do it whenever I have the chance." His dark face darkened still more.

"What you did was very dangerous," he fumed. "There are jackals outside, and you had not asked for my permission!"

I was beginning to have some difficulty with the imp, but managed to wrestle it into silence. "Professor," I said patiently, "there are no jackals out there. It was perfectly safe."

His voice rose still more. "You were supposed to sleep in the room with the women!" he bellowed. "How dare you defy me? *You did not have my permission!*"

It was getting to be a bit too much. "Professor," I said coldly, cloaking myself in whatever shreds of courtesy I could still muster, "Let us come into the real world. I am not one of your students, I am as old, if not older than you are, and I do not need to follow the rules laid down for your own women in this culture. I come from an altogether different culture, with different rules. The fact of the matter is, I am not accustomed to asking permission for anything that I do and especially not from a virtual stranger. Where I choose to sleep is absolutely none of your concern."

I pushed past him in order to collect my belongings from the women's room, leaving him sputtering indignantly. I said my good-byes to the wide-eyed young women who whispered theirs in return, hoisted my pack, and walked out the door. As I passed the chaperone, stony-faced and with my head erect, I could feel my imp wagging its ears and sticking out its tongue at him. He couldn't prove a thing, and in any event, I had hardly been guilty of robbing the cradle.

I walked to the great dome-shaped oven, bought a hot bread, and sat down to eat it. Half an hour later the lorry carrying the students rumbled by. The professor, who was still pouting, sat in the front seat and the art teacher stood at the railing in back, trying not to look in my direction. I watched the lorry disappear down the road, picked up my pack, and returned to the rest house. I found a leafy branch, swept out the largest room, and moved in.

*   *   *   *

I had one other notable encounter with a member of academia. Winter was coming to an end. I had spent my mornings for the past few months as a volunteer guest lecturer at a small, rather elitist women's college in Omdurman, the old city that lies adjacent to Khartoum along the Nile. This had given me the opportunity to obtain a significant number of valuable and telling interviews with educated young women, all of whom were quite articulate, and many of whom were surprisingly able to think for themselves.

The task yet remaining to me was to interview a man who purported to be a sworn opponent of female genital mutilation, someone whom I had been led to believe was a vigorous proponent of women's rights. He was an important functionary and professor at the little college, a member of an illustrious, intellectual, and professionally accomplished family, and a man whom I believed to command the respect of the community. He had a benevolent, grandfatherly aspect and was beautifully photogenic, with a shock of white hair that made him resemble Albert Einstein.

He readily agreed to the interview, but when I sat down with him and switched on my pocket tape recorder, he suddenly became defensive. "Before we begin this interview," he declared rather peevishly, "I want to make something altogether clear. I want to be sure that you understand that the only person who is responsible for the girl's circumcision is the girl herself. Even when her parents wish to spare her, she *insists* that it be done, and she harasses them until they agree to have it performed."

I was flabbergasted. Surely I had not heard him right! Perhaps I had misunderstood. "What are you saying to me, Professor?" I stammered, in confusion.

"What I am telling you," he repeated, "is that no one forces the girl to undergo the ritual. She herself demands it."

"But how is this possible?" I asked, realizing that I had indeed heard him right. "She is only a little child when it is done to her. What on earth would possess any small girl in her right mind to demand that a part of her body be cut away?"

"She knows from infancy on that this operation is absolutely necessary to make her ready for marriage," he explained, "and she *instinctively* knows when the time for it has come. It is then that she approaches her parents and insists that they comply with her wishes. It is our task to protect the child from her own folly."

I was reeling. *This* was the man who touted himself as being the magnanimous defender of the human rights of women and little girls? This glib man who so facilely blamed the victim for her own victimization?

"*Instinctively*, Professor?" I barely managed to answer in a voice that had somehow dwindled into an incredulous whisper. "Surely you do not mean *instinctively*. When we speak of instinct, we are talking of something that is in the genes, something that is an inherent part of the organism."

"Oh yes," he insisted. "It is instinct, and it is there in all of our little girls. They know *instinctively* when the time has come." He sat back with a satisfied smile and regarded me indulgently.

I had to somehow shock him out of his smugness. "What you are saying then," I nodded, "is that Africans are an altogether different species of animal than the rest of the human race."

At this his chin shot up self-righteously. "Africans are in no way different from any other race of humanity," he instructed me severely. "It is ignorant racism to suggest that any such differences exist."

I forced myself to smile at him brilliantly, in an attempt to mollify him. "I am *so* glad that we agree on that particular point, Professor!" I breathed a sigh of mock relief. "Just the same, I would be most grateful if you could explain something to me. Since all of us are members of the same human race, and since therefore we are subject to identical instinctual drives, how is it that I have never in any other part of the world encountered a *single* little girl who insisted that her parents have her genitalia cut off?"

Uneasily he admitted that this was also something of a mystery to him, but that nonetheless what he had told me was true. I carefully suggested that it was most likely that the differences in behavior of little girls in different parts of the world were influenced by irresistible social pressures from adults or even peers. It was also possible, I speculated, that adults sometimes seriously misrepresented things to children in order to obtain their cooperation and seeming agreement to harmful acts against themselves. I assured him that I could certainly cite many such examples from my own culture.

I forced myself to complete the interview, although I realized that it would no doubt be totally useless. When it was over I thanked him for his cooperation, put my tape recorder back into my pocket, and left. I walked down to the Nile, sat in the shade of a large tree, and listened to the tape I had just recorded.

It was all there, exactly as I had perceived it. I had imagined or exaggerated none of it in my mind. I shook my head in stunned disbelief. If *this* was the touted champion of women's rights in Sudan, who could possibly be out there to intercede for those beautiful children?

I felt too weary even to cry. My imp came tiptoeing up to me softly and put its sweet little face close to mine. When it realized how sick at heart I was, it quietly tiptoed away.

*   *   *   *

My dealings with the police in Sudan were generally quite pleasant. Whenever I arrived in a new town close to nightfall and had no immediate prospects for lodgings, I would present myself at the police station, declare that I had no place to spend the night, and after some predictable confusion and dismay, they invariably took me in. They all lived at the station, and room was always found for me in the courtyard or the garden.

In the morning, they would graciously serve me tea. Then they would write out letters of introduction to the headmistress of a nearby school or to some family member that could take me in, invite me to return for dinner, and guard my gear while I found accommodations. I had learned to expect only the best of them.

I was on my way to Kadugli, a town in the Nuban hills. A sadly ailing, ramshackle bus scheduled to arrive in El Obeid that afternoon had broken down time and time again and had finally deposited me in what I presumed to be the market square at 3 a.m. All other passengers had quickly scattered into the darkness in all directions and I was left standing alone in a moonless night.

After staggering around wearily for some time with my heavy pack on my shoulders, I found a house that looked like an inn. I pounded desperately on its door, and when a man finally opened and I asked him for a room for the night, he informed me regretfully that no accommodations for women were to be had there. He had only a dormitory for men. I tried to get him to direct me to the police station, but he failed to understand what I was trying to say.

When a tall, well-dressed man in an Islamic robe suddenly materialized out of the darkness and offered to take me to his mother, I followed him. Experience had taught me that those words constituted nothing other than an offer of the most generous hospitality.

Their utterance rendered him duty bound to deal with me honorably, as if I were his own most treasured kin.

The next morning I explored the market. A group of tribesmen freshly arrived from the desert was squatting next to their camels. On their faces I noted a type of tribal marking that I had never seen before. The usual facial scars I was accustomed to seeing had been left by strips of flesh having been gouged from the face in patterns characteristic of their particular tribe or region. These men, however, had had three strips of flesh cut, left attached on top, and then lifted from the face. The strips had then been formed into a braid, and this braid had healed back to the flesh of the cheek. The effect was exceedingly startling.

As I stood marveling at them, a man in uniform approached and asked for my papers. He inspected my passport, my visa, and then my permit to travel within the country, which I had had to obtain in Khartoum. The permit listed Kadugli and some villages that I hoped to visit, but the name El Obeid, which was merely a stopover on my way, had not been written on the form. He decided that I was in El Obeid illegally and that he would have to take me to the police station. In view of my previous pleasant dealings with the police, this was not a terrifying prospect. No doubt, only a small fine would be involved. Nonetheless, I felt a little annoyed.

We walked perhaps a quarter mile to the station, which, when we entered, was deserted. "They have all gone for breakfast," he said with some irritation. He bade me sit down while he slammed things around for several moments. Then he added, "I have not yet eaten *my* breakfast. I will go and do so now. You must sit here and wait until the proper officials return to deal with this problem."

I dutifully sat for about two minutes after the door had closed behind him. Then my imp kicked me in the ribs. "I have not yet had *my* breakfast," it announced. I cautiously walked over to the door and peeked out. The man in uniform was nowhere to be seen. Keeping a weather eye out for him, I eased my way back to the market, discovered a small tea shack well off the beaten path, and sat down to drink tea. When breakfast time was well over, I found a lorry to take me to Kadugli, retrieved my pack, thanked my gracious hostess for the night, and leaving the man in uniform behind, I was on my way.

*   *   *   *

It has been astutely noted that power corrupts, and that absolute power corrupts absolutely. One of the proofs of this regrettably accurate observation may be found in the small, rickety airport at El Fasher. This town is a government outpost in western Sudan. It is located in an isolated desert oasis many bleak and waterless miles from the closest habitable area and even further removed from the next airstrip.

I had had no more than the usual difficulty in obtaining a flight to El Fasher from Khartoum, and was told by the airline clerk that I would have to obtain in El Fasher the seat reservation for a return flight. With some show of unexplained distress on his young face, he added carefully that he had to warn me that such a seat was sometimes exceedingly difficult to obtain there.

Since it seemed obvious to me that as many flights had to come out of El Fasher as went in and I had had my choice of days on which to travel there, I did not take this warning very much to heart. Actually, in view of the fact that I did not know exactly when I would be returning to Khartoum, having an open ticket suited my convenience exactly and I completely ignored the clerk's warning.

I spent the day at the university. When I mentioned to one of my friends, a professor at the college, that I was on my way to El Fasher, she told me that she had visited there some months before. She had been forced by circumstances, she said, to make the return trip through the hot desert on the top of a lorry filled with evil-smelling fertilizer. The journey had taken several days and had been extremely hard. I sensed some sort of acute embarrassment on her part, but could not quite get to its origins. I assumed that it had to do with telling me about the fertilizer on which she had been forced to travel.

El Fasher, being a government center, was not particularly interesting to me, and after I had completed the few interviews I had been able to obtain there, I hastened on to the colorful and fascinating town of Nyala, close to the Chad border, and then on still further to the mountains of Jebel Marra.

By the time I returned to El Fasher seven weeks later, I was exhausted. I had an ear infection, was running a continuous low grade fever, had lost over 15 pounds, and worst of all, my skin was in a serious state of deterioration from exposure to the intense sun. I urgently needed the services of a doctor, some salve for my skin, sensible food, and considerable time in the shade, during which my skin would be able to heal. I had nearly run out of money and I was by now desperate to return to Khartoum.

I arrived back in El Fasher late one morning. There was no sign anywhere of any vehicle that could take me to the airstrip. In an attempt to avoid at least the noonday sun, I immediately set about hiking the two mile distance, painfully lugging my heavy pack with me.

I arrived at my destination, feverish and exhausted. After resting for an hour in the shade of a sparse little tree, I found the cubicle where flights were booked. At the desk sat a delicate-boned, young Sudanese man with enormous, expressive eyes. He looked at my ticket, looked at my papers, and then looked at me.

"Are you traveling alone?" he asked tentatively. I acknowledged that I was. A shadow of acute embarrassment crossed his sensitive face, and he said, "I cannot give you a seat on a plane without authorization by the director of the airport. You must speak to him in his office." He showed me to the appropriate room a short distance down the hall.

A toad-like man sat behind the desk of the office. He seemed inordinately pleased to see me, and immediately ordered lemonade to be brought. I told him that I would like to return to Khartoum as soon as possible, that I was ill and needed the services of a doctor. He clucked sympathetically and said that it could all be arranged very simply. Unfortunately every plane was completely booked for the next four weeks, but some sort of arrangement could surely be made. We could discuss the matter in the evening, at his house, over dinner.

I protested that I could not possibly walk the distance back to town again and he replied that this would present no problem at all. He would send a government vehicle with a driver to transport me. I would be quite comfortable at his house until a flight could be arranged.

It finally became clear to me that the Toad was after a pound of my flesh. I shook my head emphatically and stalked out of the room.

I walked wearily down the hall, trying to puzzle out what I could do to get myself out of this vile and unforeseen predicament. As I passed his cubicle the ticket clerk hailed me softly, drew me into his office, and pulled the door shut behind us. He apologized for having had to subject me to what he was certain had just happened. "It is not within my power to obtain the seat for you," he said unhappily. I told him that I understood, but that I had to find a way to get out of El Fasher, and quickly. I knew that the effects of several more days on top of a lorry in the brutal desert sun could result in quite serious consequences to my already damaged skin.

"He will let you have a seat if you give him 300 pounds," the clerk offered. "And if I don't have 300 pounds?" I asked. He looked embarrassed. "Well," I continued, "I do not have 300 pounds to give him. I do not even have 20. The money I have brought with me on this journey is all gone."

"I have an idea," he said. "A plane will come in two hours, and it is going to Khartoum. I know the pilot, and he is a fine and decent man. Stand near the gate when the plane lands and try to talk to him. Perhaps he can take you along. His name is Dilassio."

I nearly jumped out of my skin with joy. Dilassio! But I knew the man! I had met him at the Aarak Hotel, where my friend, the bush pilot lived. His suite was on the floor immediately above. He was a hook-nosed, scrawny French-Lebanese man with an eager, friendly face who, to his great happiness, had just been joined in Khartoum by his new and strikingly pretty English bride. People who knew him had all experienced his remarkable generosity and willingness to go out of his way for just about anyone.

I shook the hand of my young friend and thanked him for his kindness in helping me. He looked up and down the hall to make certain that I would not be seen leaving his cubicle and I returned to the shade of my meager little tree, waiting for the plane to arrive.

In due time I heard it circling over the airport and then it set down. The door opened, passengers emerged, and a few moments later, as I stood no more than 25 feet away by the gate, I saw Dilassio appear in its doorway. He spotted me at once and waved delightedly. I motioned to him and he immediately walked over to me. I quickly explained the situation to him.

"Oh, it is no problem at all," he said, obviously happy in the extreme to be able to help, "I am entitled to a crew of seven and I have only six on board. There is an empty seat in the cockpit."

I waited while he took care of some paperwork and when he was finished, we walked together to the stairs leading up to the airplane door. The Toad had already stationed himself at the gate and was personally taking tickets from everyone who boarded. I approached and he bodily barred my way." You do not have a seat on this flight," he sneered.

"There is a vacant seat in the cockpit. I am taking her aboard as a crew member," Dilassio said mildly.

"You cannot do that," the Toad croaked arrogantly. "I will not let you. She is not qualified."

"That is up to me to decide," Dilassio answered. "I am the captain of the aircraft. It is up to me to choose my own crew."

He started past the Toad who was hopping up and down in fury and frustration. I had never seen anyone who was actually "hopping mad," and I watched his performance in open-mouthed fascination.

"A ticket!" he shouted triumphantly. "You do not have a ticket!" Grinning from ear to ear, I whipped my ticket out of my pocket and pushed it toward him. Snarling, he snatched it out of my hand and I sailed past him up the stairs and into the cockpit of my winged liberation.

As we took off and headed toward Khartoum, I sat in the navigator's seat behind Dilassio. Over the din of the engines I shouted at him that I understood why his beautiful English bride loved him and he beamed happily. The stewardesses came to feed me quantities of lemonade, tea, and little goodies. I must have looked pretty ravenous.

My imp was in seventh heaven.

Lightfoot

I have a confession to make. I have been guilty of a lie. It was not a great lie, a gross falsehood that hurt or cheated or demeaned anyone else. It was only a little lie, born of a childhood weakness that I have long since conquered. When I look back on it now I see that it was an altogether human fabrication based on ancient, unresolved fears and on pride and an overactive imagination. True, it gained me love, but it also gave a measure of joy and pleasure to others so it was not a wicked lie. I say this not because I am trying to deny or make excuses for what I did, but because I know it to be really true. I am confident that I will be forgiven for my transgression.

When you are writing a book such as this one, you are like a raw wound. You are like a woman in childbirth. There is no way that you can fake it. You are as much at the mercy of your memory and your subconscious as you are at the mercy of your body when you go into labor. A book is like a living thing. The pain of creating life can be terrible, but pain is transcended and forgotten once you have given birth. Then it seems like a miracle, and when you behold your work, you marvel: Did this come out of *me*?

Here, then, is the source of my pain.

When I was 33 I suffered a terrible injury to my knee, and it blighted my whole life. I was transformed from a tremendously energetic, athletic young woman into a semi-cripple whose activities became progressively more restricted. My damaged leg was apt at any time to give way under me. I was told by doctors that the situation was inoperable in anyone over 14 years of age, and this was probably true given the state of the art at that time.

My husband, by then 40 years old, had developed into a perennial student, we had absolutely no money, and although no one ever thought of suggesting a prosthetic device to me, the cost of one would at that time have been pretty well out of the question. Or at least so I believed, and that was enough.

I had been crippled in another, far more significant way earlier in life. I could not ask for anything for myself. Even to this day I find it horrendously difficult to do so. I believe that the origins of this curious trait stem from the fact that one of the bones of contention between my parents lay in my mother's incessantly strident demands for things that my father was clearly unwilling (or even unable) to give her. To win his favor—for he was then the only ally and source of love available to me—it was absolutely imperative that I become her total opposite in every respect possible.

I don't recall ever asking anyone for anything as a child, except once when I was 12 years old. I was then a recent immigrant to the United States, and because I so needed a feeling of belonging, I decided one day that I wanted to join the Girl Scouts. For this I would need to buy a uniform, and I had not a single penny of my own.

For two weeks I wrestled with myself, desperately seeking an acceptable framework from which I might ask my father for the money. Finally, full of dire trepidation and in stumbling tones, I asked him for the four dollars that a uniform would cost. He thought it over for a second or two and then categorically refused, declaring that I belonged at home.

That was the last time I recall asking anyone for anything. How could I possibly ask my struggling student of a husband to materialize the money for a brace for my leg? I had two small babies, and this made him respond to my desire to find work and earn my own money as an emasculating personal insult. Living with an intense compulsion to be a perfect wife, fired by a father to whom I was still psychologically enslaved, I accepted my husband's dictum and lived on in guilt-ridden, mutely frustrated, and pain-racked poverty.

My marriage was a sexually ill-matched and quietly tormented one, but I ruthlessly repressed all feelings that contradicted the firm persuasion that I was anything other than perfectly happy, in spite of the all but complete physical and emotional rejection to which it subjected me. This was, after all, far better than the likes of me deserved, and asking for more would have been not only futile, but, I was soon persuaded, altogether abnormal and perverse. I had never learned to ask, and so my marriage served only to reinforce my feelings of unworthiness and self-loathing.

I did not realize until many years later how common this malady was among women in those times. We simply learned to stifle our own ambitions, our own talents, our own desires, in order to bolster the egos of the men on whom we thereby became helplessly dependent.

Quite recently I saw an article in a magazine which dealt with the expressed feelings of several men concerning their failed personal relationships with the important women in their lives. One nakedly honest statement caught my attention. "We got married," it said. "She treated me like gold, and I treated her like dirt. She devoted her life to buoying me up and I criticized and demeaned everything she did and dictated to her what she was supposed to think and do and feel. And I thought that this was love, that this was how things were supposed to be. And when it all fell apart, I could not understand what had gone wrong." Reading this man's account and feeling its confused sadness gave me a measure of peace.

My life went on in this fashion for ten years. I had by then begun to work as a high school English teacher, our finances had improved somewhat as a consequence, and when my leg had deteriorated to the point where it had become a handicap in my work, I consulted another doctor. This one was from some near-Eastern country, and his exposure to educated or self-sufficient women had no doubt been minimal. He said that with new techniques my leg was now operable, that it would have to be done *immediately,* and that the outcome of the operation depended on one thing, and one thing only: I must do exactly to the letter everything that he told me to do.

Holding a responsible job had by that time made me capable of enough self-assertion so that I did not like the sound of this, and so I consulted yet another doctor, who was recommended as having a high rate of success with knee conditions such as mine. What he had to say made good sense to me. He said that the condition was operable, that it did not have to be done immediately, but that it would probably be a good idea to do it fairly soon before the damaged structures underwent any further deterioration.

I was overjoyed and came to the hospital as if to a wedding. The operation involved a graft of my own bone taken from another part of the knee. I awoke from the anesthesia as soon as I reached the recovery room, with a completely clear head, immediately and effortlessly sat up, and concerned myself with comforting a small, terrified boy on the cot next to mine, much to the amazement of the nurses.

The incredibly rapid progress of my recovery surprised and delighted everyone. After seven weeks my cast was removed and I was about to return to work when turning in my sleep, I suddenly experienced a searing pain in my knee. It was the graft pulling out of its socket.

My body had failed to accept its own bone, a thing that was all but unheard of. The doctors who examined me could find no evidence of any injury, or for that matter any other explanation for what had happened. I myself would not understand the reasons until some time later.

I was returned to the operating room so that the knee could be repaired once more. This time the graft was fixed firmly into place with the aid of metal screws.

I remember trying vainly to struggle out of the anesthesia, and falling back into unconsciousness over and over again. I was entrapped in a nightmare of the deepest despair. Several times I perceived dimly that people were trying to rouse me, but could not seem to force my body back into life. I allowed myself to passively drift closer and closer to the edge of oblivion, and only an urgent voice in my head demanding that I fight for my life, insisting that I was not allowed to die like this, that I was needed by my children, kept me breathing. I tried again and again to lift my head, and when I finally forced myself back into consciousness, it was morning. The struggle for my body between the forces of death and the forces of life had taken nearly 24 hours.

Somewhere in the course of the pain-racked, sleepless night that followed I wrote on the pristine whiteness of my plaster cast: "This too shall pass." But I no longer believed it.

The trauma of having my hopes for a once more normal body blighted, in conjunction with the effects of anesthesia, had fractured the rigid self-deception that mine was the best of all possible worlds and that my marriage was as good as any marriage could possibly be. I understood with heartbreaking clarity why my leg had refused to accept its own bone graft. My body was self-destructing. The accumulated insults to my psyche of my own defective chemistry, the all-out war in my childhood home set within the bizarre framework of a society that left me no alternative but to accept its definition of myself as a subhuman, and my abysmally lonely and love-deprived marriage had irrevocably caught up with me. I no longer wanted to live.

There followed nine more years of physical and emotional disability during which various repairs to the knee failed and I had to face surgery once more. Numbly I dragged myself through life as I sank deeper and deeper into depression. I longed to die, but knew that I could not abandon my children.

I suffered acutely and progressively from sleeplessness, and whenever I finally, toward morning, sank into a troubled slumber, I dreamed incessantly the same wild, hopeless, frantic dream: I was running, running, running.

Finally, after five operations, as if by some magnanimous reprieve or pardon, the damaged knee mended and held together. One day I began in fact to run. At first it was only a thrashing, deformed hobble over perhaps 50 paces. Occasional passers-by who observed my bizarre flapping either laughed or grew angry.

To avoid these encounters I began to arrive at the track before dawn, when it was utterly deserted. As I lurched along doggedly, pushing for momentum, sudden spasms of asthma would constrict my trachea as if with an iron band, and I would rage against them, spewing curses into the wind, at the still livid ghost of my father whose presence continued to hover over me like a poisonous cloud. "Leave me alone, you vile old bastard,," I would choke. "You cannot hurt me any more, damn you! You're dead as dirt and I am still alive! You can rot in hell! The rest of my life is *mine!*"

I would feel the blessed air flooding back into my lungs and for the first time in my life, the sweet taste of victory filled my mouth.

Gradually, over a period of wildly hopeful, elated months, my body straightened, my legs grew stronger and more even, and I began to stride. Finally I was able to pant my way through an uninterrupted full circuit of track, then an even-breathing two, then four, and then more and more more. After six months I was

able to run an only slightly gimpy six miles, and the endorphins that
my unchained body generated largely freed me from depression.
For the first time in many years, I was able to sleep peacefully.

Stephanie, my sunny sylph of a daughter, daily floated silkenly
beside me as if dancing in the role of my protecting angel. Occasionally her friend Marie, an emerging champion runner, accompanied us. The precision of her gleaming, powerful legs in motion
was a constant marvel to behold. These two splendid-bodied young
women were certainly the most improbable running mates to align
themselves with the likes of me. Yet both of them steadfastly maintained the loving fiction that there was nothing at all unusual in our
training together, and that they accompanied me solely for their
own enjoyment. Their encouragement inspired me to strive all the
more.

I began to enter middle distance races, and soon noted that hardly
any other women over 50 were running in them. One day I remained after the race as winners were being announced and trophies
passed out, and was stunned to discover that I had taken second
place in the women's over-50 Masters Division. This shocking development inspired me to renewed and more highly concentrated
efforts, and soon I was taking first prize in my division for every
race that I ran. One heady, memorable, steamy Sunday afternoon
on Long Island, I even took second place in the over-40's division,
in a good-sized field of much younger and highly competitive
women.

I had by this time served enough years at my school to be entitled
to a sabbatical. My children were by now grown, my body had
mended, my relationship with my husband had evolved into a more
egalitarian, cordial, but increasingly estranged one.

I decided that this was the time to make a break for it, and applied
for the sabbatical. I resolved to spend a year backpacking my way
around the world. It was an ambitious project, considering the fact
that I had never backpacked before.

"Why don't you try it for a week-end first?" my husband suggested. "No. I am going for a year," I replied. If I could run and
win a race, I could do anything. In my mind I had become invinci-
ble.

I consulted my doctor on what precautionary shots I would have to take, and received an inoculatory cocktail of cholera, tetanus, yellow fever, and whatever else was required for Third World travel. The next day I ran my last race. I seemed to have a lot of trouble hitting my stride because the arm that had received the injection throbbed painfully with every labored step. Then I got my second wind, the unspeakable joy of running swiftly seized me, and I ran the race in my best time ever.

It was early August, and an oppressively hot and humid day. As everyone waited for the announcements of winners, the throbbing in my arm returned and I suddenly felt as if I would faint. I looked around vaguely for a place to lie down, and noted that the concrete area where I was standing was strewn with broken glass. I placed both of my arms against the raised platform in front of which I was standing in order to hold myself up. I closed my eyes, heard something that sounded like a cannon shot, and then everything went black.

The next thing I vaguely perceived was that I was lying on the ground with people kneeling over me and a wetness around my head, unable to move any part of my body. The cannon shot that I had heard was my skull striking the ground as I pitched backward onto the concrete.

Within minutes a volunteer medical unit arrived. With infinite tenderness and caring concern they lifted me onto a stretcher, after immobilizing my neck and explaining that I must under no conditions try to move it until X rays were able to determine whether I had fractured my neck and injured my spinal cord.

A nameless young runner, her shirt soaked with my blood, softly stroked my hand until I was lifted with great gentleness into the waiting ambulance. One of the volunteers rode with me, and I opened my eyes every now and then so that I could focus on his kind, reassuring face. I fought desperately to ward off spectres of the unspeakable nightmare — a lifetime of paralysis. Then I discovered that my hands and my feet faintly obeyed the command of my brain to move, and I gathered hope that perhaps all was not lost.

At the hospital I was rushed into the X-ray room, and within minutes a visibly relieved doctor informed me that I had sustained an egg-shell fracture to my cranium, but that my spinal cord was uninjured. After two more hours, I was able to feebly move my throbbing head.

I had been granted another reprieve, and my first prize trophy arrived at the hospital the next day.

Since the fracture had created an opening into my skull, I was kept on massive antibiotics for a week. Because my trained, well-conditioned body healed with surprising rapidity, I was allowed to leave the hospital at the end of that time with the warning that I could expect to suffer from episodic headaches for an indeterminate period, and that since my neck had also suffered a considerable whiplash, this would eventually cause me further problems. If I tried to continue running it could only make matters a great deal worse, and I was urgently advised to give it up.

It was a grievous loss. To keep myself from mourning it too acutely, I pored over maps of Europe where I had intended to begin my journey. I felt that I was fighting against time, and that if I was to make my break for it, I had to do it now, before the inevitable neck symptoms set in. As soon as I got out of the hospital, I continued preparations for my proposed journey as if nothing had happened. If I could run no longer I would walk, and walk over as much of this earth as was possible.

I knew that I would go back to Germany in search of roots; in search of some sort of resolution; in search of understanding, forgiveness, and peace. It had been 40 years since I left my home in Hamburg as a stateless nonperson, and I wanted to exorcise the ghosts that continued to haunt me. I realized how much unresolved fear I still felt, and decided that I would have to create an emotional crutch that I could lean on.

I had to find a new identity. I no longer wanted any part of my married name and felt only revulsion for the one my father had given me. I had to recreate myself, to give birth to a new being, and so, like a snake shedding its skin, I burst out of my outgrown casing.

All of my life people have mistaken me for a Native American. When I was working my way through college in Washington, D.C., I often wore my long, unusually thick, and very straight black hair tightly bound into two massive braids down my back. With my aquiline features, high cheekbones, and copper skin, it was not difficult to misjudge my origins. I would sometimes be stopped by some hopeful European tourist who would ask eagerly if I were a real American Indian; I never had the heart to disappoint him so I always said yes, and sent him home happy.

This is how it happened that I invented Lightfoot, my grandfather of the Cayuga tribe. In the story, my grandmother had been sent to America to prevent her running off with an adoring Russian Jewish suitor whom she loved, but who was felt by her bourgeois German Jewish family to be beneath her station in life. That part of the story was in fact true, except that the poor, timid, heartbroken young woman was not sent to the United States at all, but merely prevented from seeing the man again.

In my version of the story, however, she got her revenge by creating a far worse scandal when she met, fell in love with, and married Lightfoot, who was somehow connected with the circus.

He died shortly after their marriage under mysterious circumstances, and she, bereft and pregnant, was returned to her family in Hamburg. There she gave birth to my mother and eventually married a Dane of which her family approved, a businessman who in true life went bankrupt fully seven times before he was finally able to succeed in a modest import and export business.

My grandmother was the sixteenth child of a 52-year-old, and by that time hopelessly depleted mother. She was a delusional depressive doomed to intermittently spend a good portion of her life in mental hospitals. So much for this unfortunate woman's elevated station in life.

Her good husband, so my story went, adopted my mother as his very own child, and since she was fair of skin, light of hair, and had greenish eyes, no one ever questioned her parentage. Lightfoot's genes—or more likely the genes of a member of Ghengis Khan's hordes—did not manifest themselves until a generation later, in me. This was all I knew, since my grandmother was understandably loath to talk about that chapter of her life, and preferred to consign it to oblivion. I had only by accident found out about it when I chanced upon some old family documents, and had questioned her about them.

It was quite a story. I was rather proud of it. I went to such pains to construct it because I desperately needed an identity other than my own, and I suppose that the reasons for this would have kept a psychoanalyst busy for quite a while. The name Lightfoot itself, of course, suited my newborn legs, and acted as some sort of talisman.

As a child in Germany, I had, like everyone of my generation, enjoyed reading the stories of Karl May, an immensely popular writer of fiction, who lovingly portrayed the American Indian as an almost god-like, magnificent, noble savage. This highly idealized image was still retained by his contemporary readers, and so while Lightfoot was able to remain in her erstwhile identity as an outcast, displaced, minority unperson, one-quarter of her at least was completely transfigured into something rare and wonderful.

I cannot deny that embedded in the story there was also a small, covert element of revenge. I looked forward to laughing secretly at those whom I duped in this fashion.

Of course, it did not turn out that way at all. When I got to Germany and past the initial terror of the uniformed guards at the border, I fell in love with many of the young Germans I met, and they with me. With or without Lightfoot, we would have become friends.

But the story, when I related it, so charmed them, and it was so eagerly told and retold to their friends, that I did not have the heart to confess that I had made it all up. I do know that its invention clearly marked the beginning of my life as a storyteller. I still remember the young woman who rushed up to me in a bookstore, full of happiness at seeing me, grabbed both my hands and blurted out excitedly: "I know who you are! Your name is *Thundercloud!*"

So I resigned myself to what was obviously my fate. I no longer wanted the revenge of duping them; I only wanted to make them happy. Lightfoot became substantial flesh and blood. Lightfoot became me.

I am Lightfoot, Lightfoot the swift runner, Lightfoot who walks the Sudanese desert and mountains alone, Lightfoot the Noble Savage, the Strong Woman who sleeps on the bare African earth, She who is free to come and go like the wind.

It may be argued that I have clothed myself in false feathers, that I am not in truth an eagle, as many have believed me to be. I am only a crow. But there was no malice in my fabrication, and now I have cleansed myself of it in the waters of truth. I am indeed no more than a crow, but the simple crow is well loved by the Great Spirit, for it may speak wisdom. I have spoken.

El Shadida

Somewhere in a book written by a seasoned adventurer not unlike myself, I found an excellent piece of advice based on his own experiences with lengthy and out of the ordinary journeys. It was this: Never pass up a chance for sex and never pass up a chance to do your laundry.

I certainly never passed up a chance to do my laundry. While chances for sex were often many, they were mostly grim and saddening in one way or another. Wonderful sex comes one's way only rarely when one is constantly on the move, and so, when the ballet of the vital juices commences, one often settles for what is available.

Actually, this is not so terribly different from what one has to deal with in ordinary, everyday life. Most of us have to kiss a depressingly large number of frogs before we find a prince, but given a more normal set of circumstances, we are in a better position to bide our time and to pick and choose.

When you are on the road all of your encounters are brief, and most of them are disappointing. However, in just such a situation you find that among the mountains of dross there are some jewels that you cherish with gratitude and joy for as long as you live.

I will not burden the reader with my mountains of dross. They were ultimately nothing more than boring and distasteful episodes and I need not conjure up their tiresome ghosts here. Having all of my life suffered from an inferno of unassuaged sexuality, I do confess that there were far more of them than I care to remember, and I consign the lot to the generic category of errors in judgment.

Among my jewels there was Roy. It was only one month into my first journey and I had not before this time dared to go beyond the security of the familiar language in England. I had just learned from a fellow wayfarer how to hitchhike effectively, and I was trying out my newly acquired skill on the approach road to Dover. I had been told that vehicles took this road to the ferry that crossed the English Channel to the Continent, and a hitchhiker could make the journey without any cost by finding a lorry that would take her on board as a "second driver."

Hitchhiking was staggeringly easy in England, especially for a mature and obviously harmless woman. It never took me more than two or three minutes to get a ride, and frequently the first passing car obligingly stopped for me. Outside of the London area (and most other large cities anywhere in the world), England was well-known among backpackers to be a safe and thoroughly pleasant place to obtain rides, and my small and recent fund of experiences certainly bore this out.

I had barely stationed myself along the approach road and was taking off my backpack, when an enormous Scandia truck plowed into the shoulder along the road about 100 feet in front of me and came to an abrupt, grinding halt. There was no doubt about it, it had stopped for me. I wrestled my pack onto my back and hurried forward. The door on the passenger side swung open and when I reached it, I saw a huge bear of a man with a truck driver's beer belly, and an imposing hatchet-like nose sitting in the driver's seat. His grin was reassuringly good-humored and kind. "D'you need a hand, luv?" he asked in his thick Cockney bass voice, as I struggled with my heavy pack. His massive paw reached out and swung it easily unto the bunk behind his seat, and then pulled me up alongside him into the cab.

It was my first experience with such a huge vehicle, and my excitement at finding myself at a vantage point so high above the road and on my way onto the ferry kept my secret terror well hidden. Once on the ferry, I thanked him and made it clear that I would stay on deck to watch the Cliffs of Dover receding into the distance. Roy said that he was going to have a couple of beers at the drivers' table, and that I could find him there if I so wished. He had a cabin, and offered to take my pack there for safe keeping. He handed me a key.

I sat for two hours in solitary safety on the windy and freezing deck, and finally beat a shivering retreat to the cabin in quest of my warm sweater. I tentatively knocked on the door, and receiving no answer, knocked again. I inserted the key and carefully opened the door into a darkened room. The door closed behind me, and I could make out a pair of bunks under the porthole a few feet away. Suddenly an enormous dark shape loomed up in one of them, and I hastily fled the room. I spent the rest of the trip huddled in some remote corner of the boat, without my sweater, trying vainly to keep warm.

It was nearly night by the time the ferry docked. I had assumed that when we arrived on the other side we would be in Calais. I would thank my host and be on my way to find a room for the night. I knew nothing about the lifestyle of lorry drivers or I would have realized that that was not in the cards. Calais, I discovered, lay some distance inland from the ferry.

After disembarking we drove another five or so miles, and then pulled in at a truck stop where about a dozen lorries were already parked. Roy went out to make the truck tight for the night.

My chagrin must have shown quite plainly when he came back into the cab. How was I to resolve this quandary? Where was I to go? What was there to be gained by starting out along the road into an unknown darkness?

Roy regarded me quizzically for a moment. Then he gave me his good-natured grin and asked, "What'll y' 'ave? The upper or the lower?" For the first time I saw that there was another bunk folded into the wall above the one behind the seats. I took a deep breath. "The upper." He locked the doors and made the windows fast. The space above my face in the upper bunk was no more than that which a coffin would have afforded. "Could you please leave a window open just a little bit?" I pleaded. "I suffer from claustrophobia." I could see that the concept was strange to him, but he cranked the window down a few inches so that I could feel the chilly night breeze on my face. Then he turned off the light. I wriggled into my sleeping bag and heard him plowing around in his bunk under mine for a moment or two. Then there was silence. I was almost certain that he was asleep, when I heard his voice one more time. "You sure can move fast when you want to," he marveled. A minute later his deep, rhythmic breathing told me that he was asleep.

In the morning he made us a lovely kettle of English tea on his kerosene burner, and I began to feel comfortable with him. He was going on through Germany and into Vienna, and because he was such a gentle bear, I decided that I would continue on with him. We got used to one another's altogether strange speech and started to become friends. I began to appreciate him as a totally unflappable man with interesting, down-to-earth views of the world, and bone-dry English humor. I began to relax.

When we approached the German border I was seized by a new and totally elemental fear. I had known this would happen but I was not prepared for its magnitude. I had left Germany in 1938, 40 years before at the age of 11, in the heyday of the Nazi regime. I had never until this time returned, and I carried with me all of my childhood fears. When I caught my first glimpse of the border control officers with their German uniforms and dour public servant faces, I began to gasp for breath. I instinctively groped for Roy's hand and clutched it tightly for strength and comfort. He gave me a reassuring squeeze, and the moment of panic passed.

That night we parked near a German "Gast House" that featured live music, and Roy treated me lavishly to dinner and wine. By this time I was beginning to size him up, and for some obscure reason had decided that although he was certainly a sweet and gentle man, he was probably not very accomplished in the sack. It must have been one of those popular stereotypes of Englishmen that had per-vaded my younger days which addled my perception. At the end of the evening I retreated to my upper bunk coffin, and in spite of his slight air of puzzlement, ensconced myself in my sleeping bag, cracked the window, and escaped into sleep. Escaped almost, but not quite. My sleep was redolent with erotic dreams.

The next day we reached the Austrian border where several rows of lorries returning to the East Block already waited, their engines idling, to check through border control. I heard a truck pull up on our right and Roy muttering awestruck under his breath, "Would you look at those two blokes!"

I turned to look out the window and saw two men with tough, nightmarishly harsh Slavic faces scowling at me from under bushy and knitted brows. Naively I smiled, and the scowls deepened. Fail-ing to understand what was going on, I turned to Roy to find an explanation.

"Maybe they don't like their own women riding with lorry drivers," he suggested. "Some of these mountain people have pretty mean rules where it comes to females."

I nodded in recognition. It was an attitude with which I was more than just glancingly familiar. "That makes me a whore by their definition," I commented.

"Seems that way," he shrugged.

For a brief moment I recalled my father's singular reaction, when at the age of 18 I had escaped his stifling tyranny. I had left home, taken a bus to Washington, D.C., found a small room and a waitress job, and entered college. For some obscure reason, the fact that I worked as a waitress reinforced his conviction that I had become a whore.

Then my imp suddenly awoke. I dug into my bag and came up with a pack of American cigarettes. I had obtained these in the duty-free shop on the flight over, even though I had no personal use for them, knowing they would come in handy somewhere.

I rolled down my window and held the pack toward the scowling men. "American!" I chirped brightly. They looked both taken aback and uncertain. I gestured back and forth from myself to them, indicating that I was offering a gift and smiled hopefully.

The window on the driver's side was partially open and now it was slowly cranked down still further to allow a nicotine-stained paw of a hand to hesitantly emerge. The face nearest to me had miraculously softened into a shy smile, revealing a full row of dazzling gold teeth. The driver took the pack, each man delicately plucked a cigarette and he started to pass it back to me. I gestured that I wanted them to keep all of it, and the gold-toothed smile broadened. The second driver leaned across that one's massive barrel chest, holding out a small box of chocolates toward us. "Bulgar!" he boomed, an incongruously shy smile creeping over his murderous face as well.

We each took a piece of chocolate and started to return the box. "Nyet. Nyet," they insisted. They wanted us to keep it. Roy meanwhile had scrabbled around under his seat and had come up with a bottle of scotch. "England!" he rumbled, holding up a thumb to indicate that this was very good stuff, and it in turn was passed over. A large bottle of vodka immediately materialized from the other side. By this time they were both beaming. We toasted one another. Then the lorry in front of us started up and it was our turn to go through border control. We waved, they saluted, and we went our separate ways.

We reached Vienna shortly after. Because it was the end of the week and German law forbade lorries the use of highways on the weekend, we parked on the Prater, near the famous Viennese amusement park, along with about two dozen other trucks from all over Europe. From them we learned that immediately following this weekend there was another holiday to which the same rules applied, so that they could neither load nor drive, and it looked as if we would be stuck for four days.

Across the road from us several prostitutes plied their trade, waiting apathetically for customers who drove by in cars, picked them up, and delivered them back some minutes later. The transactions took place at such a remarkable speed that I decided to clock them. The average cycle took four and one-half minutes. I asked Roy what services were offered. He ambled over and came back shortly to report. "Blow job with a rubber," he announced. "One minute to the park, one minute back." The going price was the equivalent of 20 dollars. The other truckers spent the afternoon idly watching, making bets on which of the women would do the most business, and how many minutes each transaction would take. They found little else to do except drink and sleep.

That evening we went to a beer hall, along with three other Limey truckers, and I danced with all of them in my denim workman's suit and hiking boots. Vienna is basically a very conservative place with some very staid rules of behavior for women. Not all the looks I got were approving, but this hardly mattered.

By the time we got back to the lorry I had decided that I would spend the night with Roy, not because I expected that there would be any good sex, but because I liked him so very much, and because I knew that it would calm and comfort me just to lie next to his bear-like body.

* * * *

I had been married for many years to a man whose sexuality had been stifled and crushed in earliest childhood, and who was totally inexperienced sexually when he married me at the age of 35. For a brief interval, my own sensual nature seemed to enable him to achieve a modest measure of personal liberation, but it soon developed that he could neither fathom nor endure the fires that raged in my body. As it developed, he was in fact fully persuaded that they constituted a kind of malignant disorder, urgently requiring remedy, and so he willfully set out to cure me of them. He soon gave me to understand that sexual intercourse was physically painful and depleting to him, and consequently avoided touching me or being touched by me altogether. I could not understand why this should be happening, but allowed him to convince me that it was somehow my own fault.

Our encounters thereafter were rare, tortured, and thwarting. They ended invariably in the same humiliating fashion. He would jump up as if possessed, rush into the bathroom, and commence to scrub all traces of my essence from his body. Because of my unfortunate upbringing and because I, like other women of my generation, had been brainwashed into accepting the guilt for whatever went wrong with my marriage, such scenes left me in the end with the conviction that I was fully deserving of his revulsion and that it was I who was somehow horribly abnormal. I plunged more and more deeply into depression, which ultimately left me teetering constantly on the very brink of suicide.

I remained faithful to him for 16 tortured years and then, in a desperate, last-ditch attempt to save myself, began to find occasional snatches and bits of satisfaction elsewhere. These rare would-be escapes were with men who had similar marriage problems. The punishment for my digression was firmly built into each enslaving relationship. I was always granted just a fleeting taste of what it might be like to have what I so desperately desired, never satisfying my craving for being touched, being wanted, being worthy.

* * * *

When we reached the door of Roy's lorry, I asked, "Roy, would you like me to spend the night with you?" He looked at me wonderingly, and replied, "I thought y'd never ask!"

It was a memorable night. Somewhere in the course of it I confessed to him both that I had thought he would not have much to offer in the pleasure department, and also that no one had ever in my life given me enough. I had for some time known that I was multi-orgasmic, and I had learned that it was no use for me to count. Roy, it turned out, was also multi-orgasmic, and seemed to have a refractory period of about three seconds. I counted for *him*, and when he had reached ten, I not only had had enough, but could no longer move. "No more," I gasped. "I can't any more."

He did not stop. "Y've 'ad enough then? Are y' sure y've 'ad enough?"

"I've had enough, Roy! I've bloody wonderful had enough!" He asked me twice more, and then, seeing that I was in a state of near-collapse, he let me go to sleep.

It was a memorable night in many ways. It exploded once and for all the delusion that had been forced upon me that I was repulsively and irrevocably abnormal. I realized that I was merely unusual.

*   *   *   *

Two years later, in Khartoum, I was made aware that a gynecologist by the name of Salah Abu Bakr had made an outspoken and courageous condemnation of female circumcision on the Sudanese television. It was not easy to locate anyone in Khartoum since the telephone network left by the English colonial system was in the process of rapid and progressive disintegration, and the receivers one saw on the desks of bureaucrats were little more than nonfunctional status symbols. So for three days, I went on a series of wild goose chases by whatever vehicle I could muster, and finally wound up at a small gynecological hospital in Omdurman, directed by Dr. Salah, as he was called.

I told him about my field of interest, and when he asked how he could help me, I explained that I needed a fair-sized group of women whom I could interview. He immediately called a staff conference. He would direct his staff to cooperate with me and would supply me with two Sudanese translators who were nurses trained in London, were themselves circumcised, and like all of his nurses and midwives, carried on a flourishing practice in female circumcision on the side.

He told me that in return for their cooperation, I must tell the women anything they wished to know about myself, and that it was crucial that I be as honest with them as I expected them to be with me. Of course, I readily agreed.

The staff conference went quite predictably at first. There was a great deal of excitement at my being there, and rapt attention to everything I had to say. Dr. Salah explained my mission — that I came from a culture where circumcision was not practiced and that I would answer their questions in return for their answering mine — and then I was on my own.

There was a long moment of silence, and then tentative questions about whether I was married, (yes), if I had children (a son and a daughter), did I not miss them (of course, terribly!), and how had my daughter been circumcised. When I told them not at all, there was much shaking of heads and wonderment. I could see that this was a totally incomprehensible concept for them.

"Not at all? But *why*?" I explained that it was something that women in the Western world simply did not do. Another question came. "How are *you* circumcised?" Again I told them that I was not circumcised at all. "But *why*? Was your mother a prostitute?" No, she was not. Again, "But *why*? How could she leave you in such a terrible condition?" Again I tried to explain, and again there was much shaking of heads and wonderment.

For a long moment there was silence, then a brief, urgent, whispered conversation among the midwives. Finally one of them, her proud and secretive face lined with the most deeply gouged tribal scars I had ever seen, stood up. She took an adversarial stance, taking her time in looking me up and down. Then she turned back to the other midwives for support, while they all urgently nodded their encouragement.

I leaned forward, convinced that something important was about to happen, and held out my hands, palms upward, toward her. "Speak," I said.

"We want to know," she said, and turned once more to the other midwives for support, while they all nodded eagerly, "We want to know what is the most you have ever done it in one night."

The question crashed at me as unexpectedly as a bolt out of the blue. My face broke into a big, happy grin of rememberance, and almost reflexively I turned my two hands so that the palms were toward them, all of my fingers spread. "Ashera (ten)!" I said.

There was instant bedlam and pandemonium. They were shrieking wildly with laughter, excitement, delight, glee. It went on and on and on. After several minutes Dr. Salah gave up trying to call the meeting to order, and dismissed them.

I am sure that they thought I was the most depraved slut in all the world. I am sure that I had staggered their wildest imagination. But I had achieved what I had set out to do, and that was to win their confidence. The cooperation I got from this group was absolutely amazing. I asked them the most intimate questions, and they gave me unquestionably honest answers.

The story spread like wildfire. The next morning, as I passed the guard at the gate, he looked at me with wonderment and deep respect and asked softly, "Ashera?"

"Ashera," I replied proudly.

Then, tentatively and hopefully, pointing to himself: "Chamsa (five)!"

"Ashera!" I announced firmly, and sailed past him.

On the obstetrical ward the midwives were gathered, and the one with the remarkable tribal scars looked up from the squares of much laundered cloth that she was folding into bandages, and announced sardonically, "El Shadida fee (the Strong Woman is here)!"

I have kept that name, El Shadida. I have absolutely no idea whether it was meant pejoratively. The midwives, after all, must have viewed me with considerable ambivalence. I was tampering with their extremely lucrative livelihoods and obvious importance in the community. Whatever its intent, I like that name. It has a fine, audacious ring to it, and there were moments along the way when only my audacity pulled me through.

*   *   *   *

After four memorable days on the Prater in Vienna with Roy, we parted. He had to return to London and I was on my way to tour Europe. I had by this time met most of the other drivers that were parked on the Prater. They had come, one by one, and had offered to take me along to their various and often temptingly interesting destinations. With some of them my long and sensitive nose caught the indefinable but indisputable scent of danger. I thanked them for their kind offer and told them gently that my plans lay elsewhere.

In all the time that I spent hitchhiking, I never failed to trust my nose. It became exceedingly sensitive, and whenever a lorry or car door opened for me and I did not like what I scented, I thanked whomever sat at the wheel, said that I had forgotten something, and hurried away in the opposite direction.

Eventually Roy found what seemed to be the perfect driver for me, a young Dane with a beautifully clownish face, who was on his way to Copenhagen and whose route took him through Poland and Czechoslovakia. Roy carried my gear into the Dane's truck, helped me up into the passenger seat, and closed the door. As we drove away, I saw his bulky figure recede and then blur as the tears coursed down my cheeks.

But that was not the end of it. Life very rarely presents you with a balanced diet. More generally you must reckon with either feast or famine. There were more periods of seemingly endless famine in the course of my travels than I care to remember. Occasionally, however, there were feasts. This was one of those occasions.

Frank was one of the happiest men I have ever met in my life. He was forever bursting into song out of sheer exhuberance. He attributed his joyous outlook to a superbly happy childhood, which was immeasurably enhanced by the fact that he was one of only two boys in a class of 35 children. Due to this altogether impressive imbalance in the male/female ratio, his opportunities for childhood and adolescent sexual experimentation had been monumental.

He carried a treasure trove of Danish delicacies in a basket behind the driver's seat. When lunch time came we pulled into an enchanting forest grove and sat, pillowed by fragrant pine needles, feasting. He was half my age, and his youth was like a bubbling spring. He was as passionately happy as if I were the Prom Queen deigning to go out on a date with him.

Night fell, as night had to fall, and as he was making the truck fast I suddenly saw that above the bunk behind the seats there was no second upper bunk that folded into the wall, as there had been in

Roy's truck. The development of my depraved sluthood was not sufficiently advanced at this point for me to register this disconcerting piece of information without some chagrin, and I climbed out of the truck while I briefly but seriously considered spending the night on the cold ground outside, or at best in the front seat. But then he walked toward me.

When Frank reached for me, it was so beautifully and honestly impassioned, and at the same time so hopelessly funny, that all of my resistance melted. I allowed him to lead me back to the truck. His body was like nothing I had ever experienced before. It glowed with an almost otherworldly, intense heat, and I felt as if I were holding a burning torch in my arms. He exuded an equally remarkable odor which I have never been able to forget. It filled my nostrils and I could not seem to gather enough breath to take in all I wanted of it. The next day he sang and sang and sang. He almost burst with happiness. Frank was in love with me.

We drove through the bleak, rubble-strewn Czechoslovakian countryside, seeing bloated and malnourished peasants pushing primitive wheelbarrows along pitted dirt lanes. We stopped at an open marketplace to find some bread. At the end of the square, a multi-spired, bleakly gray stone cathedral loomed. I entered its roughly hewn portals and saw a long, snaking line of stoically waiting older peasant women which wound its way the entire length of the cathedral. Their bodies had been twisted and shockingly misshapen by hardship, cold, and malnutrition; their arthritic knuckles were swollen and raw. Dull, lifeless wisps of hair straggled from kerchiefs wound tightly around their heads.

At the end of this long line a pockmarked, emaciated priest sat coughing in a wooden wheelchair, holding an ancient ear trumpet to his ear, hearing the whispered confession of a woman who crouched on her knees beside him on the icy stone floor. I marveled at this spectacle. What conceivable sins could all of these miserable women possibly conjure up for confession to this dying, tubercular priest?

We stopped in small villages and vainly tried to find something to buy in the little shops. There was nothing to be had. At the Polish border, in front of the ferry to Copenhagen, border guards circled the truck with bloodhounds whose chilling task it was to sniff out hidden human freight.

When we arrived in Copenhagen, Frank coaxed and squeezed his immense truck through narrow streets and around impossible corners so that he could bring me to the very doorstep of the hostel. We exchanged gifts. I don't remember what I gave him. It must have been insignificant indeed. He gave me a silver spoon that I had admired, and I carried it with me for a long time, until somewhere in Africa I lost it.

Frank helped me to buckle on my backpack and I walked toward the door of the hostel. I tried not to look back. I always try not to look back, but when I heard the truck start up, I turned around for one last glimpse of that beautiful clown face. I saw that he was weeping and then I turned away.

*   *   *   *

Four years later I made my third journey to Sudan. I was by then a seasoned Africa traveler with a wealth of experience, unmitigated chutzpah, and great sophistication. I had learned to make optimally efficient use of my wits, and if there was still anything I was afraid of, I never allowed my conscious mind to find out about it. I was capable, dispassionate, efficient — and monumentally lonely to the point of utter despair. I had become so ravaged by skin hunger that I had all but lost the ability to sleep, and correspondingly, my already tenuous hold on a will to live was growing ever slacker.

It was an unusually cold winter in Khartoum, which is to say, the temperature rose to 95 degrees during the day, and fell to 50 degrees at night. It was on a Wednesday, and on Wednesday the sauna at the Hilton Hotel, enclave of Western civilization and center for all transactions of significance in Khartoum, was open to women. I had learned to make the most of the fact that my face was by then a familiar one, and did a great deal of my paperwork in the cool, luxurious comfort of the Hilton lobby or coffee shop. I had come to think of the hotel as my personal office, and most of the staff had become convinced that I lived there, and treated me like one of the guests.

For a small fee I was able to use not only the sauna, but all amenities such as hot showers and good soap, an indescribably rare luxury in Sudan. Although I sometimes spent hours shampooing my hair and grooming myself, I very rarely encountered another woman, and enjoyed these facilities in solitary splendor. This particular Wednesday, however, I was joined in the sauna by two women who were either Egyptian or Sudanese, and who seemed to be bona fide guests of the hotel.

There is no false modesty among women of these cultures. The three of us sat steaming and naked on the benches and studied one another. We must have appeared equally exotic in one another's eyes, I with my hairy white skin, imposing mammaries, and bushy triangle, they with their silken and fine bird-bone bodies and plucked, Barbie doll, anatomically incorrect pubes. They rubbed one another with oil, and when they offered, I gratefully allowed them to do the same to me. Friendship in Sudan comes as easy as the flickering of an eyelid.

When I left the sauna, with dripping hair, I entered the totally empty hotel bar and sat down to indulge myself in yet another weekly luxury, a glass of wine, while I waited for my hair to dry.

On my way to the bar I had noticed a small, ugly African, wearing a black shirt, who was staring at me intently. I have always felt an aversion to black shirts because they conjure up images of a long-ago time in Germany and of men in SS uniforms, and I quickly looked away. But when I felt someone sit down on the stool immediately next to mine, I knew without looking and with some annoyance that it could only be he.

I tried for some minutes to ignore him. It is not an easy task to ignore someone who is sitting so close to you that you can feel the warmth of his body, especially if he is the only other person in the room, and you are both facing a large mirror. Eventually I decided that it was not worth the effort, and turned rather resolutely in his direction. I looked him squarely in the face and decided immediately that my fleeting first impression had been altogether wrong. His face, rather than ugly as I first perceived it, was an intriguing composition of incongruent planes and his eyes were arrestingly alive, warm, wise, and immensely interested. We began to talk, and I very shortly found myself engrossed in an intense conversation of such scope and breadth as I had not been able to enjoy for many months.

His name was Pognon. He was a diplomat from a small West African country, spoke several languages, and had studied at a number of European universities. His manner was quietly reassuring and his voice soothing.

I cannot say how it happened, but somehow I fell into those eyes and into the essence of his African soul. He was a man that was totally out of the ordinary, with an intelligence and insight that one only rarely has the good fortune to encounter.

We talked for many, many hours, through a leisurely dinner, an excellent wine, and well into the night. The black shirt receded more and more into the distance, and finally seemed to disappear. He looked at me helplessly. "If only I had met you two weeks ago. I have been here for two weeks, and my plane leaves tomorrow. If only I had known." There was no art or artifice in his voice, only genuine sorrow.

I too was nearly overcome by sorrow and longing, and so I said humbly, "Pognon, I will stay with you tonight. I am immensely lonely. I am so desperately lonely and sick at heart that I see no way that I can go on any longer. I need someone to give me courage. If one night is all we have, then so be it. I am immeasurably grateful to have that."

He thanked me softly, and I saw him tremble with emotion.

I will never forget Pognon. Every time I awoke in that night, I felt him tenderly stroking my face, stroking it with love and caring, as a mother strokes the face of her sick child, as my own mother never stroked my face, as only one other man had ever lovingly stroked my face before.

It was after I had been in labor for three days and three nights with my son, my first born. Because I had not been able to dilate during all of that time, I was given no analgesic while the fool who was in charge of the labor room over the weekend waited for my gynecologist to return from his golf weekend. He himself was either unable to perform an emergency cesarean section, or merely lacked the courage to make the decision that this was the only thing that could be done. Obviously a forehead presentation left absolutely no other options open. The head had long since engaged and it was by then impossible to turn the baby.

By the time Dr. Big Shot returned on Monday morning, I was half dead and my poor, battered infant fared no better than I. When some days later I was able to step onto a scale, I was shocked to discover that I had lost 40 pounds during those three days, at least 20 of which had been my own body weight.

My son manifested stress for many months. Even now, so many years later, serenity comes hard to him.

By the time they wheeled me into the operating room, my contractions were so continuous that the time between them was no more than two or three seconds, and with my infant's head battering my pubic bone, it was as if both of us were being tortured.

They had to give me spinal anesthesia in order to operate, and as we waited for those precious two or three seconds between contractions during which a needle could be safely thrust between my vertebrae, a black orderly offered me his hands to hold.

Half crazed with pain, I flung my arms around his waist, buried my face in his belly, and held on for dear life. His arms encircled me lovingly and he held me, tenderly stroking my hair. They shot the anesthesia into my spine and as soon as the contractions stopped, I passed out.

That was the briefest love affair I have ever had in my life, and also one of the most intense. I never saw this man again, but I will recall the security and love I experienced, gathered up in the darkly rich tenderness of his arms, for the rest of my life.

For a long, long time I tried vainly to find him again in other men — not necessarily among Africans — and when I finally did find him again for the first time, it was Pognon, whom I also never saw again.

Such are the ways of treasures. Such are the ways of the road.

The Faces of My Beloved

The first time I fell in love with a woman was in 1950. I was then 23 years old and had just graduated from college. The object of my sudden passion was a dumpy, frizzy-haired, middle-aged female who was standing at a lectern on a podium. She was talking about some of the aboriginal peoples of the world and the chances for survival of the human race in the event of an atomic war, a topic that was then of overwhelming concern to everyone due to the particular political frictions of the time.

She voiced the opinion that civilization as we knew it would not make it through such a cataclysmic event, but that some patches and remnants of humanity would doubtlessly survive somewhere in the world to carry on the human race. Although her own cheerful serenity seemed to be quite untouched by such a prospect, her audience in the packed auditorium drew small comfort from it.

The name of this purveyor of questionable glad tidings was Margaret Mead. Most of her listeners gave the impression that they had come to hear her speak in the hope that she might relieve them of the fear that they were going to die. Her cheerful reassurance that the human race would not become extinct, that it had faced equal or worse challenges before in its long and only partially recorded past, did not seem to make them any happier.

I was totally enthralled. I had never seen such a woman before. She represented to me everything under heaven that I longed to be. She had had adventures in remote regions of the world among totally strange people who had altogether different concepts of themselves and their society. She had had the courage to find and live among these people, and yet she was a woman. I, chafing under the imprisonment of all the familial, religious and societal restrictions placed on women in my day yearned achingly to be just like her.

It was the only time in my life that I ever saw her. I can think of her now as a sister, a kindred spirit, but back in 1950 she was my idol, my heroine, and far, far larger than life.

The most vivid thing that I remember about the entire experience was that she had a particularly arresting gesture, one that I recall whenever I now bake bread. She would accept a question from the audience and before tackling it, would briskly push up her sleeves, one after the other, as if she were about to begin kneading a bowl full of dough. Then she would present her answer.

I have fallen in love many times since then and have collected many sisters and daughters along the way. There is even an extraordinary woman in Hamburg, the place where I was born, who searched me out and who became my soul mother. She had read an article that I had written about the plight of women in Sudan, published in an English journal. After obtaining my address from the publisher, she wrote to me, asking if there was any way in which she might help me.

We began to write to one another. I was delighted to find in her a remarkably interesting, witty, superbly rational, and intellectual correspondent. The age of this treasure was somewhere near 80. She was a gifted linguist and art historian and had completed a university education in her youth, in an era when such a thing was only rarely accomplished by women. Her range of interests scanned the world, and everything possible in human behavior could be discussed dispassionately between us.

We wrote to one another about our lives. She had had the remarkably good fortune of having been raised by two of the most tender and loving parents imaginable, who had also bestowed a noteworthy degree of freedom upon her. During the war they had tragically become victims of the Holocaust, and had disappeared without a trace in some Nazi death camp.

I wrote to her about my own life and told her that I realized what I wanted to do with what remained of it. In answer to her question of how she could help me, I confided that what I needed most desperately was someone who would believe in me and who would somehow assert for me my value as a human being. In short, I said, I needed a spiritual mother.

Our budding friendship turned out to be made in heaven. Although children and the sheltering of them against all forms of abuse were her overriding passions, she wrote in reply, her personal misfortune had been that untoward circumstances had prevented her from bearing any of her own. She offered to assume the role of my mother. I was elated, hopeful, and equally consumed with anxiety that she would reconsider her offer. After completing preparations for my second journey to Sudan, I conquered my agonized trepidations and traveled to Hamburg to claim her.

In my many long years of self-hatred and self-doubt, I had often tried to imagine what a mother who loved me without reservations would be like. I had constructed fantasies in my mind of impossibly wonderful creatures, but paralyzing anxiety and guilt prevented me from ever approaching them, even in dreams.

When I met Herta Haas, I realized immediately that the stuff of my dreams had been far too flimsy. She was beautiful, with electric blue eyes and a smooth, soft-skinned face. She exuded acute intelligence, gentility, self-possession, vitality, wit, and kindness. She was cultivated, charming and tenderly loving, and she became *my mother*.

She took her task of adopting a more than 50-year-old daughter serenely in stride, as if there were really nothing whatsoever unusual about this at all. She concerned herself intensely with my well-being, and when we went out to the market together, she bought me ice cream because, she said, one should always buy ice cream for good children. At night when I went to sleep, she tucked me in and I sighed contentedly and slept like a baby. We spent our days together and to my great joy, she never seemed to tire of my company. It was touching, ludicrous, adorable, and healing. It was a blinding revelation to me. I adored her shyly and longed for nothing more in this world than to make her proud of me. When I left Herta two weeks later to journey to Norway, I took with me the buds of a newly found strength and self-possession. Her healing influence continued over the years, until eventually I mended and became whole.

We continued to write, and like a loving daughter, I came to Europe to visit her whenever I had the chance. Even now these visits are to me among the highlights of a life that has become rich, happy, and filled with love.

In Norway I met BeritAs, a pioneer feminist legislator who had been the impetus behind a great deal of social and legal reform affecting women in her country. A strong, feminine vitality emanated from her stocky, maternal body, which gave the impression of her being grounded in the earth of her land. There was a quiet solidity about her that brought to mind the Eddas, those powerful and wise women of Norse mythology.

She too asked how she could help, and I foolishly replied that I needed funds to could continue my research. I had attempted to find support in the United States and my efforts had met with absolutely no success. Berit told me that she would speak to the women of Norway in my behalf, and a short while later she presented me with 3,000 dollars which these women had contributed.

Elated, I thanked them, but it was not long before I was beset with doubt. I was immensely touched by Berit's confidence and trust in me and was truly grateful to the kind and open-hearted Norwegian women for their generosity, but the money hung like an albatross around my neck. It was not by any reckoning a princely sum, yet I came to wish that I had never accepted it. Already driven by my own personal demons, I now felt that I had to work day and night, and whenever I drew breath and tried to relax and enjoy myself for a day, I was overwhelmed by nagging guilt. Only after my book was published did I feel that I had absolved myself of my indebtedness, and I vowed then never to allow myself to be beholden to anyone again.

When I left Oslo to begin my journey across Europe back to Africa, Berit wished me good fortune, took me in her arms and embraced me in farewell. I shall remember that embrace until the day I die. It was like being enfolded in the arms of the Earth Mother herself. I felt a powerful energy emanating from her body into mine, and I had the sensation that I was either dying or being born, I could not tell which. The experience was so overwhelmingly strong that when she softly released me from her arms, I feared that I would faint.

But I did not faint. I returned once more to Africa, and whenever I was weary and sick at heart, I remembered Berit's embrace and it helped me to find strength.

*   *   *   *

I have related the circumstances I lived through in my childhood to a number of mental health professionals in the course of my lifetime. These have on various occasions expressed the opinion that it would have been only logical for me to have chosen to be a lesbian. Although I have come full circle in relation to women, and I now enjoy a number of deeply enriching friendships with them, I have never made such a choice. Sexually, I have always been driven imperatively only into the arms of men.

Perhaps all such choices are made by the programming of one's inherent genetic makeup. Perhaps also the all-encompassing imprinting formed at my birth by my father set an irreversible pattern. Perhaps, even, the primal fears of abandonment and death instilled by him will always be there.

Whatever the reasons may be, they no longer matter. I shall no doubt retain my heterosexual preference. Nonetheless, I now know the faces of my beloved, and in earning my freedom, I have found the courage to love her.

Your Death Is Always with You

When I was teaching in a New York City high school, in a prison-like building surrounded on three sides by inner city slums, many of the young men I had taught died in the Vietnam War, and just as many of my students died at home from drug overdose, domestic violence, disease, murder, or suicide. I would hear about these deaths, but I never saw any of them happen. In Africa, your death is always with you, and quite often, unexpectedly, you see his no-face staring nakedly into your horrified eyes, as you watch someone die.

In Cairo I saw a man flung from an overcrammed bus careening madly around a corner on bald tires. His head hit the pavement and split open like a ripe melon. He had been one among many others clinging to window posts on the outside of this bus. The driver stopped, got out to look at him briefly, and then climbed back into the bus. Another man was already clinging to the vacated window post as he drove off.

On the way from Khartoum to Costi, a fight broke out between a number of tribesmen that were riding on top of the railroad cars and others that were trying to climb on. In the melee that ensued, a man was pushed off the car and plummeted headlong to the ground where he lay unmoving, his head at an improbable angle. The man who had pushed him leaped off the car in a vain attempt to escape into the desert, and was pursued by a pack of the others. When they caught up with him, they flailed him to death with the heavy fighting sticks they were carrying. They left his broken body lying in the dust, and climbed back up to their perch on top of the car, carrying their kinsman, whose neck was broken, with them.

Sometimes you are suddenly face to face with the unspeakable. The Aarak Hotel sits in the center of a square in downtown Khartoum near the main business street, in the shadow of a large mosque. Around the periphery of the mosque, within easy view of windows in the Aarak, a row of beggars and lepers sits silently, their begging bowls at their feet, hoping they will find favor in the eyes of Allah, praying fervently that the worshippers who frequent the mosque will be moved to charity.

I had walked to the Aarak Hotel through the blinding sun and choking dust of afternoon Khartoum. I had recently met a bush pilot who resided there, and was coming to talk with him in hopes of obtaining a lift to Juba, a town beyond the Sud along the Nile, that could be reached overland only with the greatest difficulty.

It took me a while to find his room, and when I finally knocked on the door, I heard him call in a loud voice to enter. He was standing by the window, watching some spectacle below.

There was much shouting and milling about, and every few seconds a piercing scream rent the air. In the center of the crowd we saw what looked like a police car, and some men in uniform were hacking away at something that looked like sticks of dark wood which they were stuffing into a large bag. The screams grew weaker and weaker, and finally stopped altogether. The men in uniform finished filling the bag, tossed it into their car, and drove off.

When the agitated crowd finally dispersed, we saw a large pool of blood on the ground where the scene had taken place. We went downstairs to investigate, and heard described what it was we had witnessed from the window: A car had careened into one of the lepers, an old woman, who had remained on the ground, seemingly dead. The authorities had come to collect her body, tried to stuff it into a plastic bag, and found that it did not fit. They had then taken an axe and begun to dismember the body. The woman had only been unconscious, for she suddenly revived and began to scream. They had continued their task of cutting off her arms and legs in spite of her screams, and finally, after they had decapitated her, there was silence. After throwing the bag containing her truncated body into the car, they had driven off.

Death comes readily and often to little girls when their time to be circumcised has come. The job is all too often done by old women with defective vision, in dimly lit huts or kitchens, and with kitchen knives, much-used razor blades or paper scissors. In most cases the child is totally unanesthetized, and her vain, frantic struggling may lead to even worse damage than is intended. Death may come in the form of shock due to intolerable pain. Even when she is one of the more lucky ones who is given an injection of local anesthesia by a trained midwife, she may hemorrhage, die of infection, or contract tetanus from the dirty implements that are used to inflict this terrible trauma on her. Death is never very far from little girls, those frail-armed wisps of creatures, whose enormous, wounded eyes convey a betrayal that words cannot express.

I never saw such a girl being circumcised. I was given the opportunity to witness this ritual many times, but I always refused. Every human organism has limits beyond which it cannot safely go, and that was where I drew my line. I could not willingly watch a child being tortured. It would have been impossible for me not to bodily interfere, and I knew that my desperate act would in no way have spared the child.

Driven by the demon of my own experience with a painful, near-fatal birth, I did spend a lot of time in gynecological wards, watching the tormented births that are fostered by this cruel childhood ritual. It results in hard, inelastic scar tissue that must be cut to make birth possible, for it is not able to dilate. I saw babies born dead. I saw women hemorrhage. My ears were assaulted by seemingly endless, drawn-out shrieks of pain that left me reeling and shaken.

The doctors on these wards were half mad with frustration. Depression and an overwhelming sense of futility shrouded them like a pall.

One morning I entered the delivery anteroom just as a young gynecological resident slammed his way out through the door. He stared at me with haunted eyes, his face working, his whole body shaking with rage and frustration. "How can we help them when they come here in such a condition?" he choked helplessly, vainly battling to control his tears. He slammed his tightly clenched fist into a wall. "It is useless! *We* are useless!"

A moment later he regained the control he was struggling for and turned to reenter the delivery room. I followed him. On the table lay a festively dressed young woman, her hands and feet intricately decorated with henna, befitting a great celebration. She was heartbreakingly lovely with fine, aristocratic features. Her limbs were elegantly delicate, her wrists and ankles almost impossibly slim.

She was shaking violently with shock, and the tone of her skin was already too blue to belong to a living creature. Everything else in the room glowed deep red. There was blood on the floor, along the walls, in enamel and steel pans, on her "tope" that had been vainly stuffed between her legs to stop the blood that was exploding out of her. The hemorrhage had been too massive to stem.

I went to her side, took her limp hand in mine, and tried with all my being to will some life back into her. It was to no avail. She shuddered once or twice, the shaking ebbed away, and she was dead.

No one is immune to death anywhere, but in Africa it lurks around every corner in the form of fevers, disease, and dysentery. The lone traveler may lie untended somewhere under a tree or on the floor of some stinking inn for days on end, shaking with fever, weak with dysentery, and unless some charitable soul comes to bring her water and she carries with her the medicines she needs to survive, the traveler may die there. I have myself lain for many days, shaking thus, more often than I care to remember.

Sometimes, too, death grins at you from the faces of lunatics. In Port Sudan, where I was interviewing anyone who agreed to talk to me on the subject of female circumcision, I was referred to the headmaster of a boys' secondary school. I came to the school with Dale, a young American medical student with whom I was at that time briefly traveling, and spent an hour interviewing the headmaster. I asked him many searching and emotionally charged questions about his personal life, and he answered them with touching candor. When I had finished the interview, he invited us to share the mid-day meal at the school. We readily agreed, glad to have the opportunity to meet more teachers in hopes that we might be able to interview them as well.

A history teacher with an unctuous manner and shifty eyes beckoned me aside and whispered that he would gladly enlighten me on the history of circumcision practices in Sudan if I would come to his quarters in the evening, after dark, when the school day had finished. I did not like his looks, but felt no great apprehension since Dale was going to accompany me.

We arrived at the appointed hour, and his door opened to our knock. When he saw Dale he seemed somewhat taken aback, but recovered his composure quickly and invited us in. Another man sat in the spartanly tiny room furnished only, like most rooms in Sudan, with woven string cots. He was wearing Adidas sneakers, a rarity in Sudan, and a warmup suit. The history teacher introduced him as a teacher of sports who had received his training in Germany. He knew no English but could communicate with me in a guttural south German dialect. Dale understood not a word of it.

We conversed. I asked the history teacher some questions pertaining to his area of expertise, and wrote down this information. Then he began to ask me questions concerning my own life, which, as usual, I answered honestly. Did I wish to see female circumcision end, he asked. I gladly admitted that I did. There was a way for him personally to assist, he confided in a lowered voice. He had two little daughters, and he had had the thought that perhaps they should not be circumcised.

"There is a way," he repeated.

"And what is that way?" I asked, taking the bait.

He eyed me greedily. "If someone could prove to me that sex is better with an intact woman, I will not circumcise them."

It was the cheapest trick in the world. His daughters, if he *had* any daughters, had most assuredly already been circumcised. I smiled at him enigmatically and told him that I wished him luck in finding such a person.

Meanwhile I became aware that the gym teacher had been staring unblinkingly at me in a way that made me most uneasy. He began to talk glowingly of his training in Germany and confided that some of his professors, who had been former SS officers, had much influenced his philosophy in life. He was a great admirer of Hitler, and much regretted his defeat and downfall. I smiled at him, feigning approval, and in a voice purring with indulgence, agreed that he had indeed been fortunate to have been exposed to such interesting formative influences.

Again he fixed me with his unblinking stare. I could begin to perceive the shadows of hideous fantasy playing behind his eyes. There was an American that he admired tremendously as well, someone whom he wished to emulate, he continued. I expressed my pleasure that the influences in his life had been so diverse. Who was this American that he admired so much, I asked.

"His name is Manson," he whispered, "a man of great genius, a man who has the potential to rule the world." Someone like him could not long be confined to prison, he was certain. His followers would surely engineer his escape. Manson had long been his personal hero, he confessed, fixating me with his unblinking stare. I smiled vapidly into his maniacal eyes and agreed that of course, I understood his feelings perfectly.

Dale, meanwhile, having no grasp of the language in which we were conversing, was altogether unaware of what was going on. When the teachers left the room, I grabbed his leg and managed to alert him in terse Pig Latin, which neither of the two men would have been able to understand, that there was danger, and to let me do the talking.

When the teachers reentered the room I stood up, saying that we had to return to our quarters. The gym teacher questioned me on where we were staying, and when I strategically misinformed him that it was at the hostel to the south of the school, he asked a number of more detailed questions about the duration of our stay and the location of my room. I answered everything with a perfectly straight face, we thanked our host, and left. As soon as we got to the gate of the school compound, I hissed at Dale that we must get out of there instantly and cover our tracks, and he, an experienced tracker, led our flight into the moonless night, zig-zagging and repeatedly changing our course, until we were certain that no one had followed us. Then we headed north to the other end of town, where our quarters were located, several miles away. I never went back to the school, and never saw the two teachers again.

Sometimes death toys with you, and when you gape at him in fear, laughs mockingly in your face and walks away. It was two years later in Port Sudan, in the steaming heat of spring. I had arisen at dawn to walk in the harbor while the air was yet cool. Looking toward the single narrow channel that led into the harbor, I saw a strange and shocking sight. A freighter was lying in it, dangerously tilted, its railings on the port side already submerged. More than a hundred carcasses of drowned camels and sheep floated in the sea, while others stood woefully at the railing, contemplating the water. The animals had apparently shifted, for some reason, to the port side of the ship during the night, and lacking the appropriate ballast, the boat had listed more and more, taking the animals with it.

It was a scene from Dante's *Inferno*. I took out my camera and began to take pictures. After some time, when it looked as if the crippled freighter would sink then and there and effectively disable the entire harbor, a tug boat arrived and began to tow it out to sea. I took photos of the entire operation. When the tug boat had drawn the freighter as far as the edge of a reef, it cut it loose and left it to tilt off the reef and sink. I found a vehicle to take me as close to the reef as I could go, waded an approximate quarter-mile into the shallow water, and chronicled the freighter's demise. The water continued to fill with drowning camels and sheep as the boat listed more and more. After perhaps an hour it seemed to shake, gave a gargantuan groaning gurgle and disappeared into the depths below.

I snapped my final picture, returned the camera to my pack, and waded to shore. On the way it occurred to me that the owner of the freighter might want to buy the film to prove his case with his insurance company. I began to hunt for the shipping office, and after two or three hours of searching, was finally directed to the right place.

I entered the dingy anteroom of the shipping office where several large and fierce-looking seamen sat smoking tensely. They regarded me suspiciously. I asked several times if there was someone that I could talk to who spoke English, and finally one of them went grudgingly to the door of the inner office, called, and after a considerable time another harried and unfriendly looking man emerged. He asked me brusquely what I wanted. I told him that my visit concerned a film of photographs I had taken of the sinking freighter which they might wish to purchase for use in dealing with their insurance company.

The man shot back into the inner office and emerged again within seconds with the tallest Saudi Arabian I had ever seen. The Saudi issued a tense command and I found myself surrounded by a ring of menacing seamen. I heard death close by, snickering in amusement.

"Where is this film?" the towering Saudi asked, carefully modulating his voice in an effort to appear quite casual. "Do you have it with you?"

"I am sorry," I lied, "I have left it at the house of my friends."

"I would like to buy it," he offered unctuously. "My men will accompany you to the house of your friends, and you will bring this film back here with you."

I thought in panic of my host's small children, and managed to feign a gracious Arab smile. "There is no need. I have just remembered that I have not left it where I have told you, but that it is still in my camera, right here with me. I have brought it to you as a gift."

I opened my pack and extracted the camera. He began to relax. "I would like you to take one more photograph," he purred expansively, seeing that the danger was past. "I would like a picture of myself to give to my wife." I dutifully snapped it, rewound the film, extracted it from the camera, and handed it to him. He clutched it, triumphant, and it disappeared into the folds of his robe.

"You have been most generous," he offered. "I would like to give you a gift in return." He opened a desk drawer, took out a petty cash box, extracted a 100 dollar bill, and handed it to me with an arrogant smile. "For your work." I pocketed the money and the insult and left, counting myself fortunate to have escaped with my skin intact.

Death of another kind may overtake the young and innocent in Africa. Some three decades ago, slavery was at long last legally abolished in Saudi Arabia, and theoretically at least, slavery thus came to an end all over the world. In actuality, however, the white slave trade is known to still be flourishing in parts of Africa and the Arab Peninsula.

In Kenya I met an empty-eyed young Swede who related the following story: He had been backpacking through Morocco with his newly married brother, and that young man's 19-year-old bride. She was a beautiful blond and fair-complexioned girl who attracted a great deal of attention, such physical attributes being much prized in that part of the world. Deep in the native quarter they had been walking through narrow alleyways, between the stalls and shacks of the market. Suddenly the two men's attention was arrested by a pair of old swords that were hanging deep in the recesses of a small shop. They entered to investigate while the young woman continued on ahead. When they emerged from the shop a few minutes later, she was nowhere to be seen. They searched for her more and more frantically up and down the narrow streets, but she had disappeared without a trace. A bored police conducted a desultory search, with no results. She was never found. The young husband, unable to face his lost wife's parents, committed suicide some weeks later.

Sometimes death lurks in the rivers of Africa. Unwary travelers who venture innocently into their waters may meet him in the guise of electric fish, become paralyzed, and drown. Others, bathing unsuspectingly in still, idyllic pools, are invaded by schistosomes, insidious organisms that wreak havoc in their bodies.

I found a Finnish woman wandering around the island of Lamu, her eyes shocked, her face empty. I listened to her story. She had made the journey from Costi to Juba on the barge that traveled up the Nile into the indigenous regions of Southern Sudan. A long and bitter civil war had for many years been raging between the North and the South, and it was well known that the North was committing genocide, burning out village after village of indigenous, non-Islamic peoples.

A few weeks previously I had spoken with a French mercenary who had just emerged from two years in the Sudanese bush, and who had come to Lamu for some rest and recreation. He told me that the bush was crawling with military advisers of various nationalities, who were arming the natives and testing new weapons.

Some miles before reaching Juba, the boat carrying the Finnish woman was attacked by swarms of warriors armed with modern automatic rifles, and all of the passengers on the boat, some 1,000 people, were massacred. The Finnish woman had escaped death only because her body had been covered with corpses. She was eventually rescued by the avenging troops sent from North Sudan by air, which reached the scene a day later.

Shortly after a group of barges traversing the distance between Aswan and Wadi Halfa along the Nile caught fire and sank near Aswan, in Egypt. I had traveled this same distance on these same barges a few years earlier, and although the newspapers reported that it was unclear whether 100 or 200 people had perished, I knew that it had been well over 1,000 because the barges never left the dock until they were filled to overflowing. The passengers had all been Sudanese, returning from Egypt to Sudan. There had been no survivors. Sudanese do not know how to swim. Their waters are too dangerous to enter voluntarily. Those that had clung to wreckage in the water had been picked off and eaten by crocodiles.

Sometimes death walks to the gallows beside men of principle, who prefer his company to a life of hypocrisy. Mahmoud Mohammed Taha was such a man, and although I met him only once, I shall miss him sorely. Mahmoud was the leader of an offshoot liberal Islamic sect, the Republican Brothers. Although he attracted a number of devoted followers among intellectuals in Sudan, his philosophy was not a popular one.

When I was brought to him by one of his disciples, he agreed to an interview. I asked him about his position on female circumcision, and he replied simply that he advocated spiritual enlightenment for all of Islam, equally for men and women, and that once spiritual enlightenment had been achieved, any necessary social reform would naturally follow. His philosophy thereby diverged sharply from the more stringent interpretations of Islam, which draw sharp lines between the civil rights and personal value of men and women.

His ascetic face was remarkable mostly for its eyes, which were the eyes of a visionary. They seemed to be looking into another dimension, and the feeling gripped me that I was in the presence of a great man.

About three years after this interview, President Numeiri of Sudan, who was known to be an enthusiastic drinker of alcohol, the use of which is forbidden by Islam, and who was reputed to have proclivities toward some rather unsavory sexual practices, underwent a sudden conversion to a more stringent obedience to Islamic doctrine. As proof of his transformation, he banned the use of alcohol in the entire country, under penalty of severe punishment. He then reinstituted the ancient draconian Sharia laws which decreed that the hands of thieves be chopped off publicly, and which mandated the public decapitation of adulterers.

These laws had been on the books only in ultra-conservative Saudi Arabia, but had for many years been enforced there only reluctantly and under the rarest and most extreme circumstances. In his newly found religious calling, Numeiri presided zealously over weekly public amputations and decapitations that soon threatened to become daily occurrences, in a country where thievery is practically unheard of and adultery is avenged privately, within the confines of an indulgent law.

Sudanese men of conscience, under the leadership of Mahmoud Mohammed Taha, marched through the streets of Khartoum protesting these atrocities, with the result that Mahmoud and four of his followers were thrown into prison. After some months of incarceration, during which the amputations and executions continued to accelerate, they were given the option of recanting their "heresy" or being publicly hanged on the gallows. Three of Mahmoud's followers recanted. The remaining two men were sentenced to be hanged.

On the day of execution, the fourth follower also recanted. Mahmoud however, mounted the gallows. He was given one last chance to reverse his stand. "I will not recant," he said calmly. "These practices are against the tenets of Islam. I will die a good Muslim." The rope was placed around his neck, and death snatched him swiftly.

Numeiri's madness continued for some months more. Then he journeyed to the United States for a conference with President Reagan, and upon his return to Sudan was deposed in a bloodless coup. He was simply prevented from reentering the country. The populace milled joyously through the streets of Khartoum, shouting: "No more amputations! No more executions!"

But I shall miss Mahmoud, and when I heard about his death, I wept.

Port Sudan Haute Cuisine

In Port Sudan I stayed at the apartment of Sofia, Sidahamed's second wife. She was head mistress at the local secondary school for girls and secretly aspired to becoming a midwife. She longed to become a member of this highly respected and well-paid profession so that she could leave her dismally underpaid job at the school. She wanted to learn how to perform circumcisions so that she could earn lots of money, although she denied this vehemently when Sidahamed teasingly told me about it.

Fatma, who was wife Number One, had her only slightly more luxurious quarters in the apartment next door, and as the two women hated one another vehemently, this arrangement did not exactly make for happy living all around. Sidahamed spent an obligatory evening with each of the two women and with the children born of him by them whenever their turn rolled around, which was every third day. In this way he discharged Islamic law's demand for fair treatment of all of his wives, but it was obvious that he much preferred to spend whatever free time this left him in the company of Muna, wife Number Three. Muna was young, pretty, and undemanding. She had not yet succumbed to anger or greed as had his other two wives.

Sidahamed was a doctor by profession and specialized in the treatment of malaria, which was endemic in the humidly fetid atmosphere of Port Sudan. He himself drank only beer or Nile water, which he had shipped to him at great expense from Khartoum. He shunned Port Sudan water all together. Port Sudan water, he confided, was responsible for a commonly seen syndrome among his male patients. He planned to describe it in a scientific paper under the name of "Port Sudan Morning Non-Erection Syndrome." The water, he said, contained elements that caused mental sluggishness, an inability to concentrate and a failure to experience penile erection in the morning. Being married to three women, he said, he had to avoid Port Sudan water at all costs.

The water was, in fact, brackish, and due to a totally nonfunctional sewage system, unquestionably polluted beyond all belief. In spite of all precautions on my part, it did not take me long to become ill whenever I stayed in Port Sudan. When I told Sidahamed with a perfectly straight face that I also did not experience clitoral erections in Port Sudan, he was instantaneously intrigued. He had never talked to an intact woman on this subject before, and was amazed to learn that women's normal genitalia should also contain erectile tissue.

I relayed Sidahamed's fascinating theory of "Port Sudan Morning Non-Erection Syndrome" by letter to a German physician with whom I was corresponding, mentioning also Sidahamed's three wives. I thought my correspondent might find this amusing. This man, however, was at that time experiencing some considerable difficulties in his own personal relationship with the rather unwilling lady of his choice. I received an indignant letter in reply: "Just what does that bloody fool think the damned thing is supposed to be, a perpetual motion machine?"

Sidahamed's more Westernized colleagues referred to him as an exceptionally intelligent man, but obviously considered him to be a wastrel who made poor use of his intellectual gifts. They had little to do with him socially, severely disapproving of "his many wives."

He did not, however, lack for friends. Sidahamed, it seemed, was well known all over Sudan. The mere mention of his name among civil servants and military personnel brought about instant, happy recognition and frequently opened unexpected doors for me. He seemed to be extremely popular in those circles and the stories about his clever escapades were endless.

Sidahamed was renowned for his generosity. This only infuriated Sofia all the more, since this admirable trait extended only occasionally to herself and her children, and rather more often to his many friends. He entertained lavishly on the roof of the small apartment building where his wives lived, with the two women taking turns cooking elaborate meals and timidly reaching the trays of food up to the guests through the trapdoor above their dwellings.

Sofia talked incessantly and with great vehemence behind Sidahamed's back, daily filling in for me the lurid details of her disappointment and betrayal. She had loved Sidahamed when she married him. To win her, he had promised her and her family that he would divorce Fatma, who was Sofia's nemesis. This promise had come to naught. Fatma's family had prevented the divorce. Seven years later, to compound the insult still further, he had added his present favorite, Muna, to his household. Curiously, Sofia felt no rancor toward the gentle Muna. It was only a matter of time before she too would be betrayed with a fourth wife. Sofia was certain of it. Sidahamed was simply a very bad man, she raged. She no longer loved him. He was a bad man and a liar.

In Sidahamed's presence, of course, Sofia behaved quite differently. She was meek and obsequious and served him slavishly, quite obviously still clinging pathetically to some hope, driven by desperation, that she would find favor in his eyes. A third of a husband, in her position, was obviously still better than none.

Sidahamed, whose behavior was considerably more respectful but distant toward Fatma, was clearly quite fond of Sofia. Fatma was older than he by several years, and he described her as too domineering to tolerate. Sofia's great personal flaw was greed. She seemed to be unable to stop nagging him for the many things she coveted, with which she hoped to fill her inner emptiness. Nonetheless, when the two of them were together, they did not appear to be unhappy. Each seemed to satisfy something child-like in the other. It was only when Sidahamed was next door in Fatma's house, or in Suakin with Muna, that Sofia was consumed by obsessive jealousy and she commenced to rail bitterly against him.

On mornings when it was Sofia's turn to have Sidahamed stay with her, a meekly unprotesting sheep was apt to be pulled along the crumbling outer stairs of the building and into Sofia's apartment. The man who brought it was easily recognizable as the slaughterer, for he carried also a large, gleamingly sharp knife. Knowing what was about to ensue, I would rush to make my escape to the British Club.

The British Club of Port Sudan lay along the water front, its entrance flanked by two poorly made, crumbling stone lions and a pair of small cannons. Its dismally neglected pool had obviously not been scrubbed in many years, but it was drained and refilled with fresh salt water every week. The unused, cobweb-choked women's locker room was in a shocking state of rattling disrepair. The sloping floor of the slime-covered shower featured a large resident toad, but blessed streams of water flowed freely from its taps when they were turned on. A cracked Turkish toilet could even be flushed.

No such amenities existed in Sofia's second story flat. The water pressure was never quite sufficient to elicit more than the merest trickle of water from her tap. A bucket had to be placed under it to collect the precious fluid, and it was usually noon before enough had accumulated so that it could be poured into the toilet in order to flush it. There were a sink and bathtub in the erstwhile British bathroom, but a cup of water each had to suffice Sofia and her seven children to perform their ablutions in the morning when water pressure was at its lowest and the trickle from the tap dwindled to a reluctant drip.

Membership in the British Club of Port Sudan was an altogether simple matter. One made out an application, paid the equivalent of ten dollars, and was then free to use the facilities of the club while waiting for the application to be processed. This generally took about three months, I was told. The whole procedure was a totally meaningless formality, because by the time three months had passed, all such applicants had long since left Port Sudan for someplace else. The club was always totally deserted until the late evening meal, and I was able to make use of the luxurious facilities of its pool and locker room in absolute privacy.

When I would return to Sofia's apartment two or three hours after fleeing it, the first thing to greet my sight would be the fly-covered, severed head of the sheep lying on the kitchen floor. Its blood-streaked hide sat close by, as did a bucket full of slippery gray intestines. The rest of the dismembered sheep lay on the blood-stained table.

Sofia would be happily busying herself with her favorite delicacy—the sheep's stomach lining. Both she and Sidahamed preferred this special tidbit raw, cut into chunks, mixed with slices of strong onion, and drenched in fiery pepper sauce. Both of them would devour this concoction with obvious relish and much lip smacking. The sheep's raw liver and kidneys would provide the next course. Among my altogether strange personal habits and food preferences, the one that struck them as perhaps the strangest was the fact that I steadfastly refused to partake of these delicacies, no matter how much they tried to tempt me.

I sometimes wonder if perhaps I did not miss a spectacular treat after all. The British Club at dinner time featured something absolutely wonderful, and that was genuine imported British railroad cider. It was a far milder tasting drink than warm beer, but it was also deceptively potent in the tropical heat, where thirst seduced one easily into downing one after the other.

Sidahamed had invited Sofia and me to dinner at the Club and they had ordered a plate of what both of them considered to be the ultimate Port Sudan delicacy, raw camel liver. I was on my first can of railroad cider, and watched with distaste as they devoured the liver with their customary greed, all the while urging me to join them. It looked absolutely revolting, and remembering the sheep, even the thought of touching a piece of it with my hand made me nauseous.

However, the evening wore on, dinner was not yet served, the heat was stifling and the railroad cider tasted wonderful. I was on my fourth can when Sofia and Sidahamed ordered another plate of raw camel liver. I had not eaten since morning and was aware of a gnawing feeling in my stomach. I was totally unaccustomed to alcohol even in its mildest form and was beginning to feel more than just a little bit giddy. When the raw camel liver arrived Sidahamed pushed it toward me, and without thinking I picked up a piece and popped it into my mouth.

It was one of the most delicious things I have ever tasted. Totally unlike beef liver, it had a firm, crisp texture and tasted much like walnuts fresh from the tree. Sidahamed and Sofia laughingly watched me finish most of it.

Some months later I found myself in a village near Kadugli when the sky suddenly grew dark in the middle of the day and a great droning filled the air. It got darker and still darker, the sound grew thunderous, and great numbers of locusts began to rain to the ground. The swarm that passed overhead was several miles wide, so deep that it obliterated the sun and so long that it took a full day to pass.

The next morning the marketplace was filled with vendors offering crawling piles of locusts for sale. They looked and smelled like fresh shrimp, and were no doubt an excellent source of protein, having gorged themselves on the choicest crops. Having gained courage from my Port Sudan experience I was quite prepared to taste them, but the idea of eating them raw was just a little more than I could handle. By the time I had found someone who would cook them for me, it was afternoon. The locusts had stopped crawling and were rotting in the hot African sun. They now looked and smelled like shrimp that were fresh no longer.

There are opportunities that come but once in a lifetime. There are images that are indelibly printed upon the mind forever. I have seen billions of locusts obliterate the African sun. I have heard their collective wingbeat drumming loud as thunder through the African sky. But I have never eaten a single one of them. I have resigned myself to the likelihood that I never shall. Nobody can do *everything* in this life.

Stephanie's Song

I returned to Europe many times after my African odyssey had ended.

It was the week that the Berlin wall fell, and a time of the most inspiring joy and celebration all over Germany. The whole country seemed to vibrate with an energy born of the revitalization of long-lost hope. The bookstore at the train station in Hamburg was crowded with East German youth, carrying or wearing the flowers that had been tossed to them along the way into West Germany. They were standing or sitting in the aisles of the shop, devouring books and magazines like so many bon-bons. They had long since run out of their allotted 100 D-Mark "welcome money" and were there not to buy, but only to read. It occurred to no one to stop them or to clear the shop in order to allow paying customers to enter.

I was so moved by the sight that my arms literally ached to hug them all. Instead I hastened to catch my train to Copenhagen, which was already waiting in the station, ready to leave with unfailingly predictable Germanic punctuality.

I quickly found my seat. There was only one other occupant of the compartment. As she helped me with my luggage, I saw that she was a young Scandinavian of magnificently Amazonian proportions. We smiled at one another and it was not long before we were deeply engrossed in conversation.

She told me that she was a gardener by profession and that she was on her way home to her village in Finland, having spent the autumn picking grapes in a French vineyard. Like most young Scandinavians, she spoke English. The former teacher in me quickly determined that although she must have been an apt student in high school, her formal education had ended there. Her English was scrupulously correct but halting, and the scope of her vocabulary was small.

Still, we managed quite well. I had learned to make good use of limited vocabularies in Africa, where books are often exceedingly scarce. I had also had years of training among the functional illiterates of the New York slum school where I taught for many years. I had developed the skill of being able to communicate coherently on a great variety of subjects, using only the most basic minimum of words.

My young Amazon told me that she spoke some Swedish, so whenever we got stuck, I would try substituting a German word, and frequently this worked.

We were deeply involved in a discussion of plant life in desert and semi-arid regions and along the Arctic Circle, when a third individual quietly slid into the compartment. I noted only briefly that it was a young man, and that was all. Neither of us paid much attention to him as he sat silent and unmoving in his corner.

About half an hour later there was the periodically repeated opening and closing of compartment doors along the aisle that heralds the arrival of the conductor. The young man, suddenly highly agitated, addressed the girl in rapid Swedish, seemingly pouring out some sort of story to her. I quietly observed this scene, and in the rush of words recognized some that were English or close to it: police, Hamburg, Berlin, camera, money, Stockholm.

When the outpouring stopped, she turned to me and said, "He has been robbed in the train station. He went to Berlin to see the wall come down and he was robbed of everything, his suitcases, his camera, all his money. He says he fell asleep, and when he woke up it was all gone. He says that after making him wait for almost three days, the police had given him some sort of ticket to get as far as Hamburg. We are now past Hamburg, and he is afraid the police will come and make him get off the train. He is trying to get to Copenhagen, because he says that there the police are good and they will give him food and money to get home."

I looked at him closely for the first time. He was tastefully dressed in an excellently cut business suit of softly draping material. I could not help but notice how painfully thin he was, and that his shoulders hunched in a way that was somehow incongruous with his youth. He looked to be of near-Eastern origin, his face widebrowed and gaunt, his bearing aristocratic. I saw that his hands were quite remarkably beautiful and well cared for, with long, well-

proportioned, sensitive fingers. His eyes were large, dark, and al-
mond-shaped. Behind them, I was chilled to perceive the flickering
shadows of a nightmare. He was a very frightened young man.

I asked him his nationality, and he answered that he was Swedish. "And before that?" I smiled.

"Iran."

He had been in Sweden for seven years and made his living restoring antique carpets, he told me. He spoke broken English and I
asked him where he had learned it. "One must learn many things,"
he answered. He had accomplished this by watching American
films on Swedish television.

The opening and slamming of compartment doors were coming
ever closer, and with it, his agitation increased. He seemed to be
having difficulty breathing, and for a moment it seemed as if he
were about to faint. Suddenly the whole picture became clear to me.
The tumult of thousands of East Germans pouring across the border, the overworked police, a brown-skinned young man needing
an interpreter to make them understand that he had been robbed,
appealing to the police for help in getting home. To them he was
just another young man among thousands of illiterate Turkish
"guest workers" that had long since come to present multiple social problems for the country.

"Let me give you money for a ticket to the Danish border," I
suggested. "It is not far and it will not cost much." I reached for
my purse. He pulled away from me as though he had been burned.

"No." he said. "No. I will walk to Stockholm, if I have to."

"But why? Why?" I insisted softly. "I have the money to give
you. It is nothing." And when I saw his face: "You can send it to
me when you get back home. I will give you my address."

"No," he repeated. "I will walk. People must be strong."

Stockholm was hundreds of miles away. I bit my lip, realizing
that I had made my offer too soon, and injured his pride.

We retreated back into silence and our respective corners. The
opening and shutting of doors came closer. Now it was only two
compartments away. The nightmare behind the almond eyes emerged from its shroud of shadows.

"I can only pray that they will not call the police," he said in a small, stifled voice. Then, in a hopeless whisper, "but Allah will not listen."

Suddenly he pulled off his shoe, and then his sock. "This is what the Iranian police did to me. They did it with a saw, and then they rubbed salt into the wound." The heel of his foot had been sawed to the bone. "They did the same to my shoulder, only worse. And then they beat me with a whip, 270 lashes. They did that three times in the six months that I was their prisoner.

"My entire family bought my freedom. They had to give them 120,000 dollars. I walked to the Turkish border. It took 11 nights. I could not walk during the day or they would have found me and thrown me back into jail, and tortured me again."

The door of the compartment rasped open and the conductor, forbidding and officious in his immaculately pressed gray uniform with red epaulets, held out his hand for tickets. The Finnish girl and I gave him ours. The uniform clad arm moved toward the Iranian and waited there.

After an agonized moment, the young man handed over his expired special ticket to Hamburg along with his United Nations passport. The conductor looked at all the papers, then handed them back without a word. He gave a friendly salute, and the compartment door closed behind him.

The Iranian exhaled explosively. "He will not call the police." He smiled weakly. This time I was sure he was about to faint.

"When did you eat last?" I asked softly.

He seemed to count. "Three days ago."

Beside me on the seat sat a paper bag with food packed lovingly a few hours earrlier by my friend in Hamburg. I held it out to him. "Please take this food. I have already eaten." He raised his hand in rejection. That terrible, agonized, paralyzing pride again! This time I was ready for it.

"Have pity on me.'" I cried. "*I am a mother!* I cannot stand to see you starve!"

He took the food. Almost absently he slowly unwrapped a roll and took small, painful bites as he continued to tell us his story. His brother had been incarcerated and tortured by the Shah's police. When the family was finally able to buy his freedom, he had fled to the United States, and had lived in exile in Los Angeles for many years. When the Ayatollah came to power, he returned to Iran. Within hours he was thrown back into the same police prison he had escaped many years before, and was beaten to death.

Our friend Mohammed, as he was called, was taken into custody the next day. He had just turned 22 and had been married the month before. When he finally escaped into Turkey, and from there into Sweden, he left behind him his pregnant wife, two sisters, and an old mother. He has never seen his daughter, now seven years old. His family cannot get out of Iran. His United Nations passport gives him access to any place in the world except Iran, because if he ever tries to go back home, the police will kill him, no matter who is then in power.

Gently I asked him about the residues of torture. The pain in his back and in his shoulders remains, and he cannot sleep.

But the worst thing of all is that he misses his family, and that he has little or no hope of ever seeing any of them again as long as he lives. This is the neverending torment of exile; to be sentenced to a lifetime of loneliness, yearning, and homesickness with no hope of pardon or reprieve.

There are things that those who have been tortured only rarely talk about, except to one another. Among the many tortures that are devised for young men like Mohammed there is almost invariably sexual torture. And while they are perpetrating these deeds, the torturers mock and jeer: "No woman will ever want to touch you after this. You will never have any children, and if you do, they will all be monsters." They do their fiendish worst to leave their victims nothing. The one thing that the torturers cannot destroy in them is a stubborn, fierce, unyielding pride in their own unshakable decency, strength and ability to survive. It is all they have left.

* * * *

I too have known exile. I understand the tortures that it inflicts, even though my own exile was self-imposed.

I am able to see the nightmares dancing their bizarre ballet behind the almond eyes so clearly because I too have felt the torment of yearning for my children when there seemed to be no hope of pardon or reprieve from my self-imposed sentence.

Why then did I subject myself to this self-exile? A life devoid of all freedom had become so odious to me that I no longer wished to live. In a last-ditch effort to save myself, I had shaken off all fetters and conventions and become a gypsy, a wanderer, an adventurer, a seeker after my true self. Freedom in that existence mattered more than home, more than security, more than love, more than life itself. But freedom carried a heavy price.

There were periods of up to a year when I had no fixed address, no way of receiving mail, no way of knowing whether my letters ever reached my children. Most of them never did. I suffered acutely in the knowledge that there was a fairly high probability that I would sicken and die somewhere in some remote and nameless African village, along some endless desert path, or in some fetid disease pit of an inn where I had sought shelter. I lived with the constant fear that I would never see my children again, that they would never know what had happened to me if I did not return. They would never know if I were truly dead, or how I had died.

I, too, could not sleep, and there came a time when I realized that this would have to cease, or I would go mad. And so one wakeful night I wrote a poem and set it to music. I would sing it aloud to myself when my feelings of longing overwhelmed me. I would weep as I sang it, and my voice would break and I would be unable to go on. Then I would try to sing it again, and I did this until I was able to get through it twice without breaking down and weeping, once for each of my children. After I had done this, I could sleep. I called it "Stephanie's Song," and I sang it wherever I walked and wherever I laid myself down to sleep.

Stephanie's Song

Stephanie, Stephanie,
My bright Angel!
How I long for your smile under this boundless sky!
I walk the Earth under the soaring birds,
And when the cool night falls, I lie on this earth.

Why then do I weep for you?
And why is the emptiness of my arms so great?
When this Africa calls to me to remain all my life,

When there's peace in my heart and my days promise joy,
I must hold you again
Once more
In my loving arms.

I could never get past the line, "And why is the emptiness of my
arms so great?" without weeping. Even now, when my arms are
filled with the ever constant miracle of love, I cannot sing it without
weeping.

I have confessed this because people often see me as being larger
than life. I am not larger than life at all, for my courage was born of
desperation and a conviction that my life was utterly worthless. Yet
I did not want to throw it away meaninglessly. I wanted more than
anything in this world to die free, doing what I chose to do and with
my boots on.

I was very much aware of the constant danger. What kept me
going was an overwhelming sense of purpose and determination,
and so, to ward off my uneasiness at the constant presence of death,
I wrote another poem. I called this one "Invocation."

Somewhere in the books of Carlos Castenada, Don Juan says that
your Death is always with you. You can glimpse him over your left
shoulder if you look very quickly, and you need not trouble yourself
because he has not come for you. But when you see him at your
right side, then he is *your* Death, and he has come to fetch you.

Invocation

Walk on my left side, O Death,
Walk on my left side,
And do not come too close,
For there is much that I must do.

I see you are there.
You are there.
Yes, I see you are always there.
I can glimpse your no-face
Over my left shoulder as I walk.
I know you are there,
But there is much that I must do.

Do you hear the screams?
Do you hear the wild, tormented screams
Of little African girls
With frail, helpless arms,
As they pin them down
Upon the ground,
Gouge out their sex organs
And sew them shut?

I see you sitting on their right side,
And they watch you with wildly rolling eyes,
As they bleed
And bleed
And bleed
And bleed
And bleed,
And there is much that I must do.

I know that as I walk,
You will be there with me
As my fellow wayfarer,
But I will not call you my friend.

So walk on my left side, O Death,
Walk on my left side and do not come too close.
You shall not be my friend,
For there is much
That I
Must do.

After I had written this invocation, I put it somewhere in the very bottom of my backpack and forgot that it was there. I had no need for it then. It dealt with no ambivalence. It merely defined my direction and my direction lay straight ahead. Many months later I found it again and put it away with some other papers. Every now and then it has resurfaced, and so here it is.

I had one other device that kept my sanity intact, and that was my litany. I never forgot to be thankful to my knee, which somehow held together under the stress of the totally irrational demands I placed on it. I was indescribably grateful to my sadly warped and injured neck. By some miracle it kept surviving the insults of crowded lorry rides on the top of hard and often jagged freight, through roadless gullies, along trackless wastes, on careening vehicles with totally bald tires, whose shock absorbers were a fading memory.

I was keenly aware of my surfeit of riches. I owned a pair of well-worn running shoes, that made it possible for me to walk in comfort. It was not possible to buy the likes of them for any sum in all of Sudan. I carried my gear in a sturdy Swedish backpack that minimized the stress on my overtaxed spine. When the frame finally broke and I had to carry my equipment in a sack, like the natives, I was nearly crippled within a week, and had no alternative but to return to Europe. I owned both sunglasses and reading glasses. Such enormous wealth was almost obscene in its magnitude.

Every night when I lay down to rest, I counted my blessings and I fell asleep saying my litany:

> Bless my knee. Bless my neck. Bless my spine. Bless my feet. Bless my backpack. Bless my shoes. Bless my sun glasses. Bless my sleeping bag.

Then I would sleep like a baby until the sun came up and a new day began.

Requiem for a Goliath Heron

Adjacent to the airstrip at El Fasher, within the deteriorating rectangle that houses the offices of airport officialdom, there lies a courtyard bare of all but two sparse trees struggling to survive. Under one of those trees a madwoman sits every morning, teaching an imaginary class of children how to read.

It is evident, as one watches her, that her little phantom pupils are extremely lively and responsive, as children in Sudanese schools generally are, and that they pay the most rapt attention as she teaches her lesson. She recites their multiplication tables with them, leads them in a song, asks them questions, and calls on each of them in turn. When they give the correct answer, she smiles at them with obvious satisfaction; when they do not, she gently and affectionately tries once more to guide them into understanding what she is trying to have them learn.

As I sit under the other tree at the further end of the courtyard, trying to be as inconspicuous as possible while also surreptitiously watching her, she acknowledges my presence by counting in English for her class: "One, two, three, four, five." Then she directs them to repeat the strange words. Although she alone can hear the echoing chorus of their chirping phantom voices, I know that they perform this task perfectly, for she glances triumphantly in my direction, making certain that I have noted how well they have performed.

She is a woman of no more than 30 years of age, well groomed and pleasing to the eye. I am told that she was once the head mistress of a primary school in another town. When after five years of marriage she had borne no sons to her husband, with whom she was passionately in love, his family forced him to send her back to her own family, and to wed another woman.

For one full year thereafter she sat, staring, in her hut. Then she arose one morning, picked up her books, and walked out to the airstrip. There she sat down under the tree in the courtyard, where she now sits as I watch her, and began to teach her imaginary class.

Madness is not seen often in Sudan, and when it is, it most likely makes its appearance in so benign a form that no one bothers with it. Living among the inhabitants of a country that is dominated by viciously searing heat, stark deserts and monotonously grinding hardship, those of us who come from other cultures might conclude that everyone is by necessity more than just a little bit mad here. It is difficult to comprehend the people's indomitable zest for life; their spontaneous, easy, and joyous laughter; the pleasurable excitement with which even such a modest presence as my own seems to constantly fill them; their eager hospitality and unqualified generosity; the totality of their self-abnegating surrender in obeisance to Allah.

Every day I am asked more than once if it is not a fact that Sudan is truly wonderful, and because it makes them so instantly happy, I invariably agree that Sudan is indeed wonderful. Sudan is stark, grueling, and unspeakably harsh to those who are barely able to cling to the very knife edge of subsistence in its brutally inhospitable desert settlements and towns. But because of the unique qualities of these same people, it is indeed also the most wonderful place on earth that I have ever visited.

It makes me wonder if perhaps it is I and the culture from which I come, where nothing ever seems to be enough, where hardly anyone ever seems satisfied with what life offers, that is not totally mad. Perhaps also, all of these people in Sudan constantly live in that other reality, where words are of no importance, where individual survival does not matter, where pain does not exist, where material possessions are meaningless, where only feeling and belief are linked to truth, where paradise awaits the true believer. Madness is almost purely a question of cultural definition.

*   *   *   *

El Fasher lies in Darfur Province, in western Sudan, not far from the Chad border. Water trickles through this palm-shaded oasis, which has for centuries drawn multitudes of pilgrims traveling in camel caravans that wend their way over hundreds of weary desert miles to the holy city of Mecca. It is a government outpost from which the Western provinces are administered. I found it to be filled with bored government officials who talk of little else but their burning desire to be relieved of this post and to be swiftly reassigned to what they see as the more cosmopolitan pleasures of Khartoum.

El Fasher is also the last point west from which air travel is possible in Sudan. If one wishes to go further, one must journey overland to Nyala, which lies a day's travel through the desert to the south of El Fasher. From Nyala it is possible to continue on to the cool, lush mountains of Jebel Marra, which rise to an elevation of 10,000 feet, the highest in Sudan.

Nyala, which lies scarcely more than 100 miles from the Chad border, is a colorful, vibrantly lively market town, surging with explosive energy in the brilliant sun, like an agitated beehive. Fruit is plentiful and luscious. Stall after stall shimmers seductively with multi-colored fabrics. Hobbled and tethered camels bray resoundingly in the teeming camel mart. Appraising, prospective buyers weave sharp-eyed among them, pausing occasionally to bargain ferociously with desert-toughened camel drivers.

The government rest house, where I was compelled by falling darkness to find lodging, was a stinking disease pit in which I was loath to even draw breath. Shrinking from touching the unspeakable, encrusted obscenity of a bed, I tossed on my sleeping bag in the farthest corner of the dusty floor. After two such nights I could stand it no longer. Although Nyala fascinated me, the horrifying prospect of breathing the fetid atmosphere of the rest house for one more night forced me to flee the town as swiftly as I was able. I sought out a lorry to take me to Nyertete, an agricultural settlement at the foot of Jebel Marra.

Nyertete proved to be a slow-moving, gentle village through which clear water flowed from the mountain into its irrigated orchards and fields. In its sweet, untainted air, the lungs filled gratefully and the heartbeat once more assumed a more leisurely pace. I ambled casually through its pleasant market, buying a mango here, a tomato there, studying the people. Ultimately I even cautiously produced my little camera, and when this caused no evident distress, snapped an occasional photo.

At one of the stalls a pretty young woman was selling grain. Among her plastic containers I spied an exquisitely woven basket encased in meshed leather thongs for carrying. It was obviously quite old, yet in a state of perfect preservation. Its superb workmanship leaped out instantly to amaze the practiced eye. Even before I touched it, I was able to determine that its woven lid was so artfully wrought that it formed a seal close to airtight.

This was the first basket of like quality that I had seen outside of a museum collection. Native women in the many markets I had perused had preferred to carry their wares in plastic oil containers, sacks, or cutoff metal gasoline drums, which seemed to suit their purposes far better. Most of them shunned and even despised the old native implements and placed not the least value on them.

I indicated to the woman that I wished to buy the basket, and she, disbelieving that anyone could wish to own such a worthless object, laughed deprecatingly, perhaps a little embarrassed that she was displaying her wares in such an old-fashioned "grandmother" thing. But I insisted, so she spread a cloth out on the ground and poured the grain onto it. Then she handed me the basket, with a question in her eyes. She had no idea what to ask for it. I pulled out enough money for her to buy three or four plastic containers and she smiled broadly, nodded, and stretched out her hand. I added one more coin and handed her the money. We parted happily, both of us satisfied that we had made a splendid transaction.

I bought fragrant fresh fruit and steaming bread and carried them home to the rest house in my newly acquired treasure. The next day I took it to the hut of the rest house guardian and left it with his wife for safekeeping. Then I filled my water bottle, hoisted my pack onto my back, and began to trek along the upward path that led to the next village.

By the time I had reached the village two hours later, I had begun to feel feverish and the weight of my pack caused my legs to tremble with effort as I climbed. The next village, I knew, was in the mountains, many hours' walk away. Happily, in the small market square, I saw a man squatting on the ground next to what appeared by its size to be a prepubescent camel.

I greeted him, and he invited me to rest in the shade next to him. We exchanged a few words of conversation, and I admired his young camel, of which he was understandably proud. He had only recently acquired it he explained, as he stroked its furry flank lovingly. Camels, in a village world of laboring women and donkeys, are a luxury only the fortunate few may afford. The animal looked well cared for and this gave me the confidence to ask if he would guide me, with his camel, into the mountain.

At first he showed reluctance, for there was no second camel to be found in the village, and although a mature camel is capable of carrying fearful loads, the legs of his own young beast were as yet too frail to safely carry the weight of two people. Then he agreed that the animal would carry my pack while he rode it into the mountains. I had to follow behind on foot. The climb was not a difficult one, he said, and its footing was safe enough for the camel, so it would also be safe for me.

The price he asked was not unreasonable. We negotiated for a few minutes, more because form demanded it than for any other reason. Because he was so considerate of his animal, I mentally resolved that although we settled on a lesser price than the one he originally asked, I would pay him the full amount when we reached our destination.

My pack, which had felt so hopelessly burdensome on my own shoulders, was dwarfed by the considerable bulk of even an only half-grown camel. I felt no qualms about unloading it, and the camel strode easily, unaware of this additional burden added to the slight weight of my sparse, sinewy guide. Still somewhat light-headed with malaise, I followed along the gently upward sloping road behind the camel.

The sun, still low along the horizon at our outset, rose hotly to the very center of the sky above our heads as we progressed upward. The path became increasingly more rocky and steep to climb and then all but disappeared. The camel picked its way expertly between the jagged rocks, while I reeled and stumbled more and more. My guide looked back at me, frowning; in spite of all my efforts to keep up, I fell even further behind. Finally he swung his camel around, brought it back to where I struggled, sweating and close to tears, caused it to kneel, and dismounted. Wordlessly he helped me up into the saddle, the camel rose from its knees, and he led it lightly on upward along the rocky path into the mountains.

Dizzy with fatigue, I perched high up in the saddle, the camel's hump clamped tightly between my knees. I found myself swaying easily and sensuously back and forth with its every step. It was a soothing, undulating movement and I readily surrendered to it, becoming as if one with the camel. In my feverish state I felt as if I were a branch of a pliant tree moving in a gentle wind. As my mind drifted deeper into fever, it returned again and again to the gentleness of the man who loved his camel and wished to see it grow straight and strong. Then it touched with gratitude the realization that this man had struggled with his pride of ownership and won, for he now led this camel into the mountain, allowing me to ride it, while he walked before us lightly and with a sure tread.

It was late afternoon when we arrived at the village. The meager, rocky path widened once more into a dirt road. We came upon a motley group of travelers squatting under several ample trees, next to what appeared to be a rest house. They were, even at first glance, impressively seasoned and hardy. The adjacent rest house was a windowless mud hut which apparently served for little more than a repository.

The camel knelt once more, I slid dreamily out of the saddle, and drifted toward a tree that I claimed as my own. Then I paid my guide the full amount he had originally asked, adding an additional bill to the ones that I placed in his palm. He smiled with satisfaction, bid me *salaam,* and disappeared with his camel down the mountain.

Too weak to do more than greet my fellow wayfarers in the most desultory fashion, I laid down on the bare earth and sank instantly into a stupified sleep. Some hours later I awakened, stiff and shivering with cold under a pale moon. I crawled forlornly into my sleeping bag, searched for solace from an overpowering loneliness that suddenly flooded me. Finding none, I closed my eyes.

Some moments later I felt the touch of a light hand upon my shoulder. I opened my eyes to see a bright-eyed Japanese girl in peasant dress squatting by my side. Her hair was wound up tightly in a scarf around her head and she looked like an apparition from a bygone age. In her hand she held a bowl of steaming rice which, bowing, she offered to me. For a moment I wondered vaguely where in time and space I had been transported by my feverish dreams. Then I sat up and saw that half a dozen travelers were grouped around a fire on which two small kettles were heating. The Japanese girl's energetic beckoning made it clear that she wanted me to join them.

I followed her to sit close to the fire, grateful to accept the comfort of food and human companionship. A tin cup filled with scalding hot tea was thrust into my hand and I sipped it, sighing blissfully as I gradually stopped shivering and strength began to return to my body.

Only the most seasoned Africa traveler journeys through Jebel Marra. Among the ones assembled around this fire was a pair of Dutch boys who had recently rounded the Horn, sailing on a tramp steamer. There were two itinerant Australian botanists, and a pair of Japanese backpackers, who searched out the remotest areas of the world. Such wayfarers passed one another like ships in the night and there was among them an easy and tolerant camaraderie that transcended all differences in age, background, and station in life. To a great extent they measured human value by an individual's courage to search out the unknown, by his imperviousness to hardship and by the raptness with which his attention focused only on the beat of his own drummer.

For four days I lay dreamily under my tree, recovering from fever. It was a strange malaise, for while I felt lethargic, weak and irresolute, it caused me no great pain.

The windowless mud hut, I soon discovered, served not only as a rest house, but as an infirmary as well. It was administered by the schoolteacher of the village. Medical supplies consisted of little more than several boxes of malaria medication which I observed being dispensed by the teacher to all patients, regardless of their complaint.

A small boy came to sit quietly in the fork of a tree adjoining my own, from which vantage point he studied me serenely. After some time he left and returned a few moments later, followed by a string of four even smaller sisters. They all sat closely clumped together, their large, calm eyes watching me unwaveringly. After perhaps half an hour, the boy slid out of the tree, walked over to me, and regarded me at closer range for a minute or two. Then he departed, leaving his sisters sitting like frail little sparrows in the crook of the tree.

He reappeared some moments later carrying a bowl of water, which he placed in front of me. When I had drunk it, he smiled, picked up the bowl, and pointed to his chest. "Mohammed," he said. Then he took the empty bowl and disappeared once more. Another 15 minutes passed, while the little birds continued to study me. This time when Mohammed came back and put the bowl down once more, it was half filled with wheat. He squatted down in front of me and waited.

I picked up a grain and found that it was hard and uncooked. I pantomimed pouring water over the contents of the bowl, placing it in a pot, lighting a fire, and cooking it. Then I took out a coin and handed it to Mohammed. "Lightfoot," I said, pointing to my chest. He tried several times to imitate the sound. When he had gotten it nearly right, I nodded. He walked ceremoniously over to where his little sisters were sitting, put down the bowl, and addressed them solemnly. "Lah-ee-ah-foo," he said.

The almost unnatural previous silence of the little girls exploded instantly into chirping laughter. They began chanting "Lah-ee-ah-foo, Lah-ee-ah-foo" over and over, dissolving every few moments into giggles, until Mohammed made them stop. When they were quiet once more, he picked up the bowl and walked away with great dignity. I was overcome by lethargy once more and as I dozed, heard only vaguely the occasional twitter of suppressed giggles drifting in my direction and the soft peeping of "Lah-ee-ah-foo, Lah-ee-ah-foo" behind little hands.

When Mohammed returned once more, the bowl was filled with warm, freshly cooked wheat. One after the other, the little sparrows slid out of their tree and edged closer. When I held out the bowl they came sidling over, and I gave them each a handful of the sweetly fragrant grain. Then we all sat down together, eating it.

For the next four days, Mohammed brought me a bowl of wheat each morning and I lay under the tree, gathering strength. At nightfall the travelers would gather around the fire and talk of what they had seen that day. The village lay near an enormous volcanic crater that required a full day to traverse. As one climbed upward, waterfalls dropped from a great height, and further along there were hot springs bubbling out of the earth in which one could bathe. The mere thought of seeing such a wealth of water filled me with great excitement.

I began to walk shakily about the village, looking for some place where I could buy fresh vegetables and fruit. The only establishment in evidence was the tiniest of lean-to shacks, which seemed to be the local department store. Its stock consisted of two dusty bolts of cloth, half a dozen small packets of laundry soap, several sandals made of rubber tires, some empty motor oil bottles, and two plastic pitchers. On the ground stood nearly empty sacks of tiny, dried out onions and some sort of discouraging looking grain. After some poking around I unearthed another sack, containing a few remnants of diminutive peanuts.

Suddenly aware that I was tremendously hungry, I handed the shopkeeper a coin and scooped up all of the of peanuts I could find, a small handful. Munching them, I continued on my way.

Walking along the road some time later, I saw three heavily laden women coming toward me from the opposite direction, balancing platters heaped high with *kissera*, a paper-thin sourdough bread, on their heads. Our gaze met and we examined one another curiously.

Hoping to buy a few pieces of kissera, I pulled out some coins and pointed toward it. The women laughed. One of them said something in a language that I did not understand, her voice clearly expressing contempt. What woman worth her salt could not bake her own kissera? The other two women laughed again and they all walked past me. After a few steps, one of them turned around and saw that I was still standing in the road watching them. She said something to the others, stopped, reached up, pulled a folded sheet of kissera out from under the cloth that was covering it, and held it toward me. I accepted it gratefully. When I tried to give her the coins I was holding, she shrugged me off. The others laughed uproariously and then they all disappeared chattering down the road.

That evening around the fire, discussion centered on the weekly market that was about to take place the next day in a large clearing close to the village. Food had become scarce for everyone, and we all looked forward with considerable eagerness to the prospect of buying fresh supplies. The following morning we spent the early hours selecting our fruits and vegetables for the week. Then, when we had finished eating one fresh yogurt after the other in the tea shacks, we began the climb that led up the mountain to the hot springs.

Along the way we passed some small waterfalls rumbling down through the rocks, and then, somewhere around noon, we began to hear the growing thunder of water falling massively from a great height. As we drew nearer, the sound so increased in volume that we had to shout at one another to converse.

Looking up to the very top of the fall from where the roaring water plunged toward us, I saw that a lone hut, amply shaded by one enormous tree, had been built at its very rim. While it was obviously a most superbly scenic location and had the best immediate access to a constant flow of clear, fresh mountain water, I could not help but wonder what kind of a man had built his hut there. Was he perhaps deaf so that he could not hear the relentless thunder of the water? Or had he sought out this proximity because the intensity of the sound induced some kind of ecstasy in him? I tried to imagine myself living in this hut, enveloped totally day and night by the roaring of the waterfall. The idea struck me as both wonderful and bizarre.

We climbed on into the mountain, past strangely sculpted volcanic formations and exotic vegetation, until we reached a plateau. At its very lip, steam was rising from among its dark stones, and nearby a pool of hot, clear water bubbled actively. In it, immersed up to their necks, sat a number of tribespeople. They bade us welcome, and seeing that all of them had stripped to the waist, we did likewise and joined them, men and women, in the water.

The serenity that emanated from the occupants of the pool seemed in no way disturbed by our intrusion. They indicated the most comfortable rocks on which to sit. Then all of us regarded one another with leisurely interest while sharing in our enjoyment of the spa.

Where I sat, immediately near one of the vents, I could feel sand and small stones being driven out of the earth between my legs by the force of the bubbling spring. The heat of the water and the late morning sun infused my limbs with a delicious lethargy. A gourd, with which to pour water over the head, was passed from one hand to the other, and I let the gently cooling breeze that played along the plateau wash over my head. Gratefully I surrendered my body to the healing waters of this gift from the mountain and felt the last vestiges of sickness leave my body.

At high noon we joined the tribespeople as they rested quietly in the shade of an ancient tree. Before we left and continued our climb upward, I thanked the mountain, as it had become my custom to do.

After climbing for two hours more, we arrived at the rim of the crater, which proved to be forbidding indeed. Its jagged surface was so punishing to the feet and the sun had by this time become so hot and fierce that I knew immediately that I would forego attempting to cross it, as I had planned to do within the next few days. I had seen two other travelers come staggering out of the crater, half crazed with dehydration, their feet cut and bleeding. It was not one of the ways in which I needed to prove myself.

I had heard that the most beautiful region of the mountain was an area called Sunni, and after a few more blissful afternoons in the waters of the hot springs, I made ready to descend back into the valley in order to find it.

I sought out the schoolteacher at the rest house and asked if he could negotiate finding me a guide with a donkey that would carry my pack on the return trip into the valley. The teacher told me that if I were to take another route, it would bring me to a road by which I could reach another rest house. From there a path led in the direction of Sunni. It was said to be beautiful indeed, he told me. Not many travelers went that way. It was too long a journey to attempt alone on foot, but it might be possible to hire camels.

A guide was found to lead me down the mountain. The descent was a long and weary one, which brought me ultimately, after many hours, to a lorry station along a well-traveled road. The station lay on the route to Chad, nearby across the border. When I began to ask questions, I discovered that the turn-off to the rest house I was seeking was still several hours' travel away. I found a lorry that was going in what I presumed to be the right direction and boarded it, hoping for the best.

We had not yet arrived at our destination when the late afternoon sun began its plunge toward the horizon, and I vaguely wondered just where and how I would have to spend the night. Total darkness had descended by the time the truck pulled into a small roadside settlement. The men perched atop the lorry freight speedily dismounted, scattered, and were instantly swallowed by darkness. I was barely able to determine from the driver that we had not yet reached our final destination and that the lorry would resume its journey at sunrise, before he disappeared as well. I was left standing alone by the deserted lorry, wondering what to do next.

A small market lay close by. Two tables roughly hewn out of boards leaned together against a corrugated tin shed, forming the barest semblance of a shelter. I crawled under them, lay down on top of my pack, and fell instantly into an exhausted sleep.

I awoke in the chill gray of dawn. Close by, three old men were huddled in blankets around a fire on which a battered kettle was heating. As I crawled out of my shelter, they smiled and eagerly beckoned for me to join them. I burrowed into my pack, came up with a tin of treasured Dutch milk powder, and brought it with me over to the fire. When the tea was done we laced it liberally with milk, and after pouring out a large glassful for me, the men sat slurping the unaccustomed treat in noisy appreciation, with much grunting and nodding of heads. We chatted idly as we watched the sun come up. It was a lovely way to start the morning.

As the sun rose, the market began to come to life. People appeared with baskets of fruit and vegetables. A woman walked by, carrying a large tray of kissera. There was, as yet, no sign of my lorry driver. I bought some fruit and kissera for the rest of the journey and waited. The other passengers had already jockeyed for position on top of the freight and sat there, also waiting patiently.

Two hours later, the driver reappeared. With him were four new passengers, all of them women, all of them pencil thin. He indicated to me that for a small additional sum there was room for yet another passenger in the cab of the lorry. I paid him and we all climbed in, one after the other, and sat immovably wedged together, six across, as we continued on our way.

After an hour's drive we pulled up to another, yet smaller roadside settlement from which, the driver said, a path would lead me to my destination. Perplexed, I stood forlornly in the middle of the road, watching the lorry recede into the distance. Once more I had absolutely no idea about how I would proceed.

I entered a tiny tea shack and sat down to think things out. A young man detached himself from a group of others and spoke to me in English, asking what I was looking for. Greatly relieved, I told him that I wished to find the rest house that was reputed to be somewhere nearby. I expressed surprise at the facility with which he spoke English. He told me that he worked as a driver for a European research installation that could be found further along the road. He was on his way to his village, which lay in the same direction as the rest house, no more than an hour's walk below it. He would walk with me and show me the way. He was happy to have the chance to practice his English. Lightly he picked up my pack and swung it to his shoulders, indicating that he was ready to leave.

After walking for a mile we came upon a path that led off to the right across an extensive semi-arid plain. In the distance I could see the beginnings of forested hills that formed its borders. We struck out across the plain. My guide seemed pleased by the sophisticated construction of my pack, and after I had shown him how to buckle it onto his hips, he swaggered as he carried it. When after a while I offered to take my turn carrying it, he refused, saying that its weight was nothing to him.

He told me that he was the eldest of ten children, and his name, predictably, was Mohammed. The eldest son is nearly always named Mohammed in Sudan. Whenever a voice called out "Mohammed!" in any street or marketplace anywhere in the country, it was always a secret source of fun for me to watch the many heads spin around.

We walked for many hours, well into the heat of afternoon. After some time the hills drew nearer, the ground began to slope ever so gently upward, and vegetation grew less sparse. I heard the soft bleating of goats and saw a small group of thatched huts in the distance.

"We will take our rest in my mother's hut," Mohammed told me. "My mother is a very old woman, the same as you."

Such a perception of myself, had it taken place in my own country, might have caused me a measure of grief. In Africa, however, old age is not regarded as a crime. Among women, it is only the old ones, the survivors, who are accorded respect in the community. They are regarded like old trees, sheltering and wise. They have seen the seasons come and go and there is much that they know about life.

Mohammed's mother was a frail, bent, worn-out woman who looked to be somewhere in her late sixties. It would yet be many years before my own life could be said to have spanned such an advanced number. However, I well knew that young people are notoriously poor judges of age beyond their own peer groups, and tend to group anyone who is more than 15 years their senior in the generalized category of "very old."

"What is your mother's age?" I asked Mohammed. He thought for a moment, counting silently in his head. "She is 43," he said. Then he corrected himself. "No, she is only 42." "Life has not been easy for her," I commented sadly, secretly shocked at her unexpected youth. "No," he agreed. "She has had a hard life."

When the heat of day had passed, we continued on to the next village and just beyond. The rest house lay sheltered within an idyllic grove of trees, along a ridge of flat rock, over which a stream of clear, sweet water sparkled.

The rest house was large and relatively well kept. There were several other occupants; a quiet young Sudanese couple from Khartoum, and an English girl who introduced me to her strikingly handsome but sullen Sudanese fiance. She seemed desperate to talk, and at the first opportunity led me outside to confide that she was having second thoughts about her approaching marriage to the young man. Ali, her fiance, undoubtedly no less acutely aware of the tensions growing between them, remained sitting morosely inside the house, biting his fingernails.

I asked her what had made her decide to marry him. She replied that this had not been her original intent. She had met him in Khartoum and had merely meant to travel with him. His family was relatively well off, and he had been able to attend a European university. He was quite Westernized, or so she had thought at first. Somehow things had developed, as things often do, and she had agreed to marry him upon their return to Khartoum. She did love him, she said, but things were terribly difficult between them. He seemed to have no concept of what she "was all about," and when she tried to teach him, it only made him angry. Where he had been so gentle and solicitous before, he now became bitter and sarcastic whenever she tried to talk about this matter with him.

I thought of all the European women married to educated Sudanese men who congregated regularly at a table in the American Club in Khartoum. They sat together, each complaining bitterly and at length about her husband's indifference to her feelings and desires. These husbands spent most of their free time away from their women, preferring the company of male friends, and wives were expected to find their interests and emotional support at home and among other women. It was a bipolar social structure that Western women found difficult to adjust to, and most of them were patently unhappy.

They had generally met their husbands as students at European universities, and had found them to be charming, courteous, and attentive lovers. It was only when they returned with them to Sudan that the pattern changed, for their husbands then reverted to behaviors that were the norm in their own society. The Western wives, far from home and trapped within a system that was alien and maddeningly restrictive to them, were left with only one another for consolation. This was at best a very poor substitute for the warm relationship with a loving marriage companion that they had expected to find.

I advised the English girl to put off marrying the young man for at least a year. Time, I said, would either iron out their differences or make it clear to her that she had made a disadvantageous choice. It was obvious to me that she was already beset by very serious doubts, but I also knew that young girls often allowed themselves to drift into marriage for no reason other than that they wanted to be married. This often led to tragically poor choices.

That night I heard them quarreling in their room and the next morning they were gone. The Sudanese couple left shortly after, and I remained alone in the empty rest house.

In the market of the adjacent village, I bought some fresh bananas and dried dates. I had walked back to the rest house and was brewing my solitary tea over a fire when Mohammed suddenly appeared. He was on his way to visit relatives in another village further on, he said, and had come to fetch me. I was pleased and relieved to have someone to talk to, and after I had stashed my gear inside the rest house, we set off along the road.

Two hours later, as we climbed into the hills, I began to hear the sound of drumming and the high-pitched ululation of women's voices. They continued to grow in volume and intensity as we approached the village. We emerged from the brush into a large, flat clearing where a group of people was dancing ecstatically. Some were jumping up and down, over and over, high into the air, like human pistons. Others were spinning like dervishes while several drummers circled, beating their drums with heavy, measured beats. Every few moments the women's voices broke into piercing and prolonged ululations.

I asked Mohammed what the villagers were celebrating. "It is a circumcision festival," he said. "They have circumcised all of the children this morning and everyone is very happy."

"Where are the children?" I asked.

"They are lying in their huts," Mohammed answered.

"And are they happy as well?" I asked sardonically.

He laughed. "No, of course not. They are not happy at all today. Today all of them are crying. But they will stop crying, and then they too will be very happy."

We watched the dancers for a while and then continued on along the road. As we passed by a group of thatched huts, I heard a muted chorus of childish sobs and whimpers. Grimly I plunged by, but the woeful little voices continued to pursue me even when I had hurried out of earshot.

"Do they circumcise both boys and girls here?" I asked Mohammed.

"They do it to all the children, so that they will be ready for marriage," he answered.

"Has it always been done here?" I asked.

He shook his head. "In the olden days it was not always so," he said. Then he added proudly, "My mother told me when my sisters were circumcised that she herself had been among the first girls in her village."

"And must the girl you take to wife also be circumcised?" I asked. He expressed surprise that I should ask him such a question.

"Of course she must," he said. "No man would marry an unclean girl. Everybody would laugh at him."

I mentally digested what I had just learned. Mohammed's mother was only 42 years old. This meant that the practice must have begun its spread into these villages no more than 30 years ago. It was by now fully entrenched. It happened that quickly.

Mohammed took me to a hut which even from the outside smelled strongly of fermenting grain. In it, several men and women were sitting on the floor around a wooden tub from which a foaming drink was ladled. A gourd was passed from mouth to mouth, and then to me in turn. I took a sip of the gritty liquid which, although muddy in appearance, was not unpleasant, its taste rather resembling warm beer.

It soon became evident that this was the local bar scene and that all the occupants of the hut, including Mohammed, had congregated there for some serious drinking. In spite of the exotic setting, such situations held little charm for me. After a few minutes I arose, gave my thanks to Mohammed, and left the hut, knowing that I could find my way back to the rest house alone. I returned to the clearing, watched the dancers for a little while longer and started down the hill.

I reached the rest house by late afternoon, tired and drenched with sweat from my long walk in the burning sun. I had longed for the cool quiet of the grove, and was eager to refresh myself lying in the shade of its trees. As I drew near, I saw that the grove was bustling with activity. A group of several Sudanese men was busily unloading a large pickup truck. Three sheep were tethered to trees nearby. A large prayer rug had already been spread on the ground.

I remained hidden some distance away, watching as they performed their ritual ablutions in the stream. Then, while they were lost in prayer, I edged unnoticed past them into the house, quietly closed the door to my room, and went to sleep.

By the time I awoke it was dark. A tantalizingly delicious odor played around my nostrils, reminding me that I had not eaten since morning. I poured out a cup of water from my canteen, sponged myself all over, put on fresh clothes, and prepared to make what I was certain would be a grand entrance. I knew that the pack that had remained behind in my room had enabled the men to infer that there was another occupant of the rest house. However, it could in no way have given them any clues as to my identity or gender.

My expectations were not to be disappointed. My sudden appearance at the group's campfire created what can only be described as an absolutely electric reaction among them. They fairly leaped to make me welcome, I was seated in the most comfortable spot, a cushion was thrust behind my back, and a heaping plate of succulent food materialized as if by magic.

There were eleven of them. Ten of them were childhood friends who had decided after many years to meet and make a journey through the mountains together. All of them looked to be in their early forties. Among them were an Islamic scholar, who spoke excellent English and appeared to be the owner of the pickup, a doctor, and a silversmith. The other men were merchants. The eleventh man, their cook, was considerably younger than the rest.

They asked me many curious questions, and I told them about my solitary journeys through Sudan and other parts of the world. They marveled greatly at my lifestyle and at the experiences I related to them. Then they asked me where my next destination lay. I said that I was hoping to find a way to reach Sunni, which I had heard was the most interesting and beautiful part of the Marra mountain. A blissful smile spread over the face of the scholar and he translated what I had said to the rest of the men. As he spoke, I saw that hopeful smiles were creeping across all of their faces and that they were nodding their heads in agreement.

The whole group faced my direction while the scholar addressed me ceremoniously: "We are on our way to Sunni. Welcome. We will all be tremendously pleased if you will be our guest."

It was, of course, irresistible. Greatly charmed by this performance, I told them that I would seriously consider their kind offer. They said that they had come from El Obeid, some hundreds of miles away, and had been traveling through the desert for three days. They would regather strength at the rest house and continue on to Sunni after staying for a day.

The next morning found them busily at work by the creek washing their clothes, with which they festooned the shrubs and bushes to dry when they were done. Five times a day they stopped whatever they were doing, wherever they happened to be, and did obeisance to Allah.

I was altogether charmed by their obvious enjoyment of having such an exotic guest. It was more than clear that I was going to be treated like a queen by them. After a while our discussion became freer and broader in scope. I realized how fascinated they were not only to learn about a culture that was altogether strange and alien to them, but also to converse with a knowledgeable woman. I was aware that a great number of questions hung in the air but remained unasked.

We spent the day scouting around the area and laying in supplies for the journey ahead. At sunrise the next morning I came upon them already loading their amazing mass of gear into the truck, and vaguely wondered how twelve people would be able to fit into it. Their three sheep were already huddled patiently in a corner in back.

One of the merchants mounted the driver's seat and I was wedged not too uncomfortably between the doctor and the scholar, who sat at the other window. The others somehow fitted themselves into the back of the open truck, and we were off. Our first destination was a village called Lum Lum halfway up the mountain.

We left the soothing lushness of the area in which the rest house was located and began to head across a vast, arid plain. Within two hours the sun was already so fierce and hot that I silently thanked whichever one of the men had so graciously and self-effacingly given up this agreeable, shady seat I occupied, to ride instead in crowded, dust-choked discomfort in back. When I was to later try to find out who it had been, everyone only smiled and shrugged.

By late afternoon we had not yet reached Lum Lum. The truck came to a halt, and the men made ready to spend the night out in the plain. The scholar pulled a huge blunderbuss of a gun out from under the mass of gear in back. Next somehow came an enormous tent, which took form with surprising rapidity as they labored together to set it up.

The sheep were unloaded. Two were tethered to the ground while the cook led off the third. It followed him unprotestingly, but the remaining sheep bleated mournfully as they watched it disappear from sight. Shortly after, an early evening breeze sprung up and the aroma of cooking meat wafted gently in our direction.

After dinner the cook came to sit near me. He was smiling and I conversed with him as best I could. He spoke in some strange village dialect that I, with my poor grasp of Arabic, could not make out, and his English vocabulary did not extend beyond a half dozen words.

Night fell, and I could feel that the men were waiting to see where I would sleep. I withdrew from the group, chose a spot on the other side of the truck somewhat removed from the tent, pulled out my sleeping bag, and crawled into it. The night wind was rising, swirling the desert dust around. I bound my head and face tightly into a shawl and lay down to sleep.

It must have been well into the night when I felt a rude hand shaking my shoulder. Startled, I sat up and saw the cook squatting next to me. "Seggiss!" he was muttering impatiently, and attempted to peel me out of my sleeping bag.

"Get away from me!" I fumed. Teeth bared, he thrust his face into mine. "Seggiss!" he hissed, and tried his luck once more with the sleeping bag, whose drawstring I had providentially knotted against intrusion from the wind. Frustrated by my protective armor he now began to shake me, screaming "Seggiss! Seggiss!" into my ear.

I began to curse. Among my father's varied repertoire of dubious, lesser talents there had been one for nonstop cursing for a solid five minutes, during which time he never once repeated himself. This enviable ability had been acquired, no doubt, in the Kaiser's rough-and-ready cavalry in which he had served for nearly five years during World War I. My own talent along these lines paled in comparison to my father's virtuosity, but I had managed to learn enough as an admiring pupil to make a fairly impressive showing of my own. As I began to warm to my task, I found myself able to switch volubly from English to German and back again at will.

The cook reared back in surprise. It was obvious that although the language was strange to him, its intent was more than clear. "Seggiss!" he croaked uncertainly one more time and then beat a hasty retreat. Some choice epithets suddenly bubbled volcano-like to the surface from my deepest subconscious, and gasping at the flood of memory that swamped me, I hurled them after him as he fled into the darkness.

When I finally stopped, the silence was almost palpable. I could feel the men in the tent holding their breaths. A few moments later I barely heard a quiet voice, speaking calmly but with authority. I recognized the rich baritone of the doctor and knew with certainty that I would have no further trouble with the cook. I smoothed my ruffled feathers, watched my heartbeat return gradually to normal, and lay in my protective cocoon, regarding the stars.

"Seggiss," I said to myself. "So that is what they call it in the villages." Suddenly the real meaning of the word struck me and I laughed into the darkness. The mysteries of language sounds emitting from the mouths of those to whom a word is strange! The word that the cook had bleated so insistently into my face had of course been "sex!"

The next morning another sheep was led silently to its doom. Very little had changed, except that the cook no longer smiled. We glared at one another angrily for a day and then the episode was gradually forgotten. The rest of the men acted as though nothing had happened. The only perceptible change was that the doctor took it upon himself to serve me at breakfast and for all the rest of the journey.

The tent was dismantled and we continued across the seemingly endless plain. By late morning the vegetation became more dense and we began to climb almost imperceptibly. The scholar now sat with the blunderbuss across his knees, keeping a weather eye out for game. By afternoon we had flushed out several fowl, which the truck pursued relentlessly until the scholar had expertly shot them all. The cook retrieved them in a bunch like so many red-tinged wildflowers and held the feathered bouquet aloft for all to see. The men in back of the truck were jumping up and down with excitement, amazed at their friend's skill at shooting.

By late afternoon we had reached Lum Lum, an isolated, small village lying part way up the mountain. While one of the merchants negotiated for a renewed supply of sheep, I looked into its two tiny shops, which seemed to hold some promise. There was little to be had, but hanging on the wall of one of them I spied several wallets, such as I had seen market women wear. I bought one of them.

It seemed unlikely that the group's diet was going to consist of anything other than meat from now on, and as I knew that my body did not gladly tolerate more than occasional portions of meat, I searched for any possible alternatives that the market had to offer. All I was able to find were a few dried dates, and I providentially bought them to stash in my pack.

We pitched tent some small distance from the village. Spirits ran high as we waited for the birds to roast, for Sunni was now only another few hours away. As we sat around the camp fire, I pulled out my newly acquired wallet. A knotted leather thong was attached to either side so that it could be worn around the neck. I was puzzled by the great length of the thong, and wishing to wear the wallet at chest level, I started to shorten it.

The doctor, who was sitting next to me, shook his head, wagged a prohibiting finger, and gently pulled the wallet out of my hands. He hung it about his own neck and let it slide down into his robe and out of sight. Then he seated himself on the ground, like a market woman. He lifted the hem of his robe to show me that the wallet was now resting on the ground between his legs, accessible, but well protected.

He pulled the wallet back up from out of his robe and placed several heavy coins in it. Then he handed it back to me and bade me hang it around my own neck, inside my robe. When I had done so, I found that the heavy wallet hung in such a way that it was located exactly at the height of my groin. Holding my hand, the doctor pulled me along, making me walk with him.

I laughed aloud as I realized what he had been trying to teach me. With every step I took, the heavy wallet thudded softly and sensuously against my most sensitive parts. Smiling ever so subtly, the doctor walked me all around the camp fire. Suddenly he reached behind my head, pulled the wallet out of position, and like a shock, the pleasurable sensation stopped abruptly.

The lesson was masterfully taught. The reasons for the peculiar construction of my wallet and its clever thong had become perfectly obvious. Not only did a diligent day of marketing carry more than monetary reward, but the loss of a wallet would invariably be recognized instantly by its owner. I decided not to shorten the thong.

We lolled pleasantly around the campfire, chatting about the day's events and the imminent prospect of reaching Sunni. When the servant brought the roasted birds heaped high upon a platter, the doctor selected two of them and brought them to me. Throughout the journey I was served separately, always the best morsels, and my share of food was invariably far greater than fairness dictated. All of the men ate together, sitting in a circle around a communal platter.

At sunrise we were once more on our way. We stopped briefly at Lum Lum, where two of the merchants lifted three newly acquired sheep into the truck beside our lone surviving beast. A tray stacked high with kissera materialized from the depths of one of the huts and was somehow sequestered in the back of the truck as well.

Not far from Lum Lum, the road into the mountain became more rocky. Our overloaded truck labored to negotiate its inclined curves, and our progress upward grew ever more difficult. Twice we passed heavily laden camel trains wending their slow and easy way down the mountain, their drivers rocking sensuously on the backs of the great beasts. I looked after them longingly, remembering my own dream-like journey on such a creature.

Suddenly, as we rounded a curve, we found our way effectively blocked. On our right a massive boulder rose more than 30 feet into the air, while the road's width was constricted by an enormous, half buried rock on our left. There was barely room for a car with a modestly narrow wheelbase to edge through. The width of our truck exceeded this passage by half a yard.

All of the men piled from the truck to look the situation over. A shovel and a crowbar were somehow extricated from under the impossible mass of gear in back, and they began to attempt an excavation of the rock. They energetically dug around it for some time. However, when they tried to pry it out, it failed to move, while the crowbar bent weakly into uselessness.

The men resumed their digging, and after a while four tribesmen on donkeys came down the mountain. They inspected the situation carefully, looking first at the truck and then at the partially dug out rock. There was a great deal of discussion back and forth, and after some time they left and the men resumed their efforts. A short while later the tribesmen returned, each of them carrying a long, heavy pole. By this time the rock had been excavated to some degree. The poles were inserted at strategic angles, each was manned by a number of men, and at a signal they all heaved. Reluctantly the rock lifted and rolled over. The men piled cheerily back into the truck and we continued on our way.

Sunni lay on a plateau at the top of the mountain and consisted of little more than a surprisingly well-preserved rest house, which had obviously been built by the English for their own recreation. It differed subtly from most of the rest houses I had seen in that it was not totally devoid of artistry, in spite of its customary no-nonsense concrete construction. Its most surprising and mysterious feature was electricity, a totally incongruous manifestation in an outpost of Sudan. Although each room featured its own light socket, all of them were bare of bulbs save one, which lent effective proof that the system still functioned. Some insulated cable lay along the ground beside the rest house and disappeared across the plateau somewhere into the mountain.

It was already close to evening when we arrived, and after we had taken advantage of the unaccustomed running water to cleanse ourselves from the dust of travel, we congregated on the veranda of the guest house, awaiting dinner. My attention was divided between half-heartedly scribbling long overdue entries in my journal and watching the men, who were singing and playing games. When one of the merchants started to drum on an overturned pot and I saw the doctor begin to writhe in dance, I dropped the journal and gave my fullest attention to what they were doing.

The action that was taking place, in which they all participated, seemed to follow a set formula, well rehearsed and familiar to them all. Each man played his separate role. I got the distinct impression that it was something they had learned when they were all boyhood friends together, or perhaps it was something that all male children of their particular upbringing knew. Together they chanted the words of a song, slowly at first, in an intricate and sensual rhythm. It was quite unlike other songs I had heard in Sudan, which were invariably monotonously chanted repetitions of words in praise of Allah.

The scholar was sitting with studied casualness in the center of the circle, while the doctor wove snake-like around him, clearly imitating the sensuously seductive movements of a woman in heat.

Closer and closer he wove, as the drumming became gradually wilder and the chanting of the chorus grew progressively in excitement. The scholar's face remained altogether impassive and unreadable throughout.

The doctor now circled so closely that he was almost touching the scholar, weaving his body with incredible suppleness around the seated man's shoulders. Finally, as the drum beat reached frenzy, he sank to his knees in front of him, raised his arms, inclined his upper body toward the seated man's lap, undulated ever closer, opened his mouth wide, poised — and then the drum stopped abruptly. The performance was over.

Impassively the doctor rose to his feet, moving in his normally masculine way. I, no doubt, looked somewhat stunned. He brushed the dust from his robe, and smiled at me enigmatically. Everyone acted as if nothing in particular had taken place and drifted into casual conversation until the cook brought dinner.

The next day we climbed toward the terraced fields lining the mountain, and some distance from the rest house the mystery of the electric light was revealed. Within a narrow, barred cage a waterfall pounded upon a water wheel, activating a small generator. The bars of the cage were secured by an enormous brass lock, the likes of which were commonly employed in British jails during the nineteenth century.

For the next three days we clambered around the lushly terraced mountain, diligently seeking out its each and every waterfall. The sight of these inexpressible riches of water roaring down from high cliffs into their sparkling pools below never failed to exert a force that was close to hypnotic on the men. They had lived all their lives in a barren region where water surfaced only grudgingly in thin trickles.

Early each morning we set out for new adventure. Each dusk we only grudgingly returned to the rest house as the punishing sun descended toward the horizon.

The fourth day found us at an icy crystal pool fed by a gently tumbling waterfall. The men stripped off their robes and waded into the water in their shorts, ecstatically immersing their bodies. In desert regions like El Obeid, bathing had to be accomplished with a

mere bowl of water. Total immersion of the body was an unimagi-
nable luxury that desert denizens could not even dream of.

The men lolled in the water, staying close to shore in the shal-
lows, for none of them could swim. I watched them for a moment
and then, since I had grown to trust them all, I stripped off my own
robe as well and strode into the water, naked to the waist. With
strong, assured strokes I leisurely swam the length of the pool to the
edge of the waterfall, and back again.

Their eyes never left me for a single moment, while they spoke to
one another in awed and hushed voices. When I emerged, dripping,
from the water, their eyes upon my body were as enraptured as if
they were watching the fall of water thundering from a great height.

I recalled what a gynecologist in Port Sudan told me: He had
been in his late twenties before he saw the naked body of a woman.
Most men in his culture, he added, would never see such a body in
their entire lives, not even that of their wives.

Slowly and nonchalantly I drew my robe back over my head. The
scholar sighed blissfully. "You can swim," he murmured dreamily. "We have never seen anyone swim before." I smiled at him
enigmatically. It was my turn to act as if nothing had happened.

On the fifth day, as we returned to the rest house in the early
afternoon, my head began to throb painfully. As the midday heat
descended, I lay weakly in the shade trying to comfort my painfully
burning skin, which had begun to break down under constant exposure to the punishing sun. The cumulative effects of our unrelieved
meat diet had become toxic to my system, which had for years been
accustomed to predominantly vegetarian fare. I felt inexplicably
desperate and depressed and thought of the children weeping in the
hut. Without warning, hot tears suddenly overflowed and began to
course down my cheeks.

The men were making ready for our departure the next morning,
and while the merchant driver tinkered with the engine, they began
gathering their gear to load into the truck. The doctor, who was
carrying the folded prayer rug, spotted me and ran immediately to
fetch a bucket of water. This he handed to one of the merchants,
who took it swiftly to heat on the fire. Then he sat beside me,
sponging my face, until the water had heated. He carried it to the
washroom, gently took me by the hand, seated me next to the

steaming bucket and carried in yet another bucket, filled with cold water. He indicated that I must sponge my entire body alternately with the contents of the two buckets until the water was all gone.

I followed his prescription diligently for an hour, cried a little more, and found that I felt appreciably better. When I emerged from the washroom I was smiling once more, and was touched to see relief on all the men's faces.

The driver continued for some time to tinker with the engine and then announced that we would have to seek repair at the nearest accessible town. We would turn in a westerly direction at Lum Lum and head across the desert toward the road that led to El Ganeina, no more than 20 miles from the Chad border.

At sunrise the next day the men prayed together on the veranda, while I silently thanked the mountain and bade it farewell. We filled our water bottles and began our descent. The scholar had reloaded his blunderbuss and was holding it lightly between his knees.

The air grew dry as we advanced toward the plain. Soon vegetation became progressively more sparse and we presently entered terrain in which only stunted desert shrub grew. The heat was stifling and oppressive. We had reached the exit from our paradise.

We noted that there was one final ravine through which we had to pass before the flat and arid desert stretched unbroken up ahead. Along this stretch some brush and leafy grass still grew. As we passed through it there was a sudden flurry of great wings, and like a vision in a dream an enormous bird rose phoenix-like, as if by some sort of magic, into the air. Before I could draw breath, I felt an instant, reflective movement at my side, and sensed rather than saw the scholar throw his gun to his shoulder. Even as I screamed in protest, a single barking shot assaulted my disbelieving ear like a great death knell.

The bird plummeted to earth and above the roaring of my blood I heard the wild cheering of the men as the servant leaped out of the truck to retrieve it.

For a moment my vision blurred, blotting out the image of the falling bird. I covered my face with my hands, and when I dropped them resolutely a moment later, the cook was dragging the wounded bird past us. The long, broken fan of its wing trailed uselessly along the ground. Its gracefully curving neck still held its elegant and long-beaked head erect. Its eye was large, yellow, and curiously alert. It was an eye that was miraculously unclouded by shock, the face of a creature still bent on survival.

The silversmith handed the cook his long kitchen knife, there was a brief flurry, and then all was still. The truck started up once more and we descended into the inferno of desert.

When I returned to the United States many months later, I went to the library and leafed through a number of books to learn what kind of bird it had been. After some searching, I found it. It was a goliath heron which had somehow found its way out of its more usual habitat and into the gully. It was indeed not only uniquely beautiful in its configuration, but belonged to the dwindling number of an endangered species.

I used to have some friends who are members of the Audubon Society. They have curiously avoided me ever since I related this episode to them. It could not be the death of the heron that they blame me for, because I made it very clear that I was in no way responsible for this. Perhaps the thing that they cannot forgive is the fact that I, along with all the others, ate it.

Different peoples throughout the ages have eaten far stranger things than goliath herons. Anthropological research reveals that in areas where the diet was too poor in protein to ensure the survival of a people, cannibalism frequently became the only feasible alternative, and so this practice became woven intricately into their custom and religion. In mineral-poor areas where people suffered from bone deficiencies, another type of homophagia developed. These people buried their dead and after a number of years, ceremoniously disinterred the bones. They ground these up, and in their most sacred ritual of communion with their ancestors' spirits, drank the dissolved bone meal. It kept them from dying out, and no doubt a lot more healthy than they would have been otherwise.

But what has all this to do with the goliath heron? The lamentable fact is that there are already far too many human beings populating our planet, while the goliath heron, for whom I yet weep as he plunges to earth in my troubled dreams, is on the verge of extinction.

Why then did I partake of it? That is a question that I find difficult to answer when the questioner is someone who has not experienced Africa. The only thing I can say in my defense is that the bird was already dead and there was nothing else left to do with it. It no longer existed as a mythically superb creature. Death had transformed it into food.

* * * *

El Geneina lies close to the border of Chad, which is reputed to exceed even Sudan in poverty. It is considered to be the least developed country in the world, whatever that may mean. Its greatest scourge is river blindness, a disease that is transmitted through its waters by way of a worm-like organism that invades and destroys the eye.

There was little to be had in El Ganeina's poor, dust-driven market. A few dried out, minuscule peanuts, some sadly wilted spinach, and a few overripe tomatoes rotting in the sun seemed all that it had to offer. Its butchery announced itself stridently by its stench long before I reached it, thus enabling me to assiduously avoid it. The men had already found the town's dreary little eatery, had ordered meals, and now sat in the bleak, treeless square, waiting for our vehicle to emerge from the repair shop.

I spent the time exploring some alleys near the shop and came upon a small group of people silently huddled in the shade of a nearby shack. The group was composed of men, women, and children. As I approached them I suddenly realized that all but one of their number were totally blind. They appeared to be members of a family and the only one among them that evidently had some partial remaining vision was a young girl.

I sat down quietly nearby and observed them for some moments. They barely moved. Every now and then one of their hands would creep toward another member of the group for reassurance, and then would quietly return to its original position. Their faces were empty of all expression save patience and resignation.

Acutely disturbed, I returned to where the men were sitting and told them of what I had seen. They spoke quietly among themselves for a few moments and then the doctor rose and pulled some money from his pocket. One of the merchants quickly followed suit, then all of the others did as well. The doctor, as spokesman, had me show him the way. He sat down with the family and quietly addressed its patriarch, a frail and saintly looking man. As the old man listened, a happy smile spread gradually over his gentle face, and he raised his hands to heaven, fervently praising Allah the Provider, Allah the All-Merciful, for the great blessing about to be bestowed upon him. When he finished, his weathered hands dropped quietly to his side once more and the doctor pressed a roll of bills into his palm. The old man spoke briefly to his still partially sighted granddaughter. He handed her the money for safekeeping, and it disappeared into the folds of her tope.

The men had been quite generous. The sum of money they had collectively given to the river-blind family was enough to feed them for two or three months. But what were they to do when the last sighted member among them lost what remained of her vision? What would happen to them then? It was too cruel a fate to bear contemplation.

The driver-merchant approached to tell us that the truck was once more serviceable. We said our farewells and headed back in the direction of Nyala.

By late afternoon we reached our destination. One of the merchants, a nondistinct, unobtrusive bachelor, lived in the very center of town in Nyala, close to the main market. He was the owner of a decaying but sizable house in whose spacious bare earth courtyard a single neglected tree had all but abandoned its futile struggle for survival. The evening meal already stood at hand, stoically tethered to one of its leafless branches.

Swiftly I made my escape into the market so that I would not have to see it die. I returned an hour later, happily laden with fruit. I forced myself to avoid looking into the corner where the cooking shed was located, from which I heard the concentrated buzzing of many flies and where I knew the head and skin of the dead sheep would be lying.

The next morning, after they had all prayed together for a last time, the other ten men piled into the pickup in which three newly acquired sheep were already cowering. We all shook hands and the silversmith gave me a ring that he had fashioned. I thanked the men and told them in all truthfulness that our holiday together had been the most wonderful one of my entire life and that they had all contributed to making it memorable. I said that I would never forget them or the journey that we had taken together. I looked into each of their gratified faces, and their expressions told me plainly that for them, too, it had been the experience of a lifetime.

The driver started his engine. For a brief moment the doctor's eyes met mine and we smiled at one another ruefully. Then it was as if a mask had been clapped over his face and his eyes became unreadable once more. The truck began to roll and I stood with my hands pressed to my heart while I watched it recede into the distance. All of the magic receded with it.

My host, looking somewhat lost, wandered aimlessly about the house for some minutes and then reclined on one if the string cots that cluttered his veranda and began singing verses from the Koran. I found a bucket, coaxed a trickle of water from the faucet in the courtyard, and waited until it was half full. Then I retreated to the washroom.

When I emerged half an hour later, my host was conversing with several young men who introduced themselves as students. One of them informed me solemnly that the merchant wished to marry me, but that he could not quite figure out the logistics of the bride price since I had told the group of men that I belonged to no one other than myself. If I could tell him how much bride gold I wanted, he would obtain it for me.

I told my interlocutor that I was deeply touched by his friend's offer and that I thanked him, but that marriage was not what I wanted at this particular point in my life. My suitor seemed somewhat taken aback by my refusal. Why did I not want to get married, he wanted to know. Didn't all women want a husband that would take care of them?

I tried to explain that I would not know what to do with myself in Nyala. This only created more confusion. I would not have to do anything at all if I married him, he insisted. I would simply stay in the house and be his wife. I should not have any fears that he would take a second wife. One wife would be quite enough for his needs, and therefore one was all that he wanted.

I thanked him as graciously as I was able and added that I must now be on my way. I was going once more to nearby Nyertete to pick up something I had left there, and would leave as soon as I found transportation. The merchant shrugged and then accepted my decision, although I could see that it still puzzled him. He sent the interlocutor to find a lorry for me, who after perhaps an hour came back to tell me that the arrangements had been made.

In Nyertete I retrieved my treasured basket and was told by the caretaker that the rest house had been closed because some travelers had behaved badly there. He would supply me with no further details, but took me to his own living complex to stay with his wife and mother in the women's hut.

Both women had huge goiters, caused by the absence of iodine in the diet. Goiter was a common affliction in Jebel Marra. I stayed with the family for several days, and when I left to return to El Fasher, gave them my bottle of iodine water purification pills. I went to great pains to explain to them exactly how they must use them, and tried to impress upon them that if they followed my instructions to the letter, their affliction would be cured. I have often wondered if they did.

This brings to mind a story that my father told me when I was a child. When he was a young man, iodized salt had not yet been introduced as a preventative for goiter caused by iodine deficiency. And so a man is walking with his son through the mountains when they meet a stranger on the road. "Oh look, Father," the boy whispers excitedly. "That man has no goiter!" "Stop staring," the father admonishes him. "Be grateful to heaven that you have all your healthy members!"

There is a lesson to be learned there somewhere. If only it were a little easier to persuade people to do what is good for them! But how do you win them over to your way of thinking when they have their own definition of what is normal?

Oh, my friend, it's not what they take away from you that counts — it's what you do with what you have left.

— *Hubert Humphrey*

Karen Blixen
Never Returned to Africa

During the sixties, in the early days of the civil rights and feminist movements, the following humorous story made the rounds:

A sailor was swept overboard, and by the time they recovered him he had drowned. After considerable efforts to resuscitate him, however, he began to breathe once more. He opened his eyes, which were filled with wonder. "I have seen God," he said. "Tell us quickly," his rescuers urged, "tell us what God looks like!" "It is very strange," he replied. To begin with, She is Black."

I used to like this story simply for its audacity and hope for better days to come, but lately I have come to view it in a different light. I no longer see it as a humorous story, but as a tale of mythical proportions.

Why should the archetypical godhead not be a woman, and why should she not be black? We now know that *Homo sapiens* originated in the Rift Valley of East Africa, and DNA studies suggest that every human being now on earth might well have originated from a single mutant humanoid individual. She would most likely have been a recent ancestor of Lucy, who was found in Johanson's excavations.

That would mean that we all share our DNA with, for instance, the Virgin Mary, Jesus of Nazareth, the Pharaohs, Mohammed the Prophet, the Buddha, Adolf Hitler, Hirohito and other deified or semi-deified humans in man's history. At the very bottom of all of these idolized individuals' family tree, there sits a small humanoid African female, who is god-head to us all—who is our earth mother. It is She who is seen in the drowned sailor's ecstatic vision as he passes over from death back into life.

I confess that at times I have been guilty of a kind of idolatry. It was only a passing thing, and it happened after I had been the subject of violence, when my mind was prone to strange fits of unreason, so it must be understood within the context in which it occurred. But it did happen.

I remember the first time I saw her. I was half hanging out of a native bus, stuffed to bursting with an impossible number of Africans. It was careening around a sharp corner of the tourist market in Melindi in Kenya. I was on my way to the airstrip, where a rickety four-seater shuttled from the mainland to the Island of Lamu, 30 minutes' flight away.

Melindi is a small, attractive beach resort with luxurious and only moderately expensive accommodations for disproportionately rich Europeans. They are unsparingly pampered, waited on, and served by a veritable army of uniformed, constantly smiling Africans. Guests are cautioned to avoid the beach, and to swim only in the large and scrupulously maintained swimming pools. The beach itself, they are told, is not safe, and they are warned about sharks, or undertows, or poisonous jellyfish. Since most of these tourists are out for adventure of a different sort and since, in any event, it is a very refuse-strewn beach, they have little motivation to venture out into it.

Melindi represented everything I despised about the excesses of tourists in Africa. It was indeed true; the beach was dangerous to them, but not because of sharks, undertows or poisonous fish.

In the tourist market of Melindi there was stall after stall of the same kind of cheap souvenirs, hastily executed wood carvings, gaudy baskets, and thin, badly woven "kanga" cloth. Merchants vied eagerly and often desperately for business.

It was in the tourist market of Melindi that I saw her, standing in the road in front of one of the stalls, as alien as a camel upon the moon. She was an unmistakable presence, regal in her uniqueness, quietly waiting for recognition. The bus passed within 100 feet of her, and I saw immediately that she was a personage of immeasurable dignity and importance. I clamored to be let off, and after struggling past perhaps 30 steaming and closely crammed bodies, reached the back door, and catapulted to freedom.

I forced myself to walk back to the stalls slowly and casually. I tried not to show my eagerness, but I kept my eye on the place where I had seen her. When I reached it she was still standing there, leaning against a tree stump, her feet covered in red mud, where they had been torn from the earth.

She was an ancestor figure, perhaps two and one-half feet tall. She had been carved with great artistry out of heavy ebony and was unlike anything I had ever seen before, either in museums, African art galleries, or private collections in the West. The red mud on her feet made it obvious that she had been recently stolen from where she belonged, somewhere in the bush.

I casually looked over the merchant's shoddy, nondescript wares, picked up one or two undistinguished items to examine them, put them back, and turned as if to leave. Desperate to make a sale, the merchant followed me, and I stopped in front of the figure, looking at her expressionlessly. "What a strange thing. Did you make this?"

"No, no," the man said hastily.

"Well, who has made it?" I asked, as if annoyed.

"It is not from here. It is from Tanzania," he said.

"And you went all the way to Tanzania to bring such a thing back here?"

"No, not I. I got it from my cousin, who drives a lorry."

So she had been stolen from Tanzania, from someone's grave. Her feet were beautifully articulated, so it was clear that she was one of the dead who walked. Where her hands should have been, her arms faded into vagueness. Without hands she could not feed herself, and someone had fed her. Food offered up to her had been baked by the sun into the wood around her mouth. She had been young, and had had long, elegant legs. Her teeth were large, strong, and perfectly even in her bare skull. Her arms and legs were fleshed out but wasted, as was her torso. She had a small, round belly, and seems to have been pregnant when she died. Perhaps she died in childbirth. African women's full-term pregnancies are often no larger than that.

The indignity of being in a place such as the market must have hurt her, and this caused me pain as well, so I said to the man, "This thing does not belong in a market. This thing belongs in a burial place."

He started to sweat. Tampering with what belongs to the dead is not taken lightly in Africa, where spirits may take a powerful revenge. I could see that he wanted to be rid of her, that her presence made him very, very nervous.

"Take it," he said. "I will give you a good price." He named an absurdly high figure, and I told him that he could ask anything he wanted, but all I had to give him was 40 dollars. He sweated some more, and I could see him twitching to get his hands on so large a sum of money. He consulted urgently with some friends, who told him to ask for 60. I smiled cruelly. "For 40 dollars I will take this burial thing away from here," I said.

"Give me the money," he whispered hoarsely. I counted it out and waited for him to pick her up and hand her to me. "Take it," he told me, and would not touch her himself. I took her tenderly in my arms and carried her away.

Later that day I stood with her under a spray of cooling water, and washed both our bodies clean of the indignities they had suffered.

*   *   *   *

Some years later, back in Tucson, Arizona, I saw the film *Out of Africa*. It deals with the life of a Danish storyteller, Karen Blixen, whom I much admired. The film starts with a woman's voice, full of controlled emotion, beginning the telling of a tale: "I had a farm in Africa." The voice falters, and then begins again: "I had a farm in Africa." Again there is the struggle for control, the voice tries for a third time, and is finally able to go on. It is a most effective beginning to a beautifully conceived and photographed film which transported me back to the incredible wonder of the East African landscape. It documents a young woman's struggles to maintain her farm under all manner of adverse conditions, its final loss, and her heartbroken return to Denmark.

The film ends with a written commentary, which begins: "Karen Blixen never returned to Africa." I read this sentence, and could read no further. The tears coursed down my cheeks, and I wept wrenchingly and uncontrollably. As I hid my face in my shaking hands, I heard people leave the theater. When I finally uncovered my eyes, I saw that I was alone. My heart ached as if it would break, and I finally faced my great loss. Africa, as I had known it, was gone forever from my grasp.

*   *   *   *

Along the shore of Lamu island, a strip of immaculate white sand extends for 10 miles beyond all habitation. The slope of the ground into the water is so gradual that one must walk into it for more than 200 yards before it is deep enough to swim. When the tide is low and the sand packed, a solitary jogger may run barefoot along this strip, hearing nothing but the pounding of the surf, her own heart-beat, and the cry of the seabirds.

Only slightly above the packed sand there are dunes where robbers or worse may bury themselves, their exposed heads hidden under bushes, facing the beach. There they lie in wait, lurking like spiders in their web, with their bush knives at their side.

Oh sweet Lady, Goddess, why was I not meant to run?

It was not much of a rape, when you come right down to it. On some level it was simply insultingly banal, utterly uninteresting. The real exertion of power was all in that gigantic and razor-sharp knife. It quickly became clear that the whole object was simply to penetrate and violate my person, one way or the other, the penis or the knife, it did not seem to matter much which.

I had already jogged for six miles, and my energy was depleted. He was much younger than I and wiry, and I knew immediately that there was no chance whatsoever that I could outrun him, either along the beach, or into the water, or even to make the attempt without arousing out-and-out violence.

All ambiguity and ambivalence about the value of life fell away. I had never so desperately wanted to live. I realized how easy it would be for him to bury my body in the soft sand of the dunes, so many miles away from anywhere. It would never be found.

Somewhere in my mind a tape was being replayed in agonizingly slow motion: a flurry of great wings, a shot, the broken bird plummeting to the earth, the cook triumphantly holding it aloft, its wings dragging along the ground, the knife, and then silence.

"This is too stupid and pointless a way to die. *This too shall pass!*" The thought repeated itself like a mantra inside my mind, but did not alleviate the terror that I felt. The knife at my throat became the only reality.

His personal plumbing only reluctantly obeyed his bidding, and mercifully it was all over very quickly. I realized that this was the moment for rendering the Big Lie that would prevent him from carving up my face for a memento. I smiled like a besotted fool, told him that he was such a wonderful lover that I would come back the next day, and that I would bring him money. He was so unduly pleased with himself that he removed the bush knife from my jugular, magnanimously indicated that he would allow me to keep my running shorts, and let me go unhurt.

After he had disappeared back into the dunes, I ran far, far into the water, up to my neck, all the while frantically rubbing all traces of his existence from my crawling skin. Far beyond the surf I heard for the first time what my voice had been screaming over and over, above its pounding: "Nothing happened! Nothing at all! Nothing! Nothing! Nothing!"

But dear Lady, Goddess, it *had* happened, no matter how I tried to deny it, and the knife would not leave my mind.

Somehow, I made my way back. An upheaval was taking place in my nervous system. I knew that I was plunging over the edge of sanity, and there was no way that I could stop it. But how was it possible? It had been such a little, little, insignificant rape!

A woman who has been violated has three major areas of concern: She may find herself pregnant; her husband, lover, or family may abandon her; and a venereal disease may have been forced into her bloodstream. It was 1983, and a disease of plague-like dimensions had entered the Western World. At that time it still predominantly affected male homosexuals, although a relatively small percentage of women had also contracted the disease by sharing hypodermic needles with infected drug users. The disease is thought by some to have originated in Africa, and whether this highly debatable theory was true or not, a particularly virulent strain had begun to make its appearance in the central section of Africa, of which Kenya (and Lamu) is a part. This strain differed from the

Western variety in that it attacked both men and women in equal proportions.

I was beyond childbearing age, unattached, and had been gutted of my reproductive organs. My family and friends, when they later heard about the episode, would manifest only pain and compassion for me, so the only thing that caused me great concern was the likelihood that the knifebearer had had one or more of the venereal diseases that are rampant, untreated, and often untreatable in Africa.

I ensconced myself in my hut for 48 hours, making repeated attacks of lathering and scrubbing upon my skin, until it became quite abraded. Then I grimly sought out the island medical facility where I knew some sort of local paramedic to be in residence. One quick glance around the infirmary convinced me of the error of my ways. Hastily I made preparations to journey to Mombassa, a day away down the coast, where I hoped to find a doctor who would examine me, and do whatever needed to be done.

At the ticket office near the ferry, I obtained a reservation on the four-seater to Melindi for the next day. As I walked past the dock, I saw six girls in their late teens or early twenties slumped disconsolately against the seawall. Their gear strewn all about them, they looked as if they had just arrived on the ferry from the mainland. Driven by an urgent compulsion to warn them, I walked over to them. Because they were so young, I knew that the first place for which they would head was the beach, and I had to prevent them from going out alone beyond the populated places.

I discovered that they were up-country Peace Corps workers, and that they had just been robbed of all their money. They had arrived on the island early that morning and had predictably headed for the beach immediately. They had not been there for more than half an hour when a man that fitted the description of the knifebearer had come out of the dunes, approached them as if to make conversation, and when he got close enough, seized one of them, holding her hostage with the knife at her throat. She and the rest of them were forced to surrender all of their money. When some men came walking along the beach toward them, he made off into the dunes.

They had just received six months' pay, and had come to Lamu for some sorely needed rest and recreation. All they had left now were a few coins, and they were desperately trying to think of a way to get back home. When they reported the incident, the police made the usual clucking noises, wrote everything down, and washed their hands of the whole affair.

"You were lucky that that was all that happened," I intoned coldly, a ferocious anger suddenly welling up in me. "Things could have gone far worse for the lot of you." When I told them what had happened to me within a few hundred yards of where they had been robbed, they stared at me in horror. I handed them the few shillings I had on my person, and stalked back to my hut to wait sleeplessly through the night for morning.

At dawn I boarded the ferry to the airstrip. My route took me by bushplane to Melindi, and from there by bus to Mombassa. I arrived by afternoon and walked to the train station, where I stashed my pack at the "left-luggage." I found a taxi to take me to a hospital.

The driver took me to the Aga Khan Hospital, a fairly imposing structure, and I quickly found its gynecological ward. I stated my problem at the desk, and after filling out some forms, was told to wait. People came and went, and finally, after what seemed to be an unduly long time, when the waiting room was altogether empty, I was allowed into the doctor's office.

The doctor was an Indian woman in her thirties. She had a sour, pinched face which looked as if she were smelling feces. I quickly stated my problem, and requested that I be given prophylactic antibiotics along with a diagnostic workup.

She looked at me in ill-disguised disgust. "You have your nerve coming here. Get out. I have no time for you. You are a police case. I have no time to go to court."

I could not believe what I had just heard. "Are you a doctor?" I asked, thinking I had made some mistake.

"How dare you ask me that. Get out. You have no business here."

I was trying to grasp what was happening. "There are no police involved in this," I said, "You will not be asked to go to court. All I need is that you examine me, and that you order some labwork to see if I have been infected."

Her face got still harder. "Get out before I call the guards. I am not going to touch you, and I am not going to order any labwork for you. Get out."

I stood up. "You are not a doctor," I said. "You are not even a human being." I left the room, I left the ward, and I left the hospital. I felt as if I were bleeding inside. I had been raped all over again, this time by a woman, and it had been far, far worse.

It was of no consolation for me to know that I was not alone. Thousands of innocent women who had been raped in the course of the war between Bangladesh and India had been ruthlessly cast out by their families.

I found another, smaller hospital. There was another Indian doctor, this time a male. I mentioned nothing of the rape. My reason for consulting him, I confessed with downcast eyes, was that my husband was a roustabout who consorted with women of questionable morals. His latest conquest was a known prostitute who was reputed to have a venereal disease.

He shook his head sympathetically and advised me to henceforth resist my husband's sexual advances. When I asked him for an injection of antibiotics, he said that he could not give it to me since it was not known which diseases I had been exposed to. It might be the wrong medicine. There were so many diseases in Africa, after all. Since there had been no time for any symptoms to develop, the only thing he could do for me was to send me for a blood test. Syphilis would not manifest itself for six weeks, in any event, and I would have to wait for the symptoms to appear. I said that in six weeks I would be mad, but he was adamant.

My blood was taken by a sweet, doe-eyed nurse whose single braid of silken hair hung down her back to her ankles. I was told that I should come back two days later to find out my results.

In a severely disturbed state, I somehow found my way back to the left-luggage. I retrieved my backpack with the intention of obtaining a room where I could wait out the two days.

As I left the station, a slight, diminutive figure strode aggressively toward me, and blocked my way. At first I thought it was a boy, but then I saw that it was a young woman in men's clothing. Her hair was shaved above the ears in a bizarre punk style, she assumed the rough and ready pose of a young tough, but her enormous, horrendously wounded eyes gave it the lie. "Taxi?" she asked.

I told her that I was looking for an affordable room. She heaved my backpack into the trunk, and helped me into the front seat of her trash-heap taxi. "What is wrong?" she asked softly, and I began to cry. I poured out my story of the rape, and everything that had happened to me on that day. "They are swine," she said. "They have no heart."

Her name was Rocky, she was 18 years old, and she told me that she was a lesbian. Her mother, she said, was an unusually beautiful Englishwoman, and her father had been a native of the Seychelle Islands, where Rocky and one brother had been born. The father was subject to drunken fits of enraged jealousy, in the course of which he beat both his wife and the children.

When Rocky was six years old, her mother, Sheila, in a stroke of luck seemingly orchestrated by a magnanimous fate, escaped this man with the help of her employer, Klaus, a stunningly handsome German who professed to adore her. The main base of Klaus's extensive business operation lay in Nairobi, and Sheila began to live with him there in great luxury. She became so involved in her new relationship that she paid less and less attention to her children. Rocky vied desperately and futilely for her mother's love, and finally, in search of some closeness and warmth, spent more and more time in the servants' quarters.

The placidity of Sheila's life was shattered one day two years later when she returned unexpectedly from a shopping expedition, entered the children's quarters, and saw her lover's magnificent, bronzed body covering that of her eight-year-old daughter.

Thus confronted, Klaus merely laughed at her. It was the child that he had coveted all along, he taunted. Sheila had never meant anything to him at all. She was a fool. As for Rocky, she was a slut anyway, and he had not taught her anything new. He had not been the first. One or several of the houseboys had already taken care of that.

Sheila's obsession with this man was of such a magnitude that she continued to live with him for another four years, while he quite blatantly continued to abuse Rocky sexually. Unable to free herself, Sheila suffered an agony of enraged jealousy and blamed Rocky for having taken Klaus away from her. Rocky, confused and hurt, yearned only for the mother's love that continued to elude her.

Klaus eventually tired of the domestic discord, Rocky became too old for his highly specialized tastes, and he began to spend his time with a charming Italian widow who had a five-year-old daughter. At this point Sheila pulled herself together, and along with Rocky escaped to Mombassa, where her 16-year-old son was already working as a taxi driver. He helped his mother to obtain a bookkeeper's job, and the three of them found a small but pleasant apartment that backed onto a seaside forest. They could see monkeys swinging through the trees from their bedroom windows.

One month before my meeting with Rocky, the two women had been walking along a busy Mombassa thoroughfare at nine in the morning. Suddenly a native African had rushed up behind them and plunged a knife into Sheila's back. She fell instantly as if dead, and Rocky pursued the perpetrator for about 100 yards, tackled him, and brought him down to the ground. An enraged crowd of onlookers immediately stoned and flailed him, and he escaped being killed on the spot only by the arrival of the police who, as is customary in making arrests, jammed the by then unconscious man into their trunk, slammed the door shut, and drove him off to jail.

Rocky gathered the bleeding Sheila up in her arms. In an amazing feat of strength powered by desperation, she ran with her the half mile to a nearby hospital. There she bullied, screeched, and cursed the emergency room staff into tending to her mother immediately, and the massive internal bleeding was stopped. For a week Sheila hovered between life and death, while Rocky tended her day and night like an angel. Then she seemed to take a slight turn for the better, and after another two weeks, Rocky brought her home.

Since then, she had been an invalid. Because her esophagus had been penetrated by the knife and would not heal, she had lost so much weight that Rocky once more feared for her life. Sheila could not retain food and was slowly starving to death.

The perpetrator, meanwhile, was in custody and was feigning insanity. His motive remained a mystery. No one seemed to know who he was. His papers indicated that he was a Tanzanian citizen, and the Kenyan authorities were going to extradite him to Tanzania.

There was nothing Rocky or her brother or anyone could do about it. He was going to go free.

Rocky took me home with her, to the apartment by the shoreline woods, with the monkeys that swung gibbering and screaming through the trees behind the house. Her mother was still very beautiful, with the paper-thin, ethereal aura of one from whom life had begun to ebb. She told me that she wanted very much to live, if only to be given one more chance with Rocky, who was, she had realized perhaps too late, an angel. She felt that she had sorely wronged her as a child, and wanted more than anything on earth to be able to make it up to her. I told her that Rocky had related their story to me, and that she clearly loved her more than life itself. The greatest gift Sheila could give her was to find the tenacity to hang on to life.

I spent the next two days at the apartment as friends came by to take their turn at tending Sheila. One was a regal, intense African woman in her thirties who was obviously Rocky's lover. In her presence, some of the hurt seemed to drain from those incredibly large and haunted eyes, and the tense little body softened and became sweetly child-like and feminine. Another was a middle-aged, ungainly man with a wonderfully kind face who brought little tidbits to tempt Sheila's appetite. Rocky told me that he had been a passerby when Sheila was stabbed, and that he had visited her every day at the hospital. He was a man of considerable means, and had quietly paid all of her medical bills.

At the end of two days, I returned to the hospital to obtain my test results. A clerk at the desk knew nothing about them and could not even find my records. She told me to come back in an hour, while she tried to locate them. I walked about the hospital grounds, and one hour later returned once more. This time another clerk sat at the desk. I explained what I wanted, and she went on fruitless searches for the first clerk and later, my vanished records. Again I was sent out for an hour. When I returned, the records had still not been found. I demanded to see the doctor who had ordered my tests, and was told with some agitation that he was not at the hospital that day. I demanded to see the laboratory administrator. There was some discussion in the back room, then I heard something being pecked out on a typewriter, and then a woman with a Judas smile came out

and announced they had located my test results. They were all nega-
tive. She handed me a paper.

It was no use. I decided that I had no alternative but to journey to
Nairobi and try to find a doctor there. At the post office I made a
telephone call to a man I knew in that city. He was a petty bank
official, a typical British colonial, and we had no particular liking
for each other. Like most of his ilk, his job provided him with a
magnificent, luxurious house in the European quarter, tended by a
half dozen African servants. He received my call beside his Olym-
pic-sized swimming pool.

I briefly related to him why I had to come to Nairobi and begged
him for sanctuary. Whether out of decency or curiosity, he agreed
to allow me to use his guest quarters for a week, with the proviso
that I not expect him to act the part of the host. I assured him that I
would only welcome the chance for solitude.

When I arrived at his house, it soon became clear that curiosity
had been the predominant motive — curiosity, and a kind of class-
obsessed chauvinism that made it imperative that I be informed in
what way I had been remiss.

"You should have put the blighter in his place," he declared.
"One look would have done it. You have to stare them right in the
eye, and let them know who's in charge."

"Of course," I said, "but you also have to have a gun in your
holster, and bullets in the gun. Then it's no problem at all to 'put the
blighter in his place,' is it? But suppose you do not have a gun?
Suppose you are not even wearing shoes with which you might
ward off a knife, and suppose he has the knife. Then what do you
do?"

"You simply have to have that ability," he said. "Some women
know how to do it. One look is all it takes to show them who is the
master."

Was his memory so short that he had already forgotten the Mau
Mau uprising against the British colonial system in Kenya in the
1950s? Had all the English women who were raped and massacred
in that struggle by native Africans for their independence forgotten
"how to do it?" Perhaps they were taken in their sleep, before they
could open those compelling eyes, to give that single look that
would bring their attackers to their knees and show them who was

master. Was it possible that they had simply been besieged, and finally run out of ammunition? Too beaten down to argue, I gave in to my overriding need for sanctuary, held my peace, and withdrew to my quarters. Again I spent the rest of the day in the bath, washing and scrubbing over and over every inch of my crawling skin.

The next day I sought out a Scottish doctor, having been referred to him by my host. This gentle man still did not deem it necessary to examine me, as I had not developed any symptoms. He did, however, agree to give me an injection of antibiotics, which he said would most likely take care of the eventuality of just about everything except syphilis. Then he sent me on to a laboratory staffed by a woman from British Canada to have my blood tested.

I identified myself, once more driven to mention my rape. The woman looked at me with superior distaste, and sniffed: "That will be 50 shillings." I handed her the money, and without speaking another word, she wrote out a receipt, placed it gingerly in front of me, selected a hypodermic, inserted the needle into my arm, withdrew blood, and transferred it to two glass vials. Then, wordlessly, she pointed to the door.

I stared at her for a moment and then, shaking my head in stunned disbelief, I left the room. It had begun to be more than I could bear.

I wandered about the city aimlessly for some hours while my nervous system was undergoing some serious short-circuiting. The area about my groin had begun to feel sore and tender. I felt certain that I was developing the symptoms of a disease.

My agitation and panic continued to grow. I felt as if my head would burst. Finally I decided that I had better inform the American Embassy that some people on Lamu were trying to kill me because I knew too much about their nefarious activities. If I were to suddenly disappear, having my statement on file at the embassy would at least lead to the apprehension of my murderers.

The minor official at the embassy listened to me at first with a similitude of concern, but seemed to come quickly to the quite correct realization that he was dealing with a lunatic. Nodding his head impatiently, he made notes on a pad of paper, and after about ten minutes announced that he had a luncheon engagement. When I asked him if there were an embassy doctor that I could consult, he said that there was no such person. He could, however, refer me to a Belgian doctor that Europeans generally consulted.

I telephoned the doctor's office and spoke to his secretary. My spell of madness seemed to have passed, and I asked her quite rationally to inquire of the doctor whether he had any objections to seeing a woman who had been raped and who needed to be examined. There was a moment of silence, and then she answered in a concerned voice that sounded as if she actually *cared* whether I lived or died, "Of course he will see you."

"Ask him," I insisted.

A moment later the doctor himself came to the phone. His voice was quietly kind and reassuring. He directed me to come to his office immediately. He could see me right away.

I took a taxi and arrived at the office 20 minutes later. Something in my face must have told the motherly looking receptionist who I was. Without further ado, she guided me gently to a treatment room.

The doctor was a youngish man with warm blue eyes, set in an honest face. He sat down with me and asked me to tell him what had happened, and how he could help me. I had thought that this would be an easy thing to do, but found myself choking on every word.

"I think I am developing symptoms," I said. "No one wants to examine me. They say I must wait six weeks to see if I develop symptoms of syphilis. I don't *want* to develop any symptoms. I want treatment for syphilis *now*, whether I have it or not. I am going crazy. I am all alone, my nerves are gone, and I cannot stand much more of this. If it goes on any longer, I will not be able to help myself. I will throw myself in front of a bus."

"I understand," he said. "Let's see about those symptoms first. I am going to examine you, and I will be as gentle as possible." After he had looked at me, he said with a slight air of puzzlement, "I can see no evidence so far of anything that looks like a disease, but the whole general area is quite abraded. Do you know how that has happened?"

"Yes, I do." I told him about my frantic washing and scrubbing. The soreness I had experienced had been no more than the angry protestation of my macerated skin.

He said that he realized that the first priority of treatment was to alleviate my anxiety, and that he would inject a double dose of penicillin. My agitation eased for the first time in days, I began to relax, and my skin stopped crawling.

When he was done I asked what I owed him. I knew that penicillin was not easy to come by in Africa, and that the injection would be costly. He said that I did not owe him anything, and that it was the *least* anyone could do for me. I tried unsuccessfully several times to thank him, and finally heard my voice come out in a grotesque croak. "Thank you, doctor. Thank you for restoring my faith in humanity."

I returned to my quarters and slept for 24 hours. The next day my host appeared and informed me that he was driving up-country, to the vicinity of Mt. Kenya. If I wished, he could give me a ride. A change of scene might do me good. He could drop me off at a hostel immediately adjacent to a resort hotel at the base of the mountain. I could obtain a bunk for the night quite cheaply, and go on to the mountain in the morning. It was a little late in the season to climb because the rains were imminent, but there were interesting villages and wildlife in the vicinity.

My gratitude, when I thanked him, was genuine. The mere thought of returning to Lamu flooded me with such irrational rage that I understood instinctively that my need first of all was to distance myself not only from the prospect of that journey, but from all cities, houses, and people. Nature alone would heal me.

The hostel at the foot of Mt. Kenya was deserted, and I lay in my bunk in solitude, listening to a multitude of African night sounds. I spent the next day reading in the magnificent gardens of the hotel. I walked along the paths of the narrow river adjoining it. A great monitor lizard dragged its primeval bulk to the edge of the water and drank deeply. Three hippos were lazing in the muddy waters of a deep pool with all but their alert eyes and the tops of their heads immersed. Every now and then they would lift their huge, glistening heads, open cavernous mouths, grunt like mammoth pigs, and recede once more into the water, away from the grueling sun. When late afternoon came, they rose ponderously from the depths, waddled up the bank, and moved into the brush to graze. The bushes were alive with birds. Brilliantly iridescent in the sunlight, they flew from branch to branch, calling in many voices.

I indulged myself in the expensive luxury of dinner at the hotel dining room, sharing a table with a middle-aged Canadian couple. They were on their way the next morning to Point Lenana Base Camp to pick up their two sons. The camp was located at an altitude of 10,000 feet, about an hour's drive away. The teenage boys were climbing this point on Mt. Kenya as a kind of rite of passage. The camp locale, the woman said, was singularly beautiful, with spectacular vegetation. Even more enticing, a rare and unusually tame variety of monkey could easily be observed there. They could make room for a passenger in their Land Rover, they said, and graciously offered to take me along.

The climb to Point Lenana at 16,400 feet, they told me, was arduous, especially at this time of year, so close to the rainy season. The Intermediate Camp at 15,000 feet was due to be closed in a few days because weather conditions would soon make scaling the mountain impossible. It was already extremely difficult. The major part of the climb consisted of a vertical bog, and everyone who had climbed the Point at this time of year could speak of nothing but this nightmarish bog.

They had evidently spoken true. Shortly after we arrived at the base camp lodge, a group of rugged teenagers came staggering off the path that led to the mountain. They were obviously exhausted, covered from head to toe with black mud, and glowing with achievement. "That vertical bog," they kept saying over and over again. "You'd never believe that vertical bog. It goes on and on, and all of it is knee-deep mud." The elder son, a tall, handsome 19-year-old with a hard, well-conditioned body, sat down on a tree stump and rubbed his shaking legs. "That was just about the toughest thing I've ever done," he sighed, blissfully sipping coffee.

When they had piled all of their gear into the Land Rover and left, I sat in the clearing and waited for the monkeys I had seen peering out of the trees some distance away. Gradually two of them ventured out into the open, and we sat looking at one another over a distance of no more than 50 feet. When I pulled a piece of bread out of my pocket and began to gnaw on it, the young female with a suckling infant clinging to her body moved closer. The larger male studiously ignored me. I got up slowly, walked over to the tree stump, and laid the bread on it. Then I stepped back three paces. As if I were not there, she casually hopped over to the stump, picked it up, and keeping an eye on the large male, retreated with it to the nearest tree.

Soon more monkeys came out of the trees and sat waiting in the clearing, seemingly unconcerned by my presence. After a while a woman came out of the kitchen at the back of the lodge and scattered some scraps of food among them. They gathered it all up and sat eating peacefully. Finally they retreated back to the trees at a leisurely pace.

Near the equator just before twilight, the sun falls to the horizon with amazing rapidity. I sat in the clearing, watching the movement of the lengthening shadows along the ground. My heart was heavy with loneliness, my whole body ached for a gentle touch. I thought of Pognon's warm hands tenderly stroking my face. I thought of the sweetness of the baby monkey in the arms of its mother, and the confused hunger in the wounded eyes of Rocky. I was enveloped by a feeling of abandonment and alienation so vast that it seemed to cover the entire earth. I had lost all sense of purpose, all direction. All I could feel was unassuaged, elemental need.

When I saw a dark figure come toward me in the twilight, I suddenly experienced such an overwhelming feeling of panic that I ran and hid among the trees.

"Madam!" a voice pursued me. "Madam! It is time for dinner!" It was the lodgekeeper. As I stumbled into the lodge he saw that I was trembling, and asked me if I were cold. Feeling like a fool, I told him that I was. My panic intensified when he said that he would bring an extra blanket to my room. I hastily protested that I would not need it, that I had a sleeping bag, and fled.

It was some time before I could calm my shaking nerves. I began to talk to myself aloud, saying that I would not be able to go on like this, that it was impossible. After I had cried for a while I began to talk to myself like a Dutch uncle, giving myself this advice: "If you do not get yourself together very soon, you are finished, and you will spend your whole life being afraid. You have to do something that is brave and outrageous and strong, and that will save you. You must climb the mountain." Having made that decision, I began to feel better. After a while I washed my face and went back to the dining room to eat my solitary dinner.

Early the next morning, I made arrangements for the climb. Near the lodge there were provisions for hiring a guide and porters. A sign also indicated that warm clothing and other necessary gear could be rented. I rifled through a bin of ill-assorted boots without laces, torn socks, sweat-stained shirts, and reeking, ripped sleeping bags. Finally I came up with a pair of woolen World War II British Army pants. I tried them on, found that the legs ended approximately midway down my calves, and that they were more than six inches too large in the waist. This could only be considered an advantage since I could pull them easily over my jeans. They came with a pair of serviceable suspenders, and I decided they would do just fine to keep me warm. There was no mirror, so fortunately I was unable to admire the effect.

Somewhere in that pile of misbegotten rags I also found a woolen sailor's cap, and on my way out of the none too fragrant room, I was elated to see a sturdy walking stick leaning against the wall. I had my own hiking boots, several pairs of socks, a sweater, gloves, a threadbare ski jacket, and a lightweight, none too warm sleeping bag. At the desk I saw that t-shirts with the legend "I have climbed Point Lenana" were for sale, and I bought the remaining three for the warmth their extra layers would afford.

When I went to make the arrangements for a guide and porter, a young African approached me. He said that he was one of the guides employed by the establishment, and asked if I had much gear to carry. I pointed to my backpack, and he said that he would be willing to act as both guide and porter for a lesser sum than the two together would otherwise cost me. Since the rental for my wonderful mountaineering equipment had already been quite a strain on my very limited finances, I found such an arrangement agreeable, and after we had both been signed in at the office, we began the climb.

The first two miles went along a pleasantly wooded foot path, and I began to feel quite happy. But then the path ended, and the bog began.

I have never run a marathon. In the year that began and ended my brief running career, I ran a half-marathon only once. It resulted in so much pain that I quickly realized I had better not do that again if I did not wish to do irreparable damage to my congenitally defective feet and knees. Yet there is something about a marathon that still activates all of my unfulfilled dreams and yearnings. I look upon those women who are able to run them, especially older women, with considerable awe and not a little envy. One of my greatest heroines is a little 84-year-old grandmother who has amazed the world of sports. She has completed a significant number of marathons, breaking records with each one. No more than a decade or two preceding her feats, women had not been allowed to compete in marathons at all. It was thought that running such a distance was a physical impossibility for them.

The bog was like a marathon, yet differed in a number of significant respects. It consisted of a steep, soggy incline of deep, sucking mud. To climb it one had to jump from one small clump of grass to another for footing, and there was not a single place anywhere along the entire distance where one could rest, sit, or lean against a tree. There was no shade, no respite from the broiling sun. It went on for hours, while the spaces between tiny footholds became wider and wider. My fear of twisting my defective knee grew with every leap. It was indeed a nightmare.

I was soon covered with mud. My African guide, in sneakers and dress pants that he had rolled to midcalf, carried my heavy backpack. He leaped gracefully and immaculately from one toe-hold to the other. Halfway through the bog, we were passed by several heavily laden porters on their way up the mountain, and he grumbled angrily at our slow progress. My head was reeling with altitude sickness, my stomach churned with nausea. I gritted my teeth and grimly kept going, fuelled by the realization that I had absolutely no alternative. If I gave up and sat down in the mud, no one would come to scrape me off the mountain.

After some hours the bog finally came to an end, and we emerged into a green valley with what looked like science fiction vegetation. Then we began to climb again, above the tree line, above the scrub line, into frozen snow. On and on and on. The sun was almost ready to begin its fall to the horizon, and stumbling hurriedly, unseeingly along I kept asking my guide, "How much farther? How much farther?" I was terrified that we would be overcome by darkness before we reached the camp. "It is still far," he answered every time I asked, becoming more and more angry at the slow progress of our climb.

Suddenly, as the sun began its headlong plunge to the horizon, I saw a plume of smoke up ahead, and moments later, a group of tents. There was perhaps a mile of frozen ground left to traverse, and I raced against the fading light. It had grown icy cold. My guide and backpack had disappeared somewhere up ahead. When the sun touched the horizon, I reached the first tent, staggered into it, sank to the ground, and wept with exhaustion.

An African man was standing over a wood stove, tending a number of pots. He looked at me curiously. Several minutes later, in bright moonlight, six other climbers arrived. It was their group of porters who had passed us, and the African, preparing an evening meal, was their cook. We warmed and rehydrated our cold and depleted bodies with endless cups of hot tea. Soon very much revitalized, I accepted their matter-of-fact invitation to join them at a surprisingly elaborate dinner. I still felt too ill and exhausted to do more than nibble at my food, but was glad for their easy camaraderie.

Among the yo. 'g and apparently well-seasoned group of climbers, there was o. ` member who appeared to be nearly as unlikely as I. He was perh. 's 50 years of age, and nothing about his figure suggested the sportsman or mountain climber. I discovered that he was a Boston dermatologist who had some short years before suffered a heart attack, left a troubled marriage, and accepted a job in Saudi Arabia. He was currently on holiday, and had, like I, decided to climb Point Lenana on the impulse of the moment.

Shortly after dinner, the group retired to the tents. They planned to start on the last leg of the climb at 3:30 a.m. so that they would reach the peak just after daybreak. At that time of morning the sky was expected to be perfectly clear. Later clouds generally moved in to obscure all view. I was still suffering acutely from altitude sickness and fatigue and knew that I would not be able to join them. A cold wind had begun to howl.

I found the smallest tent in the near-deserted camp, knowing that I would have to conserve as much body heat as possible. I mummified myself in every piece of clothing I had in my pack, including cap, boots, and all my socks, crawled into my thin sleeping bag, pulled its string shut above my head, and tried to sleep. As freezing gusts of wind battered my tent, I lay shaking in the dismal darkness and tried to remember what in the name of heaven had possessed me to come to this godforsaken place.

The night seemed endless, and when the equatorial sun finally rose, I crawled stiffly out of my cocoon to thaw out. I had had the foresight to leave a bucket of water in front of my tent before I retired, hoping to perform my ablutions in the morning. When I looked at it, I laughed aloud at my foolishness. At first I thought that the water in the bucket was merely covered by a sheet of ice, but when I tilted the bucket I discovered that its entire contents had frozen solid.

My head had cleared overnight and the churning of my stomach now indicated hunger, not altitude sickness. I found my disgruntled guide and told him that we would start for the Point after breakfast. The sky was still clear, the weather seemed favorable, and I realized that this would most likely be my one and only chance.

I went to the cooking tent, discovered that the cook was making tea, and found some pieces of bread left from the night before. I sat with my bread and mug of hot tea in the warming sun in front of the tent, watching the hyrax, terrier-sized rodents, scuttling about. They were searching for food, systematically going from tent to tent. Where there was a small gap in the perpendicularly zipped closings, they inserted their noses and with great efficiency forced the zippers apart. Then they entered and rifled the tent. They had not yet reached mine, and I quickly made certain that the zippers were fast, leaving no gap for them to insert their probing noses. They looked sleek and well-fed, and having checked out all the tents, they came to sit near me, looking at me with trusting expectation. I had not the heart to disappoint them, and gave them the rest of my bread.

My guide, when I collected him at the porters' tent, seemed singularly uninspired about my decision to continue on to the Point, and was grumbling under his breath as we set out. He wore his usual spotless, rolled-up dress trousers, three thin polyester shirts, and a cotton windbreaker. Perhaps his ill nature was simply due to the fact that he was cold and had looked forward to remaining in the warmth of his tent. I resolved that I would give him my ski jacket as a farewell gift when we returned to base camp.

The climb began over a long, frozen field which led into a steep, narrow scree of jagged gravel. Footing became extremely hazardous. My every step sent a handful of small stones tumbling. Up and up we went. A damp fog rolled in, obscured our vision, and after an hour more, partially receded. We turned a corner and there, on our left, a vast glacier lay between two mountain peaks. My head had once more begun to throb. Each step seemed an impossible effort. I retched with nausea, but forced myself to go on. Suddenly the fog lifted on our right and almost as if I were dreaming, I saw the vast valley, miles below. I found myself looking down into the very heart of equatorial Africa as it lay baking in the hot sun, and far, far off into the distance.

Then I saw Point Lenana just ahead, but a system of measures and balances in my body told me that I had no strength left to spend, that I must turn back now, or I would not make it. "It does not matter if you reach the Point or not," the voice in my head said. "You have *climbed* your mountain! That is all that counts."

I began my staggering descent, and wondered vaguely if I had the strength left to reach camp. A cold fog rolled in once more, obscuring the valley, obscuring the mountain, leaving only a few feet of visibility ahead. Somehow I made it down the scree, out of the fog, and into the ice field where I could see the tents in the distance. Again my guide disappeared up ahead, and I was left to finish the last two miles alone.

Close to unconsciousness, I lurched toward the nearest tent, from which a plume of smoke was rising. The porters were sitting around a blazing fire and bid me a cheery welcome. I sank to the ground. Someone thrust a mug of hot tea into my hand. I took a couple of swallows and fell immediately asleep where I sat.

Darkness had fallen by the time I awoke. The porters still sat by the fire. I became aware that one of them was racked by a painful cough. I looked into his feverish face and asked him what was wrong. "It is the altitude sickness," he said. "It comes from going up and down the mountain." He had been a porter on the mountain for five years, carrying heavy loads dressed only in thin shirts and sneakers. Now he had been told that he must stop or die. He looked at me with his fever-bright eyes and asked sadly, "And if I stop going up the mountain, who will feed my family? It is all I know." Another one of the men sighed fatalistically. "It will happen to all of us. Sooner or later it will happen."

That night the wind howled around my tent, snow fell, and I thought of the bog that I must face once more in the morning. When the sun rose I packed up my gear and made ready for my descent. As I arrived at the kitchen tent for a morning cup of tea, the dermatologist was just leaving. He told me that he and his guide were about to start their descent and that the rest of the group had already left at daybreak. The camp was being shut down, he had been informed. Bad weather was expected to close in that afternoon. I would do well to get off the mountain as quickly as I could.

I made my last minute preparations. My guide was ready to leave and we set off down the mountain. The weather was crisp and clear, giving hope for an uneventful descent. At the outset it was relatively easy going down the mountain. I felt a surge of energy as we descended into less rarefied air. But after two hours we reached the bog, and the nightmare began once more. Where it had snowed up on the mountain, it had rained in the bog, which now ran torrents of icy water. Halfway through it there was a sudden downpour, which quickly turned to icy sleet and brought my laborious progress to a virtual halt. Torrents of icy water poured past my drenched legs and into my boots.

My guide, who had until now sullenly preceded me, turned, his face contorted with fury. "Give me more money," he shouted above the howling wind, "Give me more money, or I will leave you here!"

Rage overwhelmed me. "I will give you no money!" I shrieked back. "Go back without me, and see what happens to you when they look at the book you have signed, and they ask you where you have left me." "Give me money," he repeated. I could feel my adrenaline surging.

"Do you think you can threaten *me*?" I spat, my jaw rigid with contempt, thrusting my face into his. "*I* am El Shadida. I have no need for the likes of you. I will find my *own* way!" We stood for a long moment, shaking with cold and glaring stonily into one another's face, dripping icy water. Then I saw his mouth quiver. I had won. He turned and led the way once more down the mountain. The downpour stopped as suddenly as it had come. I was flushed with victory, and angrily pushed away the nagging sense of shame that tried to edge its way into my consciousness.

After what seemed like an eternity, we came to the end of the bog. My legs were shaking with fatigue. In the afternoon sun, steam rose from the mud drying on my body.

As we reached the path that led to the lodge, my guide disappeared. I never saw him again. Halfway along the path I found my backpack, abandoned in the middle of the road. I hoisted it onto my shoulders and marched, head held high, the rest of the way. I was ten feet tall. I had conquered my mountain.

As I approached the clearing behind the lodge, I saw that a table had been set up there. It was laden to groaning with food. Several young women looked at me in surprise as I emerged into the clearing, and then embraced me in welcome. They were Israelis recently discharged from three years of military service. A group of their young men had begun the climb to Point Lenana at two in the morning, and were expected to return soon.

Within the hour a tough looking young crew of Israeli desert fighters arrived. They had actually accomplished the climb and the descent without any interruption. They were full of excitement. "That bog! That bog was beyond all belief," they said over and over. When they found out that I too had made the climb, they hugged me to their nail-hard bodies, called me "mother," and gave me a place of honor at their table.

I remembered another such group of young soldiers that I encountered when I packed through Israel in 1979. The whole country had long been an armed camp. The thing I found to be the most unnerving was the matter-of-factness with which everyone in the country accepted this: constant, naked aggression had become a well-established way of life. It made me feel sick to the depths of my being.

I had camped alone on a beach near Elat, on the Red Sea, in a piece of territory that had been wrung from Egypt in the latest war. For the moment it was No Man's Land and it was scheduled to be returned to Egypt in the near future. I had found a sheltered spot and gone to sleep.

Suddenly, in the middle of the night, I was awakened by the loud bark of engines converging on me. I found myself trapped in the harsh beam of three spotlights, and felt rude hands pulling me upright in my sleeping bag. "Who are you, and what are you doing here?" a harsh voice fired menacingly. Badly shaken, I explained as calmly as I could that I was an American and had come to snorkel on the reef. I peeled my passport out of my pack and handed it to them. When they became aware that I was a middle-aged, fair-skinned woman, they calmed down, lowered their weapons, and turned off the spotlights. My answers to their questions seemed to satisfy them. They handed me back my passport, started up their engines, and went roaring off the beach and out of earshot.

It must have taken me an hour to calm down sufficiently to fall asleep. I was on the verge of dropping off when I heard them return once more. This time they did not turn their guns or their spotlights in my direction. I watched one of them climb out of his vehicle. He was carrying two large shopping bags. "Here is some food for you," he said gruffly. He set the bags on the ground in front of me, went back to his jeep, and all three vehicles once more drove off. I looked at the bags wonderingly, and regretted for the first time that I was alone on the beach. They had brought me enough food for a good-sized party.

I signed out at the Mt. Kenya Base Camp office, mentioning nothing of what had taken place in the bog, and by nightfall my Israeli mountaineering friends had dropped me off once more at the hostel.

To my dismay, I found it crowded to bursting with a group of African Primary School pupils and their teachers. Not only the bunks, but every inch of floor space was already occupied. As heavy rain began to fall, I hiked back to the hotel, hoping to find accommodations there.

The hotel was completely booked. The weekend had begun and every room was taken. I passed the dining room, hoping to find an employee with whom I could negotiate for floor space in some storage room, when I spotted the dermatologist, sitting alone at a table. Over a cup of tea I told him of my dilemma, and he graciously offered to share his quarters with me. He had been given a large room with three beds, he said, and he was alone. Above all, his quarters boasted a private shower and lots of hot water. Gratefully, I accepted his offer.

I luxuriated in the shower. The cascading warm water washed the mud and fatigue from my body. As I slid between the cool, smooth sheets of my bed, I heard the dermatologist already snoring softly at the other end of the room.

The next morning, at breakfast, he offered an unnecessary apology. "It isn't that you aren't a very attractive woman," he said, "but I was totally exhausted last night. I hope I have not been remiss."

I smiled at him ruefully. "You were not the only one that was exhausted," I said, "and you have assuredly not been remiss." Then I added, "It isn't that you are not also a very attractive man (he was no such thing), but I have very recently been raped. It may take me some time to sort things out."

Something in my face made him quickly avert his eyes. Finally he asked softly, "Will you be all right, do you think?"

"I hope so," I whispered tonelessly. "It comes and goes. It will be a while before I know."

He sighed heavily and said that he wished me all the luck in the world.

We sat silently for some minutes and then he added that a limousine was waiting to take him from the hotel back to the airport. He offered to take me back to Nairobi if I wished to come along.

I breathed a sigh of relief. Luxury such as this did not come my way often in Africa, and when it did, it made life immeasurably easier. It was one of those moments when I had great need for ease.

On the way back to Nairobi, he talked about his work in Saudi Arabia. He confided that he loved it. It had its drawbacks, of course, and one had to get used to a strictly enforced monastic existence in rigorously segregated bachelor quarters. All forms of alcohol were strictly forbidden, and reading matter, as well as films entering the country, were most stringently censored, obliterating anything even remotely sexual in nature. His own personality was able to tolerate these restrictions, although he knew quite a number of other men who had found them totally intolerable.

His job was excellently recompensed; he was allowed three months of vacation time each year and was able to afford traveling anywhere in the world in great luxury. The thing that he really loved, however, was the fact that he saw all kinds of strange and exotic diseases such as he had never seen before. Whenever he returned to the United States to attend medical meetings and report on these cases, he was always the unabashed envy of his colleagues.

There was one case, in particular, of which he was very proud. Some 20 years before he had seen pictures of a young girl suffering from a terribly deforming, undiagnosed malady of the skin in a medical book on African tropical diseases. The disease affected this child's whole body. She was displayed nude except for her face, which was covered by a veil.

A few months ago a woman in her thirties had been brought to him, and by certain physical features he was able to recognize her. She had been the girl in the pictures. After examining her he had been able to diagnose her illness, and had treated it successfully with a combination of antibiotics and sunlight. She was, of course, so badly scarred by the disease that he felt she would never be able to marry. Still, she was without disabling pain for the first time in her life, and immeasurably happy and grateful. He planned to renew his contract in Saudi Arabia when it expired, he said. For the first time in his life he knew the joy of being a doctor in the service of humanity.

When we arrived at Nairobi Airport, he instructed his driver to take me back to the house of my banker acquaintance. We shook hands, wished one another luck, and parted. Half an hour later I was back in my quarters, cleaning my gear, and making ready to depart for Mombassa the next day.

When I arrived at Sheila and Rocky's apartment, I found no signs of life. The door of an upstairs neighbor finally opened to my insistent knocking, and she told me that the entire family had been flown to Nairobi by their benefactor. It had seemed to be the only chance for saving Sheila's life. Immediately after I left she had taken another turn for the worse, and had been close to death. The very serious risks of moving her had to be weighed against the possible benefits of the superior care she hoped to obtain in a Nairobi hospital. Knowing that she stood no chance at all if she remained in Mombassa, she had opted for the journey. I could get no further information, and decided that I had no alternative but to begin the last leg of my return to Lamu. Apprehensively, I walked to the steamy, garbage-choked bus station. I chose one of the many junkpile buses that stood filling up, waiting to wheeze its way to Melindi. I felt a pall of depression descend on me. I had no desire to return to Lamu, but a hard, stubborn core in my being that resisted being driven off forced me to go back so that I might finish my work on the book I had started there.

At the marketplace in Melindi I found an express bus to the airstrip. It was on this bus, as it careened around a corner of the tourist market, that I saw The Goddess.

After I rescued her from the thieves, I carried her to the airstrip. I was told that I would have to buy a second ticket since my luggage was now in excess of the sparse weight allowance for the small plane. I bought two tickets; one for her and one for me. There was one other passenger, who sat behind me on the four-seater. At the last moment yet another man boarded the plane, making me yield the extra seat I had paid for. I recognized him to be Ali One Eye who, it was well known on Lamu, made the trip to Mombassa every Saturday in order to fence the cameras that had been stolen there from tourists that week. He cloaked himself in an air of respectability and thought of himself, no doubt, as a successful businessman, but I knew him for what he was: a common thief.

I pulled The Goddess close to my body, buckled the seatbelt over both of us, and sat silently with my arms wrapped about her. When I alighted from the plane upon our arrival, a pack of luggage carriers lying in wait outside lunged at me, then shied away. I do not know whether it was the totem that I carried in my arms that repelled them, or the rage and determination on my face.

There are many roads in life from which to choose, but each of us can travel only one. In looking back, it is fruitless to agonize over all the other paths one might have taken at any given point. It is far more productive to contemplate the distance that one has traversed, and to learn something from the journey.

I chose, or was compelled by a series of circumstances and inner drives, to remain on Lamu for six more months. I had foolishly leased a small inn at the water's edge of the harbor. A hut had been built on its roof for me. The business end of the inn was badly managed by Ali, a native Kenyan who, while I financed it, was for official reasons its entrepreneur. While this arrangement gave me a place to live, my money was disappearing swiftly down the drain. The only way to keep electricity and water from being turned off almost daily was via an endless stream of graft, phony permits, and bribes. To compound matters, a disco opened right next door to the inn the week after my return. It blared reject American disco records over its ruined loudspeakers until 5 a.m. at nerve-destroying volume five nights a week. Sleep was impossible, and those few unsuspecting tourists that Ali enticed into the inn fled after one night.

I sat in my hut, fighting madness, recording my notes gathered in Sudan onto tape. I planned to bandage these tapes to my body as a precaution against the thieves that customarily rifled luggage at Nairobi Airport. This, in any event, was a completely rational safety precaution. Nairobi Airport was infamous for its thievery.

Many times during those six months I thought longingly of returning home, but there was no place that I could call home any longer. Repeatedly I endeavored to pack what I would need to escape the island, to continue my travels. I found myself incapable of making the simplest decisions on what to take and what to jettison. I could barely even dress myself in the morning.

There was no place I could think of any longer where I wanted to go. I was subject to sudden, unpredictable, and uncontrollable rages, most of them directed at the confused Ali. These left me shaken and afraid. My delusion that there were people on Lamu that planned to kill me asserted itself periodically, and I became highly circumspect in my comings and goings. To this day I do not know if I was subject to paranoia or if this was simply justifiable caution.

Somewhere I read the observation made in jest that just because you are paranoid, this does not mean that they are not out to get you. On Lamu it was a deadly serious matter. Every few weeks a body washed up onto the beach, having been carried there by the current from the harbor three miles over. The story was always the same. The man had been drunk. He had fallen off the seawall as he staggered home at night. Often there were unexplained bruises on the heads of these drowned men, and no one could really say how those had occurred in the moderate current and soft sand of the beach.

I do not know whether I became The Madwoman of Lamu or the Angel of Lamu. Perhaps it was both. I tried to warn every woman I could find that there were rapists hiding in the dunes. I talked incessantly — in the teahouses, at the inns, along the seawall, wherever I met one of these women. Perhaps I saved some.

In the six months that I remained on Lamu I saw five other women who had been raped by what must have been different men. One had been beaten quite badly, another had been cut with a knife about the face, a third had been robbed of more than 3,000 dollars that she had had on her person and was then raped by the thief. As she fled back toward the safety of the little beach hotel, she was accosted by a second man who had lain in wait in the dunes. He had come catapulting down when the first assailant left and had raped her a second time. I do not know how many more women left the island hurriedly without telling anyone what had happened to them, wishing only to escape and to find some doctor. The police clucked sympathetically, assured each woman that such a terrible thing had *never* happened before on Lamu, carefully wrote everything down, and did absolutely nothing more.

New visitors came to the island almost daily, and left again two or three days later. Although I told my story over and over in the hopes of finding some relief, it was like reading the first page of a well-worn book again and again. It was like going to a new psychotherapist daily, only to never see him or her again. Sometimes, over a short period of days, an emotional support system seemed to form in the person of someone who stayed on for a day or two longer. Then it vanished once more.

I spent most of my time alone with The Goddess in my hut. No matter how fervently I begged her, she gave me no sign.

Finally I learned the bitter lesson that no one would come to help me. I realized that if I ever wished to leave the island alive and to see my children again, I would have to regain my sanity by virtue of the mainsprings of strength deep within myself. It was then that she relented and sent me one of her angels.

I saw him first as he was sitting in one of the tea houses, and was immediately drawn to his beautiful, beatific smile. He was a fine-looking man in his middle years, broad shouldered and deep chested, profoundly masculine in appearance. He wore khaki shorts which revealed remarkable, muscular legs. His splendid head of hair was silken and graying, and I noticed that it was tonsured.

It did not take us long to become engaged in conversation. He told me that he was the abbot of a small monastery in San Francisco. Upon reaching his fiftieth birthday, he had been offered a vacation anywhere in the world by a wealthy relative, complete with the unlimited use of several credit cards. He had spoken to a travel agent about his desire to make a spiritual retreat somewhere in Africa, and had asked for her advice on where to go. This sadly benighted woman had looked at the map and misguidedly sent him to Lamu, one of the worst vice pits in all of Africa.

Lamu, built during the heyday of the slave trade and one of several in a chain of slave ports that stretched along the coast of Africa, was at one time an affluent and immaculately clean Islamic island town. When the tourist nowadays sets foot on it, he finds a picturesque place that still has remnants of its former charm, if he goes no further than the two main streets along the water. As soon as he leaves this, however, he finds that the rest of the island is choked with uncollected garbage. Open sewers flank the narrow paths between houses, running with evil-smelling filth everywhere.

When on the island for a while longer, one becomes aware of another kind of stench. The town of Lamu is a haven for pedophiles who flock there from all over the world. Small children may be had for a pittance, and over a period of time I learned exactly which Specialty of the House many of the little inns along the waterfront offered. Some of these inns were merely brothels of an altogether conventional nature, but the greatest demand was unquestionably for children.

When the abbot alighted from the airplane, he was immediately set upon by panderers offering him little girls, virgins, whatever his heart desired. He gently declined, saying that his religion forbade such things. This did not deter the panderers, however, who immediately began to sing the praises of another type of merchandise that they could sell him: little boys, young, tender, and of course, pure. Pain battled with outrage in the abbot's gentle face as he related this humiliating scene to me. It was to be repeated many times during his stay on the island.

We became friends and told one another our histories. He had been born into privileged circumstances and had attended some of the country's best universities. Religious training had been an unimportant part of his upbringing and he had given it little if any thought. By the time he was 32, he had built his own fortune and was very much a man of the world. He had two beautiful mistresses, both of whom loved him sufficiently to forgive each other's existence in his life. He had everything any man could ask for: good health, an athletic body, the love of beautiful women, great wealth, cultured and interesting friends, a stimulating and diverse environment.

One night he had had a religious experience, a vision — he did not know what to call it. There was no way to explain its occurrence. He had not been ill or under the influence of drugs, alcohol, or grief. He simply became aware of a force, a presence in his room. It had been so powerful an experience that he abandoned his worldly life, entered a theological seminary, and prepared himself to become an Anglican monk. Some years later he took his vows of chastity, poverty, and obedience. His family was deeply distraught. His inconsolable mistresses had not to this day been able to forgive him.

I told him that in my childhood I had been subjected to the burden of blatant personal hypocrisy by my ostensibly devout father and had been weighted down by insufferable political and social lies. Consequently, I believed in absolutely nothing. I was an unrepentant skeptic, pagan, nonbeliever. Neither one of us felt compelled to make any attempt to dissuade the other from his or her stance in life, and so our friendship deepened.

We spent many hours together. I began to heal within the benign aura of his gentle spirituality, as I also gained strength from the wisdom of his worldly experience. Because his virility was such a visibly strong component in his nature, and because it was only natural that I should ask, I inquired if his vow of chastity was not a problem to him. "It is with me every day of my life," he answered humbly. "I had been warned before I took the vow that it would be this way." I was aware of a strong erotic current between us, and there was no doubt in my mind that he felt it just as acutely as I did.

After giving me four healing weeks, he prepared to leave the island. He was returning to his monastery. There he and his monks wove cloth and sewed handcrafted shirts to support the hostel in which they fed and sheltered homeless wayfarers. I waited in his hotel suite while he readied himself for the flight back to this other life.

He emerged from his dressing room wearing a dark cowl of heavy monk's cloth, looking every inch the religious ascetic. We embraced in farewell. I felt a surge of intense longing for the warmth of his gentle, strong, acutely male body upon mine.

It later crossed my mind that while he was away from his monastery I might well have seduced him, but I also knew that such a seduction would have been as cruel as a rape. It would ultimately have caused him only pain and regret. I loved him far too much to do that to him.

I wrote to him once when I had safely returned to the United States. I thanked him for his sweetness and for helping me recover the strength that was in me. I never heard from him, as I had known I would not. His vow of poverty did not allow him even so small a luxury as owning writing paper.

Two weeks after he had gone, I randomly threw some things into my backpack, told Ali to keep everything else, wrapped The Goddess in a piece of kanga cloth, and set out for Nairobi for the last time. I found an affordable room along a road known for its dangers in the center of town. This reputation hardly mattered. I had seen tourists surrounded by armed gangs in the most exclusive part of Nairobi centrum, being stripped down while the police looked the other way. My own choice of location could be no worse.

I had a ticket from Athens to New York stashed away in my money belt, and now I needed to find the best bargain in a flight from Nairobi to Athens. I inquired the going rate at several airlines, and found that they were almost all equally out of the question for me. I remembered a piece of information that some other Africa traveler had conveyed to me somewhere along the way. Aeroflot by way of Moscow, he said, would be by far the cheapest way to go. I decided to investigate.

I found the tiny one-room Aeroflot office, furnished spartanly with a desk and two wooden chairs, in the upstairs corner of a backstreet house. The room was filled with people who were clearly from all over Europe and Asia. They waited patiently as the single agent at the desk wrote out tickets.

Finally my turn came. I sat down across the desk from the agent and told her what I wanted. An inexpensive flight to Athens was indeed possible, she informed me. I could leave in two days. Perversely, the plane would fuel in Egypt, just across the channel from Athens, while passengers had to remain on board. It would then continue on to Moscow, where after an indeterminate passenger layover in the airport transient hotel, a flight would carry us back clear across Europe into Athens. It would not be possible to obtain a transient visa on such short notice. That would take at least two weeks. I would have to remain in the transient hotel for the duration of my stay.

This was before the days of *glasnost*. I had never been inside the Russian border and it seemed like a fitting way to end my journey. I bought the ticket.

The flight was leaving, as usual, at some ungodly hour of the early morning. It would be necessary to arrive at the airport two hours before departure time in order to go through the lengthy customs procedure. It hardly seemed advisable to walk the streets of nighttime Nairobi at 3 a.m. in search of a taxi. I decided to spend the night, as I had often done before, on the floor in the airport.

I arrived at 9 p.m., selected a spot by the open door of the security guard's booth, providently lay down on top of my pack, and tried vainly to sleep. By midnight the airport had become silent. I was aware of only occasional footsteps that came and went, the whirring of a distant vacuum cleaner, the security guard in the booth being replaced by another guard. No one bothered me in my well-chosen location. Early in the morning, other passengers began to arrive. I dragged my gear over to where a family of Indians, complete with five silent, wide-eyed children and two ancient grandparents, were sitting, and slept fitfully for an hour. Then I joined a group of other passengers lining up to go through the tedious airport procedures, in preparation for boarding the plane.

It was the end of March. The night in Nairobi had been quite warm and I had donned a cotton dress and sandals for the journey. I had stuffed my warm sweater and boots into the very top of my pack, expecting to change into them when I reached Moscow airport. I boarded the plane, carrying with me on my back only a small pack containing my precious notes and films, a book, my tiny camera, a pair of glasses, a cotton scarf, and a pair of warm socks I had for some reason added as an afterthought. In my arms I carried The Goddess wrapped in a double length of kanga cloth. My tapes were bandaged tightly to my waist.

The plane lifted off and I watched without a trace of regret as Kenya retreated beneath me. Something in my mind shifted gears and I suddenly felt perfectly normal once more. Some hours later the plane landed in Cairo. We refueled, and finally, after an inexplicably long wait on the airstrip, were airborne once more on the flight across Europe to Moscow. Exhaustion overtook me almost immediately and I slept in dreamless security most of the way.

When I awoke it was late afternoon. The plane was about to land, and I stared in amazement at the strange, snow-covered world that came into view below me. A cold winter sun hung above the horizon. Trees bare of all leaves swayed in the wind. I had not seen a winter landscape in a very long time.

As we alighted from the plane, transients were immediately separated from those few passengers who were entering the country. We were herded as a group through the silent and singularly beautiful airport by three young soldiers carrying automatic weapons. They took us to a bare, unheated back room and we lined up to have our papers and carry-on luggage inspected. A trolley carrying our other luggage rolled up and stood four paces away from us. I had begun to shiver and thought longingly of my warm clothes. I could see my backpack, perched tantalizingly at the very top of the pile on the trolley.

I took two tentative steps toward it and found a gun levelled at my chest. I stopped in my tracks and asked the security guard standing next to me, "Please, would it be possible to get my coat and shoes? I have left all my warm clothes in my backpack." I pointed to it. The dough-faced woman shook her head sourly.

"Nyet. No luggage. Luggage stays here." It was immediately

apparent that there was no point in continuing the discussion. I realized that I would have to make do with what I had.

I sat down on the floor, opened my carry-on pack, and took out my cotton scarf and socks. I pulled on the socks and wrapped the scarf about my head. Then I unwrapped the kanga cloth from the Goddess, baring her, and wound it tightly about my shoulders.

The eyes in the dough face looked at her aghast. "What is *that?*" she pointed. "It is a grave stone," I smiled sweetly.

"What is it *for?*"

My look conveyed that the answer was obvious. "It is for my grave." Her jaw dropped. Glancing over my left shoulder I added lugubriously, "You never know. Your death is always with you."

She muttered something under her breath in Russian, pointed her forefinger to her temple, and rotated it slowly. The milkfaced boy soldier with the automatic rifle snickered behind his hand. I winked at him playfully and he snickered some more.

After we had been processed, we were taken outside and stood for 20 minutes in the cold wind, waiting for the bus that was to take us to the transient hotel. Shivering, I clutched my kanga cloth about me, ruefully remembering the porters on Mount Kenya.

The single, large window of the chilly room to which I was assigned was barred. The room had a private bath with an old-fashioned, full-length bathtub, whose faucets yielded seemingly limitless quantities of unexpectedly hot water. I drew a steaming bath and luxuriated in it for an hour, thawing out my stiff limbs. Then I dressed, pulled a heavy woolen blanket off the bed, and draped it around my body like a toga. Having thus girded my loins, I left my barred chamber and followed the sound of clattering dishes to the gloomy dining hall.

The layover of indeterminate length stretched into its third day, and the plane to Athens had not yet materialized. I had finished reading my book and caught up on my sleep. Although I searched earnestly, I had not found a single person that was particularly interested in conversing with me. I seemed to be the only older woman traveling alone and all of the English-speaking young people clung together in pairs. After some abortive attempts at conversation with several nondescript young travelers, I gave up. The prison atmosphere of the transit hotel had lost its initial bizarre charm, and

lacking interesting conversation, I began to look for ways to alleviate my boredom. I wandered about the two floors of the hotel on
which transients were isolated, feeling increasingly rebellious and
less and less adverse to stirring up just a little bit of trouble.

In the lobby, two elevators traveled from one transient residence
floor to the next, both of which were disconnected and blocked off
from the rest of the large hotel. Two matrons in charge of the floor
were lazily sprawled, dozing, their shoes strewn about, their arms
and legs askew, slacking off. Their attitudes, I decided, did not
befit their ponderously important official positions. Their function
was, after all, to guard the Motherland against dangerous transient
aliens. I quietly sat down in a chair facing them, pulled out my little
camera, and snapped an incriminating photograph of how they
spent their time at work.

At the sound of the shutter, they were instantly galvanized into
high-speed action. One of them cornered me bodily with her considerable bulk, fully prepared to forcibly prevent my rising from the
chair, while the other frantically spun the dial of the desk telephone,
all the while screaming *"Spion! Spion!"* (Spy! Spy!)'' at the top of
her lungs.

After a minute, someone answered. She excitedly poured out her
story, which as far as I could gather, was all about the dangerous
spion that she had just caught taking photographs in the hotel.

Finally she hung up, sat back with her arms folded across her
chest, a "Boy, are you in for it now!" expression on her face, and
we all waited for the firing squad to show up. The bulky one
reached for my camera, but the spy-catcher quickly deterred her
from taking it. It was clear she wanted me to be taken with the
goods.

I returned the camera to my pack and we waited. After perhaps
ten minutes the phone rang. The spy-catcher snatched it up, answered, and I heard a male voice barking loudly into the receiver at
the other end. The longer the spy-catcher listened, the more disappointed she looked. Apparently there was no absolute death penalty
for taking pictures of loafing matrons in the transit residence of the
hotel. Pouting she put down the receiver, rose from her chair, and
extending her arm at shoulder level, pointed a long index finger at
me. "Madam! Go to your room!" she ordered. I indicated the tele-

vision set, to show that I had come to the lobby to watch. She planted herself firmly in front of it. No television for disobedient children. "Go to your room, Madam!" she repeated sternly.

Properly chastened, I retreated to the elevator and to the television set on the next floor. There I watched a number of outstanding cultural programs until notification came over the loudspeaker that the plane for Athens was leaving in an hour.

As I passed security on the way out, I peeled off my life-saving, warm toga, folded it carefully, and handed it to one of the guards. The weather had warmed to mild early Spring, and I deeply breathed the sweet air of freedom as the bus took us to meet our plane.

In Athens the streets were unexpectedly quiet. It was some sort of long weekend holiday, and nearly everyone had left town, including, it turned out, the friends I had hoped to visit on my way back to the States. I found one of the many small hotels just off the main drag near the center of town where I could stay until my flight home could be negotiated.

The hotel too was quiet, and seemed to be practically deserted. The manager at the desk had a swarthy, greasy-looking face and gave the impression that he had just gotten out of bed. He took my passport, noted that I was an American, and looked me appraisingly up and down. His hands, I noted as he wrote, had sausage fingers with black-rimmed fingernails. His hard, black eyes emitted the kind of greedy look that made me demand a room with a strong bolt on the inside of the door.

As I wrestled my backpack down the narrow, ill-lit hall in search of my room, I saw a door open a small crack and felt, rather than saw, a pair of eyes peering out at me. Uneasily I hurried by, entered my room, and bolted the door. The room was surprisingly pleasant and large, with high white walls and a large window through which the warm Greek sun flooded.

After some time I gave in to my usual acute desire to cleanse myself of the dust of travel and went in search of a shower. Again the same door opened a crack, and I felt eyes following me down the hall. I hurriedly found the bathroom, made doubly sure that the door was securely bolted, and quickly lathered my body under the barely tepid water. Greatly refreshed, I toweled myself dry, dressed, and strode down the hall, back to my room.

This time the mysterious door was wide open, and a delicious young thing in khaki desert shorts stood in the doorway, smiling hopefully. "My name is Avi," he said, "I am from Israel. You are an American, are you not?" Then he added artlessly, "I know you are, because I went down and asked the manager at the desk where you are from." American women, I knew, were reputed among Mediterranean men to be notoriously easy to seduce.

Stepping back two paces into the room, he went on, "I was hoping you would join me in a meal so that we may talk and become friends. Welcome." I glanced past him, and saw that he had laid out a small feast of olives, dates, pita bread, hummus, and wine. "I have brought all this with me from Israel," he urged, "I have just been released from the Army." Feeling suddenly hungry and knowing I would come to no harm, I entered the room.

Avi was inordinately pleased with his catch, and his bright young eyes shone with happiness and lust. My little spider was 21. He had a mass of black, curly hair, gleaming with health, and a trim, tightly muscled body. He had been in the desert for three years and was ravenous for experience. It did not seem to occur to him to call me "mother." His enthusiasm was boundless, he was sweet, and his pathetically naive approach was definitely high comedy. After we spent some time together, I discovered that my body was once more capable of lust, and feeling healed, I let it have its way.

After a few days I was able to negotiate the flight back to the United States. The holiday was over, workaday Athens had once more filled with people, noise levels had reached their usual insane pitch, and the tortured air was again more clogged and polluted with unbreathable fumes. I was happy to make my escape. I kissed my ecstatically well-experienced lover goodbye, and flew away.

When I reached United States customs, my luggage, as has happened to me each time, was not inspected, but because I looked like a woman out of the wilds, everyone wanted to know where I had been and what I had done. The Lady had once more been wrapped in her kanga cloth. Only her skeletal feet showed. "What is *that*?" the customs agent asked, misgiving showing plainly on her face.

"It is only a wood carving," I said. "Would you like to see it?"

"No, no." she answered emphatically, and waved me past.

When I reached my room I unwrapped the Goddess, took off all my clothes, and carefully oiled both our bodies. Then I sat down naked, opposite her on the floor, and gently stroked her dark gleaming wood.

"Mother," I said. "It is time we had a woman-to-woman talk. I am tired of exile. I must find a place that I can call home, and I desperately need to find love. Tell me what I must do."

Across the millennia, I heard her voice, like a silver bell, laughing sweetly. "You know the road," she told me, "and you will find your way. You will find what you are looking for."

And I did. In truth, I did.

Kristallnacht Revisited

Some years later, in 1988, I was once more on my way from Hamburg to Copenhagen. I had formed my strongest friendships in those two fateful cities so that my heart as well as circumstance kept pulling me back.

It was November, and in many places in Germany there had been commemorative celebrations of the fiftieth anniversary of the infamous "Kristallnacht," which marked the official beginning of the extermination of nearly all of European Jewry by the Nazis. I sat pensive and alone in my compartment, scarcely aware of the barren, cold autumnal landscape rushing by. I thought of how it had all been so long ago and of how the nightmares had at long last faded from my mind.

When the train stopped at a small station, the door to my compartment opened. A young couple with two small children looked in hopefully, and asked if there were room. "I am the only passenger so far," I smiled. And then, as if transported back to Sudan where I had heard that word so very often and under similar circumstances, I added: "Welcome."

Gratefully they piled into the compartment, explaining that they had no reservations and that they were most happy to be able to find seats for all of them together. They were going home, two hours away, having been on a brief holiday with the children. They asked me where I was going, and I told them that I had been to Hamburg and was on my way to Copenhagen.

They busied themselves with the children with great interest, seeing to it that the two were happily occupied with their books and games. I was immediately entranced by the whole family. Each of them exuded an aura of warmth and respect equally toward the others. The parents answered all of their children's questions with seemingly endless patience and honesty, and there was about these children a sense of freedom and easy self-control unmarred by parental coercion. I could not help but marvel. I must have beamed at them all, because soon they were all beaming back at me.

A few moments later I left the compartment in search of a water fountain, and when I returned, the father addressed me apologetically: "Please, we do not wish to intrude, but while you were gone we tried to puzzle out where you are from. You speak perfect German, and yet we are certain that you must come from someplace else. You look so interesting and unusual that we are very curious and you seem so friendly that we felt you would not mind if we asked."

I explained that I was an American, had spent some recent years traveling in Africa, but had been born in Hamburg which I had left as a child in 1938.

The young couple looked suddenly alarmed and stricken, and the woman asked tentatively, "Did you leave for *political* reasons?"

I nodded assent. "Yes, you might say that," I answered, and added gently, "Those were bad times for *everyone*."

It was as if a pall had fallen over them, and the children looked back and forth between us wonderingly. "What is it?" I asked. "It was all so long ago. Why are you so troubled?"

"We have often spoken of it together," he said haltingly. "We feel such guilt for what our fathers did to you and to the whole world."

"No!" I almost shouted. "You must not do that! You must not do that to yourselves and to those beautiful children! That all happened before any of you were born! That has nothing to do with you at all! Nothing! There is no such thing as *collective* guilt. You must wipe such thoughts from your mind whenever they come, and remember instead what I tell you: You are not responsible for any part of the past. It is dead and gone, and you were not even alive when it all happened. Live for the present, live for the future, and do not waste your energies on borrowed guilt. I understand what you are saying. I understand what you are feeling, but you must fight it, and tell it when it comes that it has no place in your lives."

Then I told them of the many years of "survivor's guilt" I had suffered simply because I was still alive, simply because I had not endured the horrors that nearly all of my contemporaries had experienced. I had dragged myself through life, unable to feel joy, because so many, so much more deserving than I, had perished. One day, much as these young people, I had confessed these feelings to an older woman and she too had shouted at me to stop this heresy, to fight this delusion, to confront it with the reality that I personally had not been responsible for *any* of those deaths, that I had not been the perpetrator of a single one of them. I had done this and slowly, gradually, the delusion eroded away.

The children asked what it was all about, and the parents related to them the sad history of their land, taking to heart what I had just said, admonishing them that it was not their fault and that it had happened long before they were born. Their eyes glowed with gratitude as they spoke.

Then they asked me about Africa, and I told them what I had done there, what I had learned there, and about the book I had written. I told them about my wanderings, and how they had changed my life.

By the time we arrived at their destination, they were full of excitement. "What an encounter," they kept saying. "You have made our whole trip. We will never forget what you have told us." We all shook hands and they piled out of the compartment.

The train began to move once more. I settled back into my seat and suddenly heard an urgent tapping on the window. I looked out, and there they all were, like old friends, their faces radiant, waving me goodbye. I placed both my hands over my heart in a universal gesture of love, and as the train gained in speed, watched them fade into the distance.